Stanley Lane-Poole

Coins and Medals

Their place in History and Art. Second Edition

Stanley Lane-Poole

Coins and Medals
Their place in History and Art. Second Edition

ISBN/EAN: 9783337322090

Printed in Europe, USA, Canada, Australia, Japan

Cover: Foto ©Andreas Hilbeck / pixelio.de

More available books at **www.hansebooks.com**

COINS AND MEDALS

THEIR PLACE IN HISTORY AND ART

BY THE AUTHORS OF
THE BRITISH MUSEUM OFFICIAL CATALOGUES

EDITED BY
STANLEY LANE-POOLE

79231

SECOND EDITION

WITH NUMEROUS ILLUSTRATIONS

LONDON: ELLIOT STOCK,
62, PATERNOSTER ROW, E.C.
1892.

PREFACE.

THE present work is intended to furnish an answer to a question that is often and properly asked about any study of which the use and advantages are not immediately obvious. In the following chapters we have attempted to show what coins can teach us; what is their value as documents of history and monuments of art; and what relations they bear to other branches of historical, artistic, and archæological research. The book will be found of service to the antiquary and the collector of coins; but it is primarily intended for the general student who wishes to know what he may expect to learn from any particular branch of numismatics.

The writers are or have been all Officers in the Department of Coins and Medals in the British Museum, except Professor Terrien de la Couperie and myself, who, however, have been entrusted with the task of preparing the Chinese and Mohammadan

Catalogues for the Department. A feries of effays which appeared in the *Antiquary* in 1883 forms the nucleus of the volume; but thefe have been revifed and enlarged, while additional chapters and illuftrations have been incorporated. A few misprints have been corrected in this fecond edition, which is otherwife a reprint of the firft.

In the abfence of any general guide to the ftudy of coins, of a popular character, in our language, it is hoped that the prefent work may prove of value to many who have been accuftomed to regard the fcience of numifmatics as little better than a diftraction.

STANLEY LANE-POOLE.

ATHENÆUM CLUB,
    June, 1892.

CONTENTS.

CHAPTER	PAGE
PREFACE	v
I. THE STUDY OF COINS	1

By Reginald Stuart Poole, LL.D. Cambr., Yates Professor of Archæology at University College, London; author of the Catalogues of the Greek Coins of *Alexandria, the Ptolemaic Kings*, and *the Shahs of Persia*.

II. GREEK COINS - - - - - - 10

By Barclay V. Head, D.C.L. Durham; Ph.D. Heidelberg; author of the Catalogues of the Greek Coins of *Macedonia, Central Greece, Attica, Corinth*, and *Ionia;* and *Guide to the Coins of the Ancients*.

III. ROMAN COINS - - - - - - 42

By Herbert A. Grueber, F.S.A.; author of the Catalogue of *Roman Medallions*, and *Guide to English Medals;* and joint author of *Medallic Illustrations of the History of Great Britain and Ireland*.

IV. THE COINAGE OF CHRISTIAN EUROPE 74

By Chas. F. Keary, M.A., F.S.A.; author of the Catalogue of *Anglo-Saxon Coins*, and *Guide to Italian Medals*.

CHAPTER		PAGE
V.	ENGLISH COINS	99
	By CHAS. F. KEARY, M.A., F.S.A.	
VI.	EARLY ORIENTAL COINS	141

By PERCY GARDNER, LITT.D., F.S.A., Lincoln Professor of Archæology, Oxford; author of the Catalogues of the Greek Coins of the *Seleucid Kings, Thessaly, Peloponnesus*, and the Catalogue of the Indian Coins of the *Greek and Scythic Kings*.

VII. MOHAMMADAN COINS - - - - 156

By STANLEY LANE-POOLE, B.A., Oxford; author of the Catalogues of the Oriental Coins of the *Eastern Khalifehs, Mohammadan Dynasties, The Turkumans, Egypt, The Moors, The Mongols, Bukhara, The Turks*, and *Additions* thereto; the Catalogues of the Indian Coins of *The Sultans of Dehli, The Mohammadan States of India, The Moghul Emperors of Hindustan*; and the Catalogue of *Arabic Glass Weights*.

VIII. COINS OF INDIA - - - - - 175

By PERCY GARDNER
AND STANLEY LANE-POOLE.

IX. COINS OF CHINA AND JAPAN - - - 190

By TERRIEN DE LACOUPERIE, author of the Catalogue of *Ancient Chinese Coins*.

X. MEDALS - - - - - - - 236

By WARWICK WROTH, F.S.A.; author of the Catalogues of the Greek Coins of *Crete, Pontus*, and *Mysia*.

INDEX - - - - - - - - 271

LIST OF ILLUSTRATIONS.

	PAGE
SILVER COIN OF THASOS	20
SILVER COIN OF TARENTUM	22
SILVER COIN OF GELA	24
SILVER COIN OF SELINUS	25
SILVER COIN OF AGRIGENTUM	26
SILVER COIN WITH HEAD OF MITHRADATES	33
SYRACUSAN MEDALLION	37
SEXTANTAL AS	47
DENARIUS	51
COIN OF BRUTUS	53
SESTERTIUS OF VESPASIAN	62
MEDALLION OF ANTONINUS PIUS	72
COIN OF CHLOVIS II.	79
COIN OF CUNIPERT	79
COIN OF POPE ADRIAN I.	80
CARLOVINGIAN DENARII	82
FIORINO D'ORO	88
COIN OF THE FIFTEENTH CENTURY	91
BRITISH GOLD COIN	101
PENNY OF OFFA	105
NOBLE OF EDWARD III.	110
ANGEL OF EDWARD IV.	113
SOVEREIGN OF HENRY VII.	119
OXFORD CROWN OF CHARLES I.	135

List of Illustrations

	PAGE
COIN OF AN EARLY PARTHIAN KING	147
COIN OF ARTAXERXES I.	149
EARLY JEWISH SHEKEL AND HALF SHEKEL	153
COIN OF SIMON BAR COCHAB	154
GOLD COIN OF 'ABD-EL-MELIK, KHALIF OF DAMASCUS	164
REFORMED GOLD COIN OF 'ABD-EL MELIK	165
SILVER COIN OF THE KHALIFATE	166
MARAVEDI: GOLD COIN OF ALMORAVIDES	170
MILLARES: SILVER COIN OF ALMOHADES	170
SILVER COIN OF HOSEYN, SHAH OF PERSIA	171
GOLD COIN OF ALMOHADES	173
COIN OF ANTIMACHUS, INDIAN KING	176
COIN OF HIPPOSTRATUS	178
COIN OF HERAUS, KING OF THE SACAE	178
GOLD MOHR OF JEHANGIR	189
KNIFE MONEY	205
ITALIAN MEDAL: PORTRAIT OF MALATESTA, BY PISANO	241
GERMAN MEDAL: PORTRAIT OF RINGELBERG	247
DUTCH MEDAL: PORTRAITS OF THE DE WITTS	252
ENGLISH MEDAL: PORTRAITS OF PHILIP AND MARY	253

COINS AND MEDALS.

CHAPTER I.

THE STUDY OF COINS.

F all antiquities coins are the smallest, yet, as a class, the most authoritative in record, and the widest in range. No history is so unbroken as that which they tell; no geography so complete; no art so continuous in sequence, nor so broad in extent; no mythology so ample and so various. Unknown kings, and lost towns, forgotten divinities, and new schools of art, have here their authentic record. Individual character is illustrated, and the tendencies of races defined.

To be a good Greek numismatist one must be an archaeologist; and it is a significant fact, that the only archaeological book of the last century which still holds its own is the *Doctrina Numorum Veterum* of Eckhel, now near its centenary. To

B

be a great general numifmatift is beyond the powers of one man. Some may know Greek and Latin enough, with fuch maftery of Englifh, French, German, and Italian as the modern commentaries demand, to begin the ftudy of Greek and Roman money. Thofe who would enter the vaft field of Oriental numifmatics muft be fortified with Arabic, Hebrew, Sanfkrit, and Perfian, befides adding Spanifh and Ruffian to the other European languages ftill neceffary for their work. Even they muft paufe beneath the Himalayas, nor dare to crofs the Golden Cherfonefe, unlefs they are prepared to mafter the uncouth languages and intricate characters of the further Eaft. So vaft a fubject, and one needing fuch high training, has between Eckhel's time and ours attracted few great ftudents. Coins have been ufed as helps by archaeologifts; but the great numifmatift, who could mafter the richeft provinces of the Eaft or the Weft, or even both, and dignify his fcience as no longer fervile but mafterly, is of our contemporaries. Such was De Saulcy, who has but lately left us to lament how much remained untold by a mind fignally fruitful in giving forth its manifold treafures. He has had his rivals, and he has his followers, fome, like François Lenormant, who have already followed him, others, like Mommfen, ftill living to maintain the high pofition recovered for numifmatics.

Greek Coins. Thanks to their attractive beauty, and the fkill of Eckhel, Greek coins have been beft examined, and moft carefully defcribed; yet much remains unknown and unrecorded. Befides the treafures we are conftantly digging out of well-known collections, every year brings to light from under the earth coins of new kings or cities, coins with frefh types of divinities and reprefentations of famous ftatues. Moft of thefe works, whether familiar or new in type, have the charm which the great gift of the Hellenic race, artiftic power ruled by meafure and form, threw over all that it handled. Thus Greek coins are the grammar of Greek art. In them we may trace its gradual growth, the ftern grandeur of the laft days of archaifm, and the fudden outburft of full fplendour, more marked in coins, however, by the influence of the contemporaries and followers of Pheidias than by that of the great fculptor himfelf. While the original fculpture of this age, in marble and bronze, might be contained within the walls of a fingle mufeum, the coin-types may be counted by thoufands. No reftorer has touched them, nor are they late copies, like the Latin tranflations of Greek originals which confufe the judge of ftatues. Small indeed they are; yet large in treatment, and beautiful in material, whether it be rich gold, or the fofter-toned electrum, or cold filver, or bronze glorified by the unconfcious colouring of the earth in which the coins have lain for centuries. Sometimes we can fee the copy of a ftatue,—no fervile reproduction, but with fuch proof of free work in varieties of attitude as fhows that the artift, ftrong in his power, was working from memory. Such is the Herakles of Croton, recalling a kindred statue to the so-called Theseus of the Parthenon. Bolder masters took a theme like the winged goddess of Terina, and varied it with an originality which showed they were worthy peers of the sculptors and painters. Croton is a town with some place in history; but who, save a numismatist, has any thought for Terina, famous only for the survival of her exquisite coinage?

Schools of Art.

While the sequence of styles is thus recorded, the study of coins unexpectedly reveals the existence of local schools; shows in the marked mannerism of the Italians, and still more of the Sicilians, that they worked under the influence of gem-engravers; while the strong central school of Greece was ruled by sculpture; the gentler and more sympathetic rival of Western Asia Minor obeyed the taste of painters; and the isolated Cretans, leading a simpler and less cultured life, expressed their feeling in a free naturalism. The larger schools again had their divisions, marking such local differences as those with which the study of mediæval Italian art has made us acquainted.

Portraits.

With the age of Alexander all art is centralized in royal capitals, and provincial feeling disappears. The great styles can still be traced in the money of the kings, the lofty naturalism of Lysippus, the dramatic force of the Pergamene masters, the theatrical tendency of their successors. This we see in royal portraits; while the decline and the commercial tendency of art is witnessed by the heraldic quality of the less important types.

The eye, dazzled with the beauty of Greek

money, is apt to take little heed of the knowledge lying beyond the province of art which is held within the narrow circle of a coin. Yet the mythological intereſt is only ſecond to the artiſtic; and when the artiſt had loſt his ſkill he produced thoſe neglected pieces of inferior work, the Greek money of the Imperial age, which preſerve the forms of famous temples, of great ſtatues, and even of pictures otherwiſe finally loſt to us.

The artiſts who engraved the Greek Imperial money, called to Rome, worked there for alien maſters. Mere copyiſts they were; yet more exact in portraiture, and better hiſtorians than their great predeceſſors. Too weak to be original, they were more faithful in rendering the preſent. To them we owe the marked lineaments of the earlier ſeries of Emperors, the cold Auguſtus; the coarſe Vitellius; Trajan, the ſimple ſoldier; Hadrian, the polite man of the world; and the philoſophic Antoninus and Aurelius, with their wayward and luxurious wives. Theſe engravers have left us a record of the art produced at Rome, and the art that was ſtored at Rome from the ſpoils of Greece, great buildings and famous ſtatues, with here and there a ſubject foreſhadowing in a new turn of ſtyle, of Roman birth, the future ſplendour of the Renaiſſance. But for hiſtory theſe men worked beſt, telling the ſtory of the firſt two centuries and a half of the Empire with a fulneſs that has entitled their money to be called an Imperial Gazette. Thus while Hadrian was viſiting the diſtant provinces, the Roman people,

Roman Coins.

when they went to market, faw in the new feftertii, the magnificent bronze currency, the portrayal of the movements of the diftant Emperor.

The Middle Ages. The tranfition from Roman to mediaeval money is not fudden. The one decays, and the other rifes from its ruins, owing as much and as little to it as the architecture of the Middle Ages owed to that of the Empire—as much in form, as little in fpirit. Here hiftory divides with art the claim to our attention. At firft the intereft is centred in the gradual introduction of Roman money among the barbarian conquerors of the Empire; but by degrees the growth of art attracts us, and we watch the fame procefs that marked the hiftory of Greek coinage—the fame fucceffion of ftyles, the fame peculiarities of local fchools. But the art of the Middle Ages in the coins never rifes beyond the limits of decoration; and it is not till the claffical Renaiffance that we difcover a worthy rivalry of the ancient mafters. The beginning of medals is of the time, if not due to the genius, of Petrarch; and the earlieft works are of his friends *Italian Medals.* the Lords of Carrara; but it was not till the middle of the fifteenth century that the great medallic art of Italy had its true origin. Pifano of Verona, who glories in the name of painter, was at once the founder of the art, and by far its greateft mafter. His works are larger in fize than the coins of antiquity and the Roman medallions, and are caft, not ftruck, in fine bronze. Defpite an inferiority to Greek money in the fenfe of beauty, the beft Italian medals have a dignity of portraiture, and a felicity of compofition, that places them in only the fecond rank, below the Greek works indeed, yet above the Roman. For if the Italian medallift had not the fame fenfe of beauty, he had the power of idealizing portraiture, not with the view of elevating the phyfical fo much as the moral qualities. Pifano, notably, reprefented a man with all the poffibilities of excellence that lay within his compafs; and thus he is the greateft of thofe medallifts who worked in portraits.

Modern coins of the European ftates and their colonies are the loweft in intereft, and the medals of their great perfonages the leaft lively in portraiture. But they have an hiftoric value that entitles them to a place in all reprefentative collections, as at leaft ufeful illuftrations of the contemporary annals, and the readieft means of bringing before the eye the chief figures of the times. A clofer ftudy reveals new and curious facts, and the character of the king or the tendencies of the ftate receive an unexpected illuftration. *Modern Coinage*

Oriental money, of larger range and more individuality than European, is worthy of more attention than it has received. The great branch of Mohammedan coinage is invaluable for a period of hiftory when written records are often wanting or little to be trufted. Its decorative art has a charm in the fineft work of the Shahs of Perfia and the Indian Emperors, but rarely is it more than a delicate rendering of an ornamental writing. The infcriptions give the coins their *Oriental Coins.*

true value, the dates and mints fixing the extent of a king's dominion, or recording the fact that he actually exercised the royal prerogative of coining. These legends have a bearing on the differences of race and faith, and even of literature and manners. The western Arabs coined their money with elaborate religious formulas, the heretical Khalifs of the race of 'Aly used myftical inscriptions, the Persians, the Indian Emperors and the Afghans inscribed poetic couplets, hard to decipher, from the occasional disregard of the order of words, and difficult to interpret, from the high-flown phrases in which royalty turned the language well-called the Italian of the East. Despite the general absence of figures, the result of the law of the Koran, there are some notable exceptions, as in the Turkoman coinage of the age of the Crusades, and the famous zodiacal coins of Jehángír and his still stranger Bacchanalian money, on which we see the emperor seated, holding the forbidden wine-cup in his hand.

Yet earlier in origin than the Mohammedan coinage, the native money of India has, like it, survived to our time. Beginning with the interesting Indian coins of the Greek princes, the so-called Bactrian money, and the contemporary rude punch-marked square pieces of native origin, it passes into the gold currency of the Guptas with interesting mythological subjects, Greek, Roman, and Indian, including a representation of Buddha, and closes with the Sanskritic money of our own time. Beyond India, China and the neighbouring lands have their money as unlike that of the reſt of the world as all elſe in the Far Eaſt, valuable alone for hiſtory, and for it moſt valuable; and curious for the occaſional departure from the forms which we aſſociate with the idea of coined money.

CHAPTER II.

GREEK COINS.

Bullion Money.

ANY centuries before the invention of the art of coining, gold and filver in the Eaft, and bronze in the Weft, in bullion form, had already fupplanted barter, the moft primitive of all methods of buying and felling, when among paftoral peoples the ox and the fheep were the ordinary mediums of exchange. The very word *pecunia* is an evidence of this practice in Italy at a period which is probably recent in comparifon with the time when values were eftimated in cattle in Greece and the Eaft.

The Invention of Coinage.

"So far as we have any knowledge," fays Herodotus,[1] "the Lydians were the firft nation to introduce the ufe of gold and filver coin." This ftatement of the father of hiftory muft not, however, be accepted as finally fettling the vexed queftion as to who were the inventors of coined money, for Strabo,[2] Aelian,[3] and the Parian Chronicle, all agree in adopting the more commonly received tradition, that Pheidon, King of

---

[1] i. 94.   [2] viii. 6.   [3] *Var. Hift.*, xii. 10.

Argos, first struck silver coins in the island of Aegina. These two apparently contradictory assertions modern research tends to reconcile with one another. The one embodies the Asiatic, the other the European tradition; and the truth of the matter is that gold was first coined by the Lydians, in Asia Minor, in the seventh century before our era; and that silver was first struck in European Greece about the same time.

The earliest coins are simply bullets of metal, oval or bean-shaped, bearing on one side the signet of the state or of the community responsible for the purity of the metal and the exactness of the weight. Coins were at first stamped on one side only, the reverse showing merely the impress of the square-headed spike or anvil on which, after being weighed, the bullet of hot metal was placed with a pair of tongs and there held while a second workman adjusted upon it the engraved die. This done, a third man with a heavy hammer would come down upon it with all his might, and the coin would be produced, bearing on its face or *obverse* the seal of the issuer, and on the reverse only the mark of the anvil spike, an *incuse* square. This simple process was after a time improved upon by adding a second engraved die beneath the metal bullet, so that a single blow of the sledge-hammer would provide the coin with a *type*, as it is called, in relief, on both sides. The presence of the unengraved incuse square may therefore be accepted as an indication of high antiquity, and nearly all Greek coins which are later than the age of the Perfian wars bear a type on both fides.

<small>Scientific Value of Greek Coins.</small> The chief fcientific value of Greek coins lies in the fact that they are original documents, to which the experienced numifmatift is generally able to affign an exact place in hiftory. The feries of the coins of any one of the cities of Greece thus forms a continuous comment upon the hiftory of the town, a comment which either confirms or refutes the teftimony which has been handed down to us by ancient writers, or, where fuch teftimony is altogether wanting, fupplies valuable evidence as to the material condition, the political changes, or the religious ideas of an interval of time which, but for fuch evidence, would have been a blank in the chart of the world's hiftory.

Perhaps the moft attractive fide of this enticing ftudy lies in the elucidation of the meaning of the objects reprefented on coins, in other words, in the explanation of their types.

The hiftory of the growth, bloom, and decay of Greek art may alfo be traced more completely on a feries of coins which extends over a period of clofe upon a thoufand years than on any other clafs of ancient monuments.

<small>Types.</small> Greek coin-types may be divided into two diftinct claffes: (*a*) Mythological or religious reprefentations, and (*b*) portraits of hiftorical perfons.

<small>Religious Aspect.</small> From the earlieft times down to the age of Alexander the Great the types of Greek coins are almoft exclufively religious. However ftrange this

may seem at first, it is not difficult to explain. It must be borne in mind that when the enterprising and commercial Lydians first lighted upon the happy idea of stamping metal for general circulation, a guarantee of just weight and purity of metal would be the one condition required. Without some really trustworthy warrant, what merchant would accept this new form of money for such and such a weight without placing it in the scales and weighing it according to ancient practice? In an age of universal religious belief, when the gods lived, as it were, among men, and when every transaction was ratified by solemn oath, as witness innumerable inscriptions from all parts of the Greek world, what more binding guarantee could be found than the invocation of one or other of those divinities most honoured and most dreaded in the district in which the coin was intended to circulate?

There is even good reason to think[1] that the earliest coins were actually struck within the precincts of the temples, and under the direct auspices of the priests; for in times of general insecurity by sea and land, the temples alone remained sacred and inviolate. Into the temple treasuries offerings of the precious metals poured from all parts. The priestly colleges owned lands and houses, and were in the habit of letting them on lease, so that rents, tithes, and offerings would all go to fill the treasure-house of the god. This accumulated mass of wealth was not left to lie idle in the

Temple Coinage.

[1] Prof. E. Curtius, *Numismatic Chron.*, 1870, p. 92.

sacred chest, but was frequently lent out at interest in furtherance of any undertaking, such as the sending out of a colony, or the opening and working of a mine; anything, in fact, which might commend itself to the sound judgment of the priests: and so it may well have been that the temple funds would be put into circulation in the form of coin marked with some sacred symbol by which all men might know that it was the property of Zeus, or Apollo, or Artemis, or Aphrodite, as the case might be. Thus coins issued from a temple of Zeus would bear, as a symbol, a thunderbolt or an eagle; the money of Apollo would be marked with a tripod or a lyre; that of Artemis with a stag or a wild boar; that of Aphrodite with a dove or a tortoise—a creature held sacred to the goddess of Love, in some of whose temples even the wooden footstools were made in the form of tortoises.

State Coinage. In this manner the origin of the stamps on current coin may be explained. But throughout the Greek world the civic powers almost everywhere stepped in at an early date, and took over to themselves the right of issuing the coin of the state. Nevertheless, care was always taken to preserve the only solid guarantee which commanded universal respect, and the name of the god continued to be invoked on the coin as the patron of the city. No mere king or tyrant, however absolute his rule, ever presumed to place his own effigy on the current coin, for such a proceeding would, from old associations, have been regarded as little short of sacrilege. In some rare cases, indeed, the right of coinage would even seem to have been retained by the priests down to a comparatively late period; for coins exist, dating from the fourth century B.C., which were issued from the famous temple of the Didymean Apollo, near Miletus, having on the obverse the head of Apollo laureate and with flowing hair; and on the reverse the lion, the symbol of the sun-god, and the inscription ΕΓ ΔΙΔΥΜΩΝ ΙΕΡΗ, "sacred money of Didyma."

We will now select a few of the almost innumerable examples of ancient coin-types in illustration of the religious signification of the symbols which appear upon them.

First in importance comes the plentiful coinage Aegina. of the island of Aegina, issued according to tradition by Pheidon, King of Argos, probably in the sanctuary of Aphrodite, in Aegina, the first European mint. These coins bear the symbol of the goddess, a tortoise or turtle; and they were soon adopted far and wide, not only throughout Peloponnesus, but in most of the island states, as the one generally recognised circulating medium. When Pheidon first issued this new money, he is said to have dedicated and hung up in the temple of Hera, at Argos, specimens of the old cumbrous bronze and iron bars which had served the purpose of money before his time.

Passing from Aegina to Athens, we have now Athens. before us the very ancient coins which Solon struck when he inaugurated that great financial reform which went by the name of the Seifachtheia, a meafure of relief for the whole population of Attica, then overburdened by a weight of debt. By the new law then enacted (circ. B.C. 590), it was decreed that every man who owed one hundred Aeginetic drachms, the only coin then current, fhould be held exempt on the payment of one hundred of the new Attic drachms, which were ftruck of a confiderably lighter weight than the old Aeginetic coins.

The type which Solon chofe for the new Athenian coinage was, like all the types of early Greek money, purely religious. On the obverfe we fee the head of Athena, the protecting goddefs of the city; and on the reverfe her facred owl and olive-branch. Thefe coins were popularly called *owls*, γλαῦκες, or *maidens*, κόραι, πάρθενοι. Ariftophanes, who not unfrequently alludes to coins, mentions thefe famous owls in the following lines, where he promifes his judges that if only they will give his play their fuffrages, the owls of Laurium fhall never fail them:

> Firft, for more than anything each judge has this at heart,
> Never fhall the Laureotic Owls from you depart,
> But fhall in your houfes dwell, and in your purfes too
> Neftle clofe, and hatch a brood of little coins for you.[1]

Delphi. Paffing now into Central Greece, let us paufe for a moment at Delphi, the religious metropolis of the Dorian race. Delphi was effentially a temple-ftate, independent of the Phocian territory

---

[1] *Birds*, 1106 (Kennedy).

in the midst of which it was situated. It was, moreover, the principal seat of the sacred Amphictyonic Council. Here were held the great Pythian Festivals, to which all who could afford it flocked from every part of the Hellenic world. The town of Delphi, which grew up at the foot of the temple of Apollo, on the southern slope of Parnassus, was in early times a member of the Phocian Convention; but as the temple increased in wealth and prestige, the Delphians claimed to be recognised as an independent community; a claim which the Phocians always strenuously resisted, but which the people of Delphi succeeded at length in establishing. The town, however, as such, never rose to any political importance apart from the temple, upon which it was always *de facto* a mere dependency.

As might be expected, the coins issued at Delphi are peculiarly temple coins; and were probably struck only on certain special occasions, such as the great Pythian Festivals, and the meetings, called Πυλαία, of the Amphictyonic Council, when many strangers were staying in the town, and when money would consequently be in request in larger quantities than usual. At such times markets or fairs were held, called πυλατίδες ἀγοραί, for the sale of all kinds of articles connected with the ceremonies and observances of the temple; and at these markets a coinage issued by the priesthood, which all alike might accept without fear of fraud, would be a great convenience.

The usual type of this Delphian temple money

was a ram's head; the ram, κάρνος, being the emblem of Apollo, καρνεῖος, the god of flocks and herds. There is also another emblem, which, although it is usually only an accessory symbol, and not a principal type, must not be passed over in silence, the dolphin (δελφίς). Here we have an allusion to another phase of the cultus of Apollo, who, as we read in the Homeric hymn to Apollo,[1] once took the form of a dolphin when he guided the Cretan ship to Crissa, whence, after commanding the crew to burn their ship and erect an altar to him as Apollo Delphinios, he led them up to Delphi, and appointed them to be the first priests of his temple.

On another coin struck at Delphi we see the Pythian god seated on the sacred Omphalos, with his lyre and tripod beside him, and a laurel-branch over his shoulders; while around is the inscription AMΦIKTIONΩN, proving the coin to have been issued with the sanction of the Amphictyonic Council.

Boeotia.

In the coinage of the neighbouring territory of Boeotia, the most striking characteristic is that it is a so-called *Federal Currency*; that is to say, that the various Boeotian cities possessed from first to last sufficient cohesion to be able to agree upon a common type, which might serve to distinguish the Boeotian currency from that of other states. This is the more remarkable when we remember the fierce political feuds which from the earliest times divided Boeotia into several hostile camps.

[1] l. 390, *seqq.*

Here then we have a clear proof that the *Buckler*, which is the type from the earlieſt times to the lateſt of all Boeotian money, is no mere political emblem, but a ſacred ſymbol, which friends and foes alike could unite in reverencing; juſt as in mediæval times all Chriſtians, however hoſtile to one another, and to whatever land they might belong, were ready to pay homage to the ſign of the Croſs. To what divinity this Boeotian ſhield eſpecially belongs we do not know for certain, but the Theban Herakles has perhaps the beſt claim to it.

The cities of Boeotia, however, while they all agreed to accept the buckler as the diſtinctive badge of their money, nevertheleſs aſſerted their ſeparate and individual rights on the reverſe ſide of their coins. On the obverſe we here get uniformity, on the reverſe variety, and yet among all the various types on the reverſes of the coins of the Boeotian cities, there is not one which is not diſtinctly religious, whether it refer to the worſhip of Herakles or Dionyſos at Thebes, to Poſeidon at Haliartus, to Apollo as the sun-god at Tanagra, or to Aphrodite Melainis as a moon goddeſs at Theſpiae. Sometimes the god himſelf is directly portrayed, ſometimes his preſence is veiled under ſome ſymbolic form, as when the amphora or the wine-cup ſtands for Dionyſos, the club for Herakles, the trident for Poſeidon, the wheel for the rolling diſk of the ſun-god, and the creſcent for the goddeſs of the moon.

Proceeding now northwards through Theſſaly Thrace.

and Macedon, we come upon a region where silver money was coined in very early times, probably long before the Persian invasion, by the mining tribes who inhabited the mountainous district opposite the island of Thasos. Here again we find the same close connection between the religion of the people and the types of their coins. The subjects represented on the money of this northern land are Satyrs and Centaurs bearing off struggling nymphs, rudely but vigorously executed, in a style of art rather Asiatic than Hellenic.

SILVER COIN OF THASOS.

Such types as these bring before us the wild orgies which were held in the mountains of Phrygia and Thrace, in honour of the god Sabazius or Bacchus, whose mysterious oracle stood on the rugged and snow-capped height of Mount Pangaeum, while around, among the dark pine forests, clustered the village communities of the rude mining tribes who worked the rich veins of gold and silver with which the Pangaean range abounded.

Ephesus. We will now take an example from Asia Minor, where we shall find the same invariable connection between the coinage and the local religious cultus.

The coins of the great city of Ephesus, "first

city of Asia," are from very early times marked with a bee on one side, and a stag and palm-tree on the other. The hierarchy of the Ephesian Artemis consisted of a college of priests, at the head of which was a High Priest called Ἐσσήν (the king bee), the leader of the swarm, while his attendant priestesses bore the name of Melissae or Bees; and however difficult it may be for us to seize the exact idea which was intended to be conveyed by this symbol, there can be no doubt that it was one of the most distinctive emblems of the Ephesian goddess in her character of a goddess of nature. The stag is a symbol which every reader of the Greek poets will at once recognise as belonging to Artemis, as is also the sacred palm-tree, πρωτόγονος φοίνιξ, beneath which Leto was fabled to have brought forth Apollo and his sister Artemis.

In the West, no less than in Greece and Asia, the religious aspect of the coin-types is very striking. Thus on Etruscan coins we meet with the head of the gorgon Medusa and of Hades. Here, too, we see Cerberus and griffins and sphinxes and chimaeras, as well as the head of a priest or augur —types which are symbolical of those gloomy and fantastic ideas connected with death and the world of shades which were peculiarly characteristic of the strange uncanny beliefs of the Etruscans. *Etruria.*

In the fertile and vine-growing Campania, on the other hand, the most frequent reverse type is a human-headed bull, a tauriform Chthonian divinity or Earth-god, worshipped very generally throughout *Campania*

Southern Italy under the name of Dionyſos Hebon; a god whoſe nature partook both of that of Hades and of Dionyſos, and who was aſſociated with a female divinity, reſembling both Perſephone and Ariadne, a perſonification of the eternal renewal of nature in the ſpring-time. The beautiful head of this goddeſs is the conſtant obverſe type of the money of Neapolis (Naples).

SILVER COIN OF TARENTUM.

Magna Graecia. Tarentum

In Magna Graecia the ſplendid ſeries of the money of Tarentum offers the curious type of a naked youth riding on a dolphin. This is Taras, the founder of the firſt Iapygian ſettlement on the Calabrian coaſt, who was ſaid to have been miraculouſly ſaved from ſhipwreck by the intervention of his father Poſeidon, who ſent a dolphin, on whoſe back Taras was borne to the ſhore. At Tarentum divine honours were paid to him as oekiſt or founder, and hence his preſence on the coins. The rider who appears on the reverſe of the coins of Tarentum may be taken as an example

Agoniſtic Types.

of what is called an *agoniſtic* type, *i.e.*, a commemoration on the ſtate-money of victories in the games held at Tarentum in the hippodrome. All Greek games partook of a religious nature, and were held in honour of one or other of the gods:

at Olympia, for example, in honour of Zeus, at Delphi of Apollo, and at Tarentum probably of Poseidon.

Another, and a very remarkable early example of one of the agonistic types is furnished by a coin of Metapontum, in Southern Italy: on the reverse is the figure of the river Acheloüs in human form, but with the horns and ears of a bull, just as he is described by Sophocles,[1] as ἀνδρείῳ κύτει βούπρῳρος; and around him is the inscription in archaic characters ΑΧΕΛΟΙΟ ΑΘΛΟΝ, showing that games were celebrated at Metapontum in honour of Acheloüs, king of all Greek rivers, and as such revered from the time of Homer onwards. The coins with this type were doubtless struck on the occasion of the festival held in honour of Acheloüs, and may even have been distributed as prizes, ἆθλα, among the successful athletes.

Metapontum.

At least one side of every Metapontine coin was always dedicated to Demeter, to whose especial favour was attributed the extraordinary fertility of the plain in which the city stood. The ear of corn was the recognised symbol of the worship of this goddess. On this ear of corn is often seen a locust, a bird, a field-mouse, or some other creature destructive to the crops, which was probably added to the main type as a sort of propitiation of the daemons of destruction, and the maleficent influences in nature.

The Acheloüs on this interesting coin of Metapontum may serve to introduce us to a whole

Sicily. River-gods.

[1] *Trach.* 12.

series of river-gods as coin-types on the money of many of the towns of Sicily. River-worship would seem, indeed, judging from the coins, to have been especially prevalent in that island in the fifth century B.C., during which the Sicilian coasts were girdled by a chain of magnificent Greek cities, all, or nearly all, of which were shortly afterwards either destroyed by the Carthaginians, or delivered by the tyrants of Syracuse into the hands of a rapacious foreign soldiery.

In Sicily we see the river Gelas at first as a rushing man-headed bull, and later as a beardless youth with horns sprouting from his forehead.

SILVER COIN OF GELA.

The Crimissus on a coin of Segesta takes at first the form of a dog, and later that of a hunter accompanied by two dogs. The Hipparis at Camarina is seen as a young horned head emerging from the midst of a circle of waves. The Hypsas at Selinus is a naked youth offering a libation at the altar of the god of health, in gratitude for the draining of the marsh, which had impeded the course of his stream, and for the cleansing and purification of his waters. On the reverse of this coin we see Apollo and Artemis in a chariot, the former as ἀλεξίκακος discharging his radiant arrows and flaying the Peſtilence as he ſlew the Python, while his ſiſter Artemis ſtands beſide him in her capacity of εἰλείθυια or σοωδῆνα, for the plague had fallen heavily on the women too, ὥστε καὶ τὰς γυναῖκας δυστοκεῖν.[1]

SILVER COIN OF SELINUS.

From the cultus of rivers we may paſs to that of nymphs, of which we may again find examples among the beautiful coins of Sicily. One of the moſt charming of theſe repreſentations is that of the nymph Camarina on a coin of that city, who is pictured riding on the back of a ſwan, half-flying, half-ſwimming acroſs the waves of her own lake, as ſhe holds with one hand the corner of her peplos or garment, which, filled by the breeze, ſerves the purpoſe of a ſail.

More famous ſtill is the fountain-nymph Arethuſa, on a tetradrachm of Syracuſe, a work which, in delicacy of treatment, and in the ſkilful adaptation of the ſubject to the ſpace at the diſpoſal of the artiſt, leaves nothing to be deſired. On this coin the head of the nymph is ſeen facing the ſpectator—a true water-goddeſs—

With her rainbow locks
Streaming among the ſtreams;

[1] Diog. Laert., viii. 2, 70.

while dolphins are playing around her, darting and leaping about among the rich maſſes of her floating hair. The artiſt has here ſtriven to convey the idea of the ſweet waters of the fountain in the iſland of Ortygia riſing out of the midſt of the ſalt waves of the harbour of Syracuſe, the ſalt ſea being ſymbolized by the dolphins.

As in the caſe of the river-gods, the head of the nymph is on this coin accompanied by her name, ΑΡΕΘΟΣΑ.

Eagles devouring a Hare.

Another Sicilian coin ſtands out as a truly powerful work. It is a ſilver coin of Agrigentum, on which two eagles are ſeen on a rocky height, the one ſcreaming with uplifted head, the other with raiſed wings and head ſtretched downwards. The two birds ſtand ſide by ſide on the dead body of a hare, which they are about to tear in pieces. As a coin-type, ſuch a ſubject ſeems hard to explain: perhaps it refers to some local myth long loſt; but it is ſcarcely poſſible to conceive that the artiſt

SILVER COIN OF AGRIGENTUM.

who engraved the die had not ringing in his ears the grand chorus in the *Agamemnon* where Aeſchylus depicts the " winged hounds of Zeus " in juſt ſuch a ſcene as the engraver, with equally imperiſhable touches, has handed down to us acroſs the ages:

> On lofty ſtation, manifeſt to ſight,
> The bird kings to the navy kings appear,
> One black, and one with hinder plumage white,
> A hare with embryo young in evil hour
> Amerced of future courſes they devour.
>   Chant the dirge, uplift the wail,
>   But may the right prevail.[1]

From the coinage of free and autonomous towns, we will now paſs to that of Philip of Macedon, the founder of that vaſt monarchy which was deſtined, in the hands of his ſon and ſucceſſor Alexander the Great, to ſpread the arms, the arts, the literature, and the civilization of Greece as far as the ſhores of the Caſpian and the banks of the Indus and the Nile. But abſolute as was the power of Philip and Alexander, theſe monarchs were ſtill eſſentially Greek, and as Greeks they were careful never to place upon their money any effigy leſs auguſt than that of ſome one of the gods of Greece. Thus Philip, when he had united in his ſingle hand the whole of northern Greece, and when he reorganized the currency of his empire, had recourſe to the two great religious centres of Hellas, Delphi and Olympia, for the types of his gold and ſilver money. On the gold money appears the head of the Pythian Apollo, and on the ſilver that of the Olympian Zeus. The reverſe types are in each caſe *agoniſtic;* that is to ſay, they com-

Coinage of Philip and Alexander the Great.

---

[1] *Agam.*, 115 (Swanwick).

memorate in a general way Philip's succeſses in the great Greek games, in which, we are told, it was his eſpecial pride to be hailed as a victor. Pallas and her attendant, Victory, with Herakles and the Olympian Zeus, are the gods under whoſe auſpices Alexander's gold and ſilver went forth from a hundred mints over the vaſt expanſe of his heterogeneous empire. But, more than mortal as Alexander was conceived, and perhaps almoſt believed himſelf to be, never once during his life-time was his own portrait ſeen upon his coins, though it had been the cuſtom in the Eaſt, from the very foundation of the Perſian monarchy which Alexander overthrew, for the great king to place his own effigy upon the royal *Daric* coins. What clearer proof can be required that none but religious ſubjects were at that time admiſſible on the coin?

Introduction of Portraiture.

But after the death of the great conqueror a change is noticeable, gradual at firſt, and then more marked, in the aſpect of the international currency inſtituted by Alexander. The features of the god Herakles on the tetradrachms little by little loſe their noble ideality, and aſſume an expreſſion in which there is an evident ſtriving on the part of the engraver towards an aſſimilation of the god to Alexander, now himſelf regarded as one of the immortals and the recipient of Divine honours.

Alexander's Succeſſors.

The firſt real and diſtinct innovation was, however, made by Alexander's general, Lyſimachus, when he became King of Thrace. The money of this monarch bears moſt unmiſtakably a portrait of the great Alexander—of Alexander, however, as a god—in the character which in his lifetime his flatterers had encouraged him to aſſume, of the ſon of the Lybian Ammon with the ram's horn over the ear. This was the firſt ſtep towards the new faſhion of placing the head of the ſovereign on the coin of the realm; but ſo antagoniſtic does this practice ſeem to have been to the religious ſuſceptibilities even of this late time, that it was only by ſlow degrees that it came to be adopted. When the centre of gravity, ſo to ſpeak, of the Greek world was no longer to be found in Hellas, but in the various capitals of thoſe ſemi-oriental monarchies which aroſe out of the ruins of the Perſian empire, Alexandria, Antioch, and the reſt, all Greece received an indelible taint of oriental ſervility. In compariſon with theſe new ſelf-conſtituted Βασιλεῖς and their deſcendants, Philip and Alexander ſtand forth as Hellenes of the old type. Only in ſuch degenerate times did it become poſſible for a king to uſurp on the coinage the place of honour reſerved of old for gods and religious emblems; nay, even to give themſelves out as very gods, and to adopt ſuch titles as Θεὸς ἐπιφανής or Νέος Διόνυσος.

The firſt of Alexander's ſucceſſors who ſubſtituted his own portrait on coins for that of the deified Alexander was Ptolemy Soter, the founder of the dynaſty which ruled Egypt for two centuries and a half. Both he and his queen, Berenice, were deified after their deaths, and appear with the title Θεοί on the money of their fon, Ptolemy Philadelphus; and the portrait of Ptolemy Soter was perpetuated from generation to generation on the coins of fucceffive rulers of Egypt down to the time of the Roman conqueft, although not to the exclufion of other royal portraits.

Greek coins, from the age of Alexander onwards, poffefs an intereft altogether different from that with which the money of the earlier ages infpires us. The intereft of the præ-Alexandrine coins is twofold. In the firft place, they illuftrate local myths, and indirectly fhed much light on the political revolutions of every corner of the Greek world; and in the fecond place, they are moft valuable for the hiftory of art in its various ftages of development. The intereft of the poft-Alexandrine coins is that of a gallery of authentic portraits. "Here," fays Addifon,[1] "you fee the Alexanders, Caefars, Pompeys, Trajans, and the whole catalogue of heroes who have, many of them, fo diftinguifhed themfelves from the reft of mankind, that we almoft look upon them as another fpecies. It is an agreeable amufement to compare in our own thoughts the face of a great man with the character that authors have given us of him, and to try if we can find out in his looks and features either the haughty, cruel, or merciful temper that difcovers itfelf in the hiftory of his actions."

Among the fineft portraits on Greek coins we

[1] *Dialogues upon the Ufefulnefs of Ancient Medals.*

have space only to mention a few. First comes that of the great Alexander himself, on the coins of Lysimachus, idealized no doubt, but still the man in the likeness of a god. In many of these coins we may note the peculiarities recorded as characteristic of his statues by Lysippus, the slight twist in the neck and the ardent look in the eyes.

Then there is Demetrius Poliorcetes, the de-stroyer of cities, that soldier of fortune, terrible in war, and luxurious in peace, whose beauty was such that Plutarch says no painter could hit off a likeness. That historian compares him to Dionysos, and as Dionysos he appears on the coins, with the bull's horn of the god pointing up from out the heavy locks of hair which fall about his forehead. *Demetrius Poliorcetes.*

Another highly characteristic head is that of the eunuch Philetaerus, the founder of the dynasty of the Attalid Kings of Pergamus. Here, at last, is realism pure and simple. The huge fat face and vast expanse of cheek and lower jaw carry conviction to our minds that this is indeed a living portrait. *Philetaerus.*

To those who are familiar only with Greek art in its ideal stage, such faces as this of Philetaerus, with many others that might be cited (Prusias, King of Bithynia, for example), from among the various Greek regal coins, will be at first somewhat startling. We have become so thoroughly imbued with the ideal conceptions of godlike humanity perpetuated in Greek sculpture and its derivatives, that when we first take up one of these portrait- *Realism.*

coins of the third or second century B.C., we find it hard to persuade ourselves that it is so far removed from our own times. This or that uninspired and commonplace face might well be that of a prosperous modern Englishman, were it not for the royal diadem and Greek inscription which designate it as a King of Pontus or Bithynia, of Syria or of Egypt.

Nevertheless, although an almost brutal realism is the rule in the period now under consideration, there are instances where the artist seems to have been inspired by his subject and carried away out of the real into the ideal. Thus the majority of the coins of the great Mithradates are probably unidealized portraits, somewhat carelessly executed, of a man scarcely remarkable unless for a certain evil expression of tigerish cruelty. But there are others of this same monarch on which, it is true, the likeness is unmistakably preserved, but under what an altered aspect! Mithradates is here the hero, almost the god, and as we gaze at his head on these coins, with flying locks blown back as if by a strong wind, we can picture him standing in his victorious chariot holding well in hand his sixteen splendid steeds, and carrying off the prize; or as a runner, outstripping the swiftest deer, or performing some other of those wondrous feats of strength and agility of which we read. This type of the idealized Mithradatic head also occurs on coins of Ariarathes, a youthful son of Mithradates, who was placed by his father on the throne of Cappadocia. The head, like that of Alexander, was afterwards perpetuated on the money of various cities on the fhores of the Euxine.

SILVER COIN WITH HEAD OF MITHRADATES.

We have fpace only to mention one other *Cleopatra* portrait, that of the famous Cleopatra on a coin of Afcalon. This is certainly no ordinary face, and yet we look in vain for thofe charms which fafcinated Caefar and ruined Antony. The eyes are wide open and eager, the nofe prominent and flightly hooked, the mouth large and expreffive, the hair modeftly dreffed and bound with the royal diadem. The evidence afforded by the coins, taken in conjunction with a paffage of Plutarch, who fays that in beauty fhe was by no means fuperior to Octavia, leads us to the conclufion that Cleopatra's irrefiftible charm lay rather in her mental qualities and alluring manner, than in any mere outward beauty.

Quite apart from the intrinfic importance, *Styles of Art and* mythological or hiftorical, of the fubjects repre- *Chronological* fented on Greek coins, lies their value as illuftra- *Sequence.* tions of the archaeology of art. Of all the remains of antiquity, ftatues, bronzes, terracottas, fictile vafes, engraved gems, and coins, thefe laft alone can, as a rule, be exactly dated. The political conditions and viciſſitudes of the autonomous coin-ſtriking ſtates render it comparatively eaſy for us to ſpread out before our eyes the ſucceſſive iſſues of each in chronological ſequence. In the ſeries of each town we may thus at once obtain a few definite landmarks, around which, by analogy of ſtyle, we ſhall have no great difficulty in grouping the remaining coins. The characteriſtics of Greek art, in the various phaſes which it paſſed through, we do not propoſe, nor indeed is this the place, to diſcuſs. It will be ſufficient to indicate the main chronological diviſions or periods in which the coinage of the ancient world may be conveniently claſſified. Theſe are as follows:

I. Circa B.C. 700-480. The *Period of Archaic Art*, which extends from the invention of the art of coining down to the time of the Perſian Wars.

II. " " 480-415. The *Period of Tranſitional Art*, from the Perſian Wars to the ſiege of Syracuſe by the Athenians.

III. " " 415-336. The *Period of Fineſt Art*, from the Athenian expedition againſt Sicily, to the acceſſion of Alexander the Great.

IV. Circa B.C. 336-280.   The *Period of Later Fine Art*, from the acceſſion of Alexander to the death of Lyſimachus.
V. „   „ 280-146.   The *Period of the Decline of Art*, from the death of Lyſimachus to the Roman conqueſt of Greece.
VI. „   „ 146-27.   The *Period of continued Decline in Art*, from the Roman conqueſt to the riſe of the Roman Empire.
VII. B.C. 27—A.D. 268.   The *Period of Graeco-Roman Art*, from the reign of Auguſtus to that of Gallienus.

It is almoſt always quite eaſy to determine to which of the above periods any given coin belongs; and as a rule it is poſſible to fix its date within the period with more or leſs preciſion, by comparing it in point of ſtyle with others of which the exact date is known. Even a ſmall collection of well-choſen ſpecimens thus mapped out in periods forms an epitome of the hiſtory of art ſuch as no other claſs of ancient monuments can furniſh. It is true that not all coin art is of the higheſt order for the age to which it belongs. Often, indeed, it is extremely faulty; but, good or bad, it is always inſtructive, becauſe it is the veritable handiwork of an artift working independently, and not of a mere copyift of older works. The artift may have been unknown, perhaps, even in his own day, beyond the narrow circle of his fellow-citizens; but he was none the lefs an artift who expreffed to the beft of his ability the ideas of his age and country, and he has handed down to all time, on the little difk of metal at his difpofal, a fpecimen, on a fmall fcale, of the art of the time in which he was at work.

<small>Die Engravers.</small>

There is good reafon, moreover, to think that the perfons employed to engrave the coin-dies were by no means always artifts of inferior merit. During the period of the higheft development of Greek art it is not unufual, efpecially in Magna Graecia and Sicily, to find the artift's name written at full length in minute characters on coins of particularly fine work; and it is in the laft degree improbable that fuch a privilege would have been accorded to a mere mechanic or workman in the mint, however fkilful he may have been. That artifts known to fame were (at leaft in the fourth century) entrufted with the engraving of the coins, is indeed proved by the fact that we find feveral cities entirely independent of one another having recourfe to the fame engraver for their money. For inftance, Evaenetus, the engraver of the fineft of thofe fplendid medallions of Syracufe, bearing on one fide the head of Perfephone crowned with corn-leaves, and on the other a victorious chariot, places his name alfo on coins of two other Sicilian cities, Camarina and Catana; and what is ftill more remarkable, the Syracufan artift, EYΘ . . . ., appears alfo to have been employed by the mint of Elis in Peloponnefus.

SYRACUSAN MEDALLION.

In Magna Greacia alfo we note that an artift, by name Ariftoxenus, figns coins both of Metapontum and Heracleia in Lucania; and another, who modeftly figns himfelf Φ, works at the fame time for the mints of Heracleia, Thurium, Pandofia, and Terina.

In Greece proper, artifts' fignatures are of very rare occurrence; but of the town of Cydonia, in Crete, there is a coin with the legend in full ΝΕΥΑΝΤΟΣ ΕΠΟΕΙ; and of Clazomenae, in Ionia, there is a well-known tetradrachm, with a magnificent head of Apollo facing, and the infcription ΘΕΟΔΟΤΟΣ ΕΠΟΕΙ.

Enough has been faid to fhow that in the period of fineft art there were die-engravers whofe reputation was not confined to a fingle town, artifts of the higher order, whofe fignatures on the coin were a credit to the cities for which they worked. Unfortunately, not a fingle ancient writer has thought of recording the name of any one of these great masters of the art of engraving. How, indeed, could they know that thousands of these, in their time insignificant, coins would outlast the grandest works of architecture, sculpture, and painting, and would go down from age to age, uninjured by the lapse of time, sole witnesses to the beauty of a long-forgotten popular belief, or to the glory of some splendid city whose very site is now a desert or a swamp? Yet we must not regret that the old Greek engravers worked without any idea of handing down either their own, or their city's, or their ruler's glory to posterity. Had they thought of these things, the coins would have furnished far less trustworthy evidence than they now do, and we should probably have had many ancient examples of medals like that famous piece of modern times which Napoleon I. ordered to be struck with the inscription, *Frappée à Londres*.

Magistrates' Names.

Not to be confounded with artists' signatures on coins are the names of the magistrates under whose authority the money was issued. All such names are usually written in large conspicuous characters intended to catch the eye, while the names of artists are often purposely concealed; and are indeed sometimes so small as to be hardly visible without a magnifying-glass. About the end of the fifth century B.C., at some towns, though not generally before the middle of the fourth, magistrates begin to place their signatures on the money. Sometimes we read their names at full length, sometimes in an abbreviated form or in monogram; while not unfrequently a symbol or signet stands in place of the name. It is a matter of no small difficulty to distinguish such magistrates' signets in the field of a coin from religious symbols which are to be interpreted as referring more or less directly to the principal type. Thus, for instance, an ear of corn might refer to the worship of Demeter, or it might stand in the place of the name of a magistrate Demetrius. As a rule, all such small accessory symbols before the end of the fifth century have a religious motive; and the same symbol will be found very constantly accompanying the main type. But in later times, while the type remains constant, the symbol will be frequently varied. It must then be understood as the private seal of the magistrate entrusted with the supervision of the coinage. Unfortunately we know very little of the organization of the mints in the various cities of the ancient world. It has been proved that at some cities the chief magistrate placed his name on the money issued during his tenure of office; thus, in Boeotia, the name of the illustrious Epaminondas occurs; and at Ephesus we find the names of several of the chief magistrates, who are mentioned as such by ancient writers or in inscriptions. This was not, however, the universal rule: at Athens, for instance, the names of the Archons are not found on the coins; and at some cities the high priest, and occasionally even a priestess, signs the municipal coinage.

Under the Roman Empire, from Augustus to Gallienus, the Greek cities of Asia, and a few in

Greek Imperial Coinage.

Europe, were allowed to strike bronze money for local use. These late issues are very unattractive as works of art, and their study has been consequently much neglected. In some respects, however, they are even more instructive than the coins of an earlier age, which they often explain and illustrate. It is to these Greek Imperial coins, as they are called, that we must have recourse if we would know what local cults prevailed in the outlying provinces of the Roman Empire, and especially in what strange and uncouth guises the half-Greek peoples of Asia clothed their gods.

Only in this latest period do we find on the coinage actual copies of ancient sacred images of Asiatic divinities, such as that of the Ephesian Artemis, with stiff mummy-like body, half human, half bestial, with her many breasts. It is not to be questioned that many such monstrous statues existed in various parts of Greece, sacred relics of a barbarous age, and that on great festivals they were draped in gorgeous attire, and exhibited to public view; but Greek art, as long as it was a living art, shrank from the representation of such images, and always substituted for them the beautiful Greek ideal form of the divinity with which it was customary to identify them.

These Greek Imperial coins are also valuable as furnishing us with copies of famous statues of the great period of art, such as that of the chryselephantine Zeus of Pheidias at Olympia, the Aphrodite of Praxiteles at Cnidus, and many others; and they are particularly interesting for the light which they fhed upon the facred games, Pythia, Didymeia, Actia, Cabeiria, and other local feftivals and religious ceremonies, of which, but for our coins, little or nothing would have been known.

CHAPTER III.

ROMAN COINS.

HE coinage of Rome falls naturally into two great claffes: (1) the Family or, as it is often mifcalled, the Confular feries, ftruck under the Republic; and (2) the Imperial feries, of the period of the Roman and Byzantine Emperors, from Auguftus to the capture of Conftantinople by the Turks in A.D. 1453.

Introduction of Coinage. The date of the firft iffue of a coinage at Rome is uncertain. The prefence of roughly caft lumps of metal in treafure offered to divinities of fountains, mixed with large quantities of coins, feems to indicate that the firft attempt at a metal currency at Rome confifted of rude lumps or ingots of copper of uncertain weight and fize, Aes rude. called *aes rude*. Thefe pieces are without any mark of authority, and could only have circulated by weight. The introduction of a coinage at Rome has by ancient authority been attributed to Servius Tullius, and he is faid to have been "the firft to mark copper pieces with the repre-

Introduction of Coinage.   43

sentations of an ox or some other animal or symbol." No coins of this remote period have, however, been preserved, and the tradition is doubtless without foundation. Considerably later than the time of the Kings are those quadrilateral or brick-shaped pieces of copper, having on one or both sides a symbol, from which they have been called *aes signatum*. These pieces must have been issued in considerable quantities, as they are not uncommon at the present time. They are of uncertain sizes and thickness, and were originally cast in large blocks, and afterwards divided into smaller portions. Like the aes rude, these pieces must have circulated by weight. They appear to have been in use up to a late period, even after the coinage had passed into another stage. To these rough pieces there succeeded a much more regular coinage, circular in shape, called *aes grave*. It consisted of a large copper coin, the *as*, the unit of the monetary system, and, being of a pound weight, called the *as libralis*, and of a number of fractional parts, called the *semis* (half), the *triens* (third), the *quadrans* (fourth), the *sextans* (sixth), and the *uncia* (twelfth). Multiples of the as were the *dupondius* (double as), the *quincussis* (five-as piece), and the *decussis* (ten-as piece); but these do not appear to have been issued at Rome, but only by the neighbouring cities, which adopted this heavy copper coinage. All the pieces of this new coinage are cast (not struck), in high relief, and without any kind of legend or inscription excepting the marks of value: for the as 1, for

_{Aes Signatum.}

_{Aes Grave}

the femis S, and for the other divifions four, three, two, or one dot or knob. The type of the reverfe, a prow, was the fame throughout, but that of the obverfe varied with each denomination. On the as was the double-headed Janus, to whom the firft coinage was mythically attributed; on the femis the head of Jupiter, the protector of the Capitol; on the triens the head of Pallas, the protectrefs of Aeneas, or Minerva, the inventrefs of numbers; on the quadrans the head of Hercules, the tutelary genius of the farmyard, and thus in general the god of property and riches; on the fextans the head of Mercury, the god of traffic and commerce; and on the uncia the head of Roma, herfelf the tutelary goddefs of the city. The weight of the as was nominally that of the Roman pound of 12 oz., but very few fpecimens extant come up to the full weight; they range generally from 11 to 9 oz. This may be the refult of a firft reduction of a pound of copper from the condition of aes rude, or large quadrilateral pieces of metal, aes fignatum, circulating by weight, to the form of a real and fyftematic currency.

The origin of this libral fyftem is affigned by Mommfen to the decemvirs, and more particularly to the influence of the Lex Julia Papiria (B.C. 430), which ordered that fines fhould not be paid in cattle but in money. But in ftyle and fabric the libral coinage cannot be of fo early a date. Anyone accuftomed to the ftudy of numifmatics can fee at a glance that thefe coins bear no trace of archaifm, and cannot be imitations of types that originated in the fifth century. They belong rather to a time that correfponds with the fine period of Greek coinage. The Romans borrowed all their ideas of painting and fculpture from the Greeks, and no doubt reforted to the fame fource for the types of their coinage. It muft therefore be fuppofed that the fines ordered by the Lex Julia Papiria were paid in metal by weight, and that the as libralis was an eventual but not an immediate effect of this law.

Befide this rather complicated feries of copper coins, no attempt appears to have been made by the State to introduce either of the finer metals, gold, or filver. In fixing the as to the weight of a pound, the State had, however, made it poffible to accept in circulation the gold and filver coinages of neighbouring cities. At that period the pound of copper was worth a fcruple of filver, a relative value which had for fome time exifted in Sicily, whofe inhabitants for convenience of trade were defirous that their filver money and the rude copper coins of Latium fhould have a joint circulation. The coins that chiefly fupplied this want were the gold and filver money of Campania, with the name ROMANO· or ROMA. The gold coin had for the type of the obverfe the head of Janus, and on the reverfe two warriors taking an oath over a youth facrificing a pig.[1] The filver coins vary in type, but the moft common have on the obverfe the head of Janus,

Early Gold and Silver Coins in Circulation at Rome.

Campanian Coins.

---

[1] Caefa iungebant foedera porca.—*Aen.*, viii. 641.

and on the reverse Jupiter in a biga, or two-horse chariot, accompanied by the divinity Victory. Both gold and silver coins of these types are inscribed ROMA. The relative value of the coins in gold, silver, and copper is a very difficult question. At this period the usual proportion between gold and silver was 1 to 12, and between silver and copper 1 to 250; but, in order to increase the value of their copper coins, the Romans appear to have estimated them above their usual worth, thus making the silver and copper at a ratio of 1 to 183, and reducing in an equal degree the ratio of the gold.

Reduction of the As Libralis. Although this large copper coinage must have proved most inconvenient for commercial transactions, a considerable period elapsed before there was any decided change in the Roman monetary system. The authorities of the Imperial age state with a very considerable uniformity of opinion that the change took place during the period of the first Punic war (B.C. 264-241), and that the as libralis fell suddenly to 2 oz., the weight of an as sextantalis. According to Mommsen, however, whose opinion is borne out by the coins themselves, the fall was not so rapid; and what took place appears to have been as follows. From a weight of 10 oz. (nominally 12), the as fell to 8 oz., and at length was reduced to 4, or to that *Triental As.* of a triens, and thus became *triental*. This probably occurred about B.C. 269, when the silver coinage of Rome begins. The evidence afforded by the coinages of neighbouring cities subject to

Rome bear out this statement. In B.C. 291 Venusia was founded, and struck coins of the libral standard; and in B.C. 289 Hatria followed her example; but in B.C. 251, when Lipara became a Roman colony, we find that city issuing a triental coinage. It is therefore between these dates that the reduction of the as must be placed, and in fixing it to B.C. 269 we make it simultaneous with the introduction of the new silver

SEXTANTAL AS.

coinage. The dupondius (2 asses), tressis (3), and decussis (10), were now issued at Rome, and also the semuncia ($\frac{1}{2}$ oz.) and quadruncia ($\frac{1}{4}$ oz.). These two last coins, together with the sextans and uncia, were now no longer cast but struck, and bore on the reverse the inscription ROMA; the other coins were all cast as before. The triental as did not long preserve its full weight, but about B.C. 250 fell to 2 oz., and was called the *as sex-* Sextantal *tantalis.* When the coinage became *sextantal,* casting was abandoned, and all coins were struck, and bore the name of the city. Also the multiples of the as were discontinued, as well as the semuncia and quadruncia.

First Roman Silver Coinage.

In B.C. 269 the first silver coinage was issued at Rome, and consisted of the *denarius*, its half the *quinarius*, and its quarter the *sestertius*. The legal weight of the early denarius was 4 scruples (72 grains), which gave a convenient number of scruples for each Roman coin. Thus the quinarius = 2 scruples, and the sestertius = 1 scruple, and the Roman pound of silver produced 72 denarii, 144 quinarii, or 288 sestertii. The reason for adopting this new standard for the silver coins is obvious, when we consider what had happened with the copper coinage. This, as has been shown, was reduced to one-third its original value, and the new sestertius was therefore an equivalent to the as libralis, of which many specimens must have still remained in circulation. In all indications of sums fixed at the period of the introduction of the new coinage, the Latin writers use as synonymous terms the words *sestertius* and *aes grave*. The relative value of silver and copper was by this arrangement maintained, although it did not long keep so, as the weight of the copper coins soon fell, and they became mere pieces of account or tokens, like the bronze coinage of the present day. In B.C. 217 the standard of the silver was reduced, and the as became uncial. The denarius was struck at 80 to the pound, and the quinarius at 160. The issue of the sestertius ceased, and was not again struck in silver, excepting at occasional intervals during the first century B.C. The quinarius, after a very short time, fell into disuse, and was only occasionally reissued. The denarius remained at this new standard for nearly three centuries, and maintained its purity throughout.

Another silver coin was also in circulation: this was the *victoriatus*, so-called from its type, which showed on the obverse the head of Jupiter, and on the reverse Victory crowning a trophy. This coin was first issued in B.C. 228; it was in weight 3 scruples, or three-fourths of the denarius, and was originally a Campanian coin; but after the fall of Capua, B.C. 211, the coinage of the Victoriatus was transferred to Rome, itself, where it continued to be coined for the use of the Provinces. It was also current at Rome, perhaps, however, to no great extent. When the weight of the denarius fell in B.C. 217, that of the victoriatus was reduced in like proportion, but after a few years its issue ceased. The type was afterwards adopted for the quinarius. {Victoriatus.}

When the as fell from sextantal to uncial, its value was also changed from one-tenth to one-sixteenth of the denarius. As the soldiers were paid after the old standard of ten asses to the denarius, that coin retained its mark of value X. By this reduction the relation of silver to copper fell to 1 to 112, less than half the original ratio. Thus the copper coinage became still more a money of account; and when in B.C. 89 it was again reduced to a *semuncial* standard no ill-effects were produced. In B.C. 80 the copper coinage {Uncial As.}

ceased; and, excepting a few pieces struck in the eastern and western provinces, it was not revived during the period of the Republic. In B.C. 16 Augustus introduced a new copper coinage consisting of a sestertius of four asses, a dupondius of two asses, an as, a semis, a triens, and a quadrans.

<small>Gold Coins, after B.C. 269.</small>

The only other pieces which remain to be mentioned are the gold. The early coins of 3, 2, and 1 scruple, marked LX., XXXX., and XX., with the helmeted head of Mars on one side and an eagle standing on a thunderbolt on the other, are usually considered a Campanian issue. These were first struck soon after B.C. 269; but from their extreme scarcity their issue could only have extended over a very short period. The first purely Roman gold money was struck by Sulla in B.C. 84-82. They bear his own name and that of his proquaestor, L. Manlius, and from their fabric appear to have been issued in Greece, probably as rewards to his veterans. The gold coins struck by Julius Caesar in B.C. 49 are of the same character as those of Sulla; and it is not till after Caesar's death that a gold coinage is firmly established, which consisted of an *aureus* and a *half-aureus*, the former struck at forty to the pound, and representing in value twenty-five denarii.

<small>Types.</small>

The original type of the denarius is, on the obverse, the head of Roma wearing a helmet adorned with wings, and a griffin's head for the crest; behind is the mark of value X; and on the reverse, the Dioscuri on horseback, charging, their spears couched, their mantles floating behind, and their conical hats furmounted each by a ftar, emblematic of the morning and evening; below, is the infcription ROMA.

DENARIUS OF THE FIRST ISSUE.

This is no doubt a reprefentation of thefe demigods as they were feen, according to the legend, fighting for the Romans at the battle of Lake Regillus. Any change of type was at firft very gradual. After a time the mark of value is removed from behind the head of Roma and placed under her chin, and the infcription is transferred from the reverfe to the obverfe. About B.C. 125 the mark of value changes to ✱., and in one inftance to XVI., the latter to reprefent fixteen affes, the true value of the denarius at that time. About B.C. 90 the mark of value is no longer ftamped on the filver coins. The firft inftance of a change in the head on the obverfe can be fixed with certainty to B.C. 100. In that year the Quaeftors Pifo and Caepio, having been ordered by the Senate to purchafe corn and to fell it to the people below the market value, received a fpecial privilege to iffue coins to cover this extraordinary expenditure. To diftinguifh their coins from thofe ftruck by the officers of the mint, they varied the type by placing on the obverfe the head of Saturn, probably in allufion to L. Appuleius Saturninus, who had propofed the Lex Frumentaria. Seven years later, in B.C. 93, the monetarii iffued two fets of coins having the fame reverfes; but on the obverfe of one fet was the head of Roma, and on the other that of Apollo. After this time the head on the obverfe changed year by year, being either that of a divinity, fometimes but rarely of Roma, or of a traditional or hiftorical perfonage. Thefe types were generally in fome way connected with the family of the monetarius. In B.C. 44, by order of the Senate, the head of Julius Caefar was placed upon the coins; and after a few years the ufual type is that of fome living perfonage, generally of him who iffued the coins.

The firft change in the type of the reverfe occurred about B.C. 217, when Diana in a two-horfed chariot is fubftituted for the Diofcuri. But this was an exception, and it is not till after a further interval of more than fifty years that we again meet with any variation. From about B.C. 160 the coins fhow a delight in recording the great deeds of Rome's heroes in the paft, in reprefenting the mythological and hiftorical traditions of the nation, and in illuftrating public events after the manner of medals. One of the earlieft hiftorical types is to be found on the coins, already referred to, of the Quaeftors Pifo and Caepio, who are reprefented diftributing largeffe to the public. A ftill more remarkable coin is that ftruck by Brutus after the murder of Julius Caefar, having on one fide his own head, and on

Historical and traditional types.

the other a cap of Liberty between two daggers, and the infcription EID. MAR.

DENARIUS OF BRUTUS.

Brutus had already, when a monetary triumvir, recorded the famous deed of his anceftor L. Junius Brutus, the banifher of the Tarquins, by placing his head upon the coins. To the fame clafs belong the coins of Sextus Pompeius, who for a time defied the efforts of Octavius to fupprefs his piratical excurfions. Thefe have on one fide the pharos of Meffana furmounted by a figure of Neptune, and on the other the monfter Scylla, half-dog, half-fifh, fweeping the fea with her rudder. They refer either to the defeat of Octavius at Meffana in B.C. 38, or to the deftruction of his fleet off the Lucanian promontory in the following year, on which occafion Pompeius offered facrifices to Neptune for his timely affiftance, and even ftyled himfelf the fon of Neptune. Of the traditional types, perhaps one of the moft interefting is that on a coin of the Poftumia gens, with the buft of Diana on the obverfe, and on the reverfe a rock on which is a togated male figure before a lighted altar extending his hand towards a bull. It illuftrates the worfhip of that goddefs at Rome, to whom, for the ufe of the inhabitants of Latium, then under Roman rule, Servius Tullius founded a temple on the Aventine. At their annual feſtival the augurs foretold the domination of Rome over all the Latin race, which was accompliſhed by Aulus Poſtumius at the battle of Lake Regillus B.C. 496. In conſequence of this victory, the Poſtumia gens claimed for itſelf the fulfilment of the prophecy. On a coin of the Marcia gens are the heads of Numa Pompilius and Ancus Marcius, and a naked warrior (*deſultor*) riding two horſes; theſe allude to the traditional deſcent of the Marcia gens from Mamerces, ſon of Numa, and the celebration of the games in honour of Apollo, which were inſtituted by the ſoothſayer Marcius. We have alſo ſuch legendary ſubjects as Tarpeia cruſhed beneath the bucklers, Aeneas carrying Anchiſes on his back and holding the Palladium, Ulyſſes returning from Troy and recogniſed by his dog, and the rape of the Sabines. Still more numerous are the ſimple repreſentations of the divinities of the Roman Pantheon.

The gold coins of Sulla and ſubſequent iſſues have types ſimilar to thoſe of the denarius. The copper coins of the reduced ſtandard preſerved their original types.

Moneyers' Marks and Names. An important feature in the gradual development of the types is the moneyers' marks and names, which serve to indicate the ſucceſſive iſſues from the mint. At firſt this mint officer only placed a ſymbol, a fly, cap, ſpear, or prow, to diſtinguiſh his iſſue from thoſe of previous years. Later on he added his initial, then his name, firſt in monogram

Moneyers' Marks and Names. 55

and finally in full, the prenomen on the reverfe, and the cognomen on the obverfe. Thefe infcriptions are always in the nominative cafe. They cease about B.C. 36, when, after the defeat of Sextus Pompeius, and the fubmiffion of the triumvir Lepidus, amongft the many honours which Octavius received from the Senate, not the leaft was the commemoration of his victories in the types on the coins. To thefe was added his portrait, and from B.C. 29, when he was created Imperator, the coinage becomes imperial.

The right of iffuing the coinage at Rome, as elfewhere in all Republics, belonged to the State, which fixed by decrees the ftandard and the various denominations. At an early period the duty of carrying into execution thefe regulations was delegated to three officers, who were called the *tresviri auro, argento, aere, flando, feriundo.* The word *flando* may fhow that thefe officers were nominated before the reduction of the as to the sextantal ftandard. The office certainly exifted before the adoption of the uncial as in B.C. 217, as we begin to meet with the initials and monograms of the moneyers before that change took place. It was an occafional office at firft, and appears only to have been filled up when frefh iffues were needed for the ufe of the State. About B.C. 104, the more frequent occurrence of the moneyers' names fhows that thefe officers were then appointed at clofer intervals. Julius Caefar increafed the number of this magiftracy to four, and thefe continued to be nominated annually till the dif-

_{Conftitution of the Mint, Officers, etc.}

fenfions caufed by the fecond triumvirate. In B.C. 39 the office was quite fufpended, and does not appear to have been reinftituted till B.C. 16, when Auguftus, before his departure for Gaul, re-appointed the quatuorviri. The office was abolifhed about the year B.C. 3, and the Roman coinage then entered on a new phafe. According to law, each officer of the mint was independent of the other, and could iffue his coins feparately or in conjunction with his colleagues. Thefe monetarii were not the only magiftrates who could ftrike money. The urban quaeftors, ediles, and praetors were fometimes charged with extraordinary commiffions; but thefe cafes were exceptional, and generally in virtue of fome unufual expenditure. Such pieces were marked with a fpecial formula, as Ex. S. C. (*Ex Senatus Confulto*), or S. C. (*Senatus Confulto*), formulas never ufed by the regularly appointed monetarii. The curule ediles were alfo occafionally allwed to ftrike coins to cover the expenfes of the great public games.

Local Mints and Iffues. Befides the coins iffued in Rome, there were others ftruck outfide the city. Thefe may be divided into two claffes: the coinage of the neighbouring cities, and the *monetae caftrenfes* or *nummi caftrenfes*. It is evident from monograms and letters on certain pieces of rude fabric that a few cities, after they came under Roman jurisdiction, were allowed to retain the right of coinage. Amongft thefe places were Luceria, Canufium, Crotona, and Hatria. Thefe coins were of the same standard as those struck at Rome. This privilege appears to have ceased during the second Punic War, or shortly afterwards. The monetae castrenses or nummi castrenses are coins issued by the general for payment of his soldiers, whether as dictator, consul, proconsul, or imperator. This right could be delegated by the commander to his quaestor or proquaestor, who usually added his own name, and in some instances placed it alone, without that of his superior officer. These coins circulated throughout the Republic with the State coinage, although the authority of the Senate was not usually inscribed on them. Finds in Spain, Cisalpine Gaul, and elsewhere, show that the nummi castrenses were struck as early as the middle of the second century B.C.; but their issue was suspended for a time after the outbreak of the Social War. They are again found in large quantities from the time of the Civil War between Pompey and Caesar till the death of Mark Antony. They may be classed under the following districts: Sicily, Spain, Africa, Gaul, the East, which includes Greece and Asia Minor, and Cyrenaica.

To the coins issued *extra muros* belong those struck by the revolted Italian States during the Social or Marsic War. These are of the denarii class, and many bear the same types as the State coinage of the time, but they are of rude fabric. The greater portion have the inscriptions in the Oscan character, and bear the names of the leaders, Papius Mutilus, Pompaedius, Minius Jegius, and Numerius Cluen-

<small>Oscan Coins.</small>

tius. Others, fimply infcribed ITALIA, are eafily recognifable as belonging to this clafs.

Claffification.

The coins of the Roman Republic may be claffified in two ways, (1) by families, under the name of the gens to which the monetarius belonged, or (2) chronologically. In large collections for facility of reference, the arrangement under families is perhaps the more practicable, but by this fyftem the hiftorical intereft of the coinage is almoft entirely loft. There are a large number of pieces which have no moneyer's name, others with only a fymbol, a letter, or a monogram. In the arrangement by families, many of thefe coins would find no diftinct place. By a chronological arrangement, each coin has its place, and we are able not only to trace the fequence of the coinage, and fee how the types gradually developed, but alfo to follow the extenfion of Roman domination, as it fpread throughout Italy to the Weft, to the Eaft, and onwards into Afia, and acrofs the Mediterranean into Africa. The large feries of coins of Julius Caefar, Pompey, Brutus, Caffius, and the triumvirate, would teach us very little if arranged under the Julia, Pompeia, Junia, Caffia, Antonia, and Aemilia gentes. For affiftance in a chronological arrangement, we have the evidence afforded by the growth of the types, by hiftory, and by the various finds. To this ftudy Mommfen has given much attention, and the refults of his labours are embodied in his learned work on the Roman coinage.[1] But more can be accomplifhed than

[1] *Gefchichte des Römifchen Münzwefens.*

even Mommsen has done as regards a local classification, and this was done by the late Count de Salis, who arranged the Roman coins in the British Museum, both republican and imperial, in chronological and geographical order.

When Augustus in B.C. 3 abolished the office of the monetarii, he reserved to himself all rights connected with the gold and silver coinages, and these remained with all succeeding emperors. To the Senate, however, belonged the power of striking the copper money, and its authority was denoted by the letters S. C. (*Senatus Consulto*), which also served to distinguish the copper coins of Rome from those issued in the provinces.

Imperial Coinage.

The coinage in circulation in Rome from that time was—in gold, the aureus, of forty to the pound, and the half-aureus; in silver, the denarius, of eighty-four to the pound, and its half, the quinarius; and in copper, the sestertius, of four asses, its half the dupondius, the as, the semis or half-as, the triens or one-third-as, and the quadrans or quarter-as. The aureus was worth twenty-five denarii, and the denarius sixteen asses. The as was nearly equal in weight and size to the dupondius, but it was distinguished by being of red copper; whilst the sestertius and the dupondius were of yellow brass or *orichalcum*, being a composition of copper and zinc. The earliest deteriorations in the Imperial coinage took place in the reigns of Nero and Caracalla; and in A.D. 215 the aureus was only the fiftieth of a pound, and the denarius became so debased that it contained

Argenteus. only 40 per cent. of pure silver. When Caracalla had thus corrupted the coinage, he introduced a new silver piece, called the *argenteus Antoninianus*, of sixty to sixty-four to the pound, which was worth a denarius and a half, and which soon became the principal coin of the Empire. This piece may be easily distinguished from the denarius by its having the head of the emperor radiate and the bust of the empress upon a crescent or half-moon.

From the reign of Caracalla to that of Diocletian the greatest disorder prevailed in the coinage, and the period of the so-called Thirty Tyrants was one of complete bankruptcy to the State. Each Emperor debased the coinage more and more, so that the intrinsic value of the silver currency was not one-twentieth part of its nominal value. The argenteus supplanted the denarius, and after a short time, from a silver coin became only a copper one washed with a little tin; and, having driven the copper money out of currency, became itself the only piece in circulation with the exception of the gold. Diocletian, in A.D. 296, put an end to this confusion by withdrawing from circulation all the coinage, and issuing another entirely fresh one, based on the standard of the currency of the first

Diocletian's Reforms. century A.D. The aureus was struck at sixty to the pound, and a new coin in silver, called the *cententionalis*, took the place of the denarius; whilst in copper two new pieces were issued, called the follis and the denarius. Special interest is attached to this new coinage, as it affords the means of explaining the prices marked in the great tariff of the Roman Empire which was publifhed in A.D. 301, and which fixed the "maximum" price of almoft every article of food or produce that found its way into the market. It was the abrogation of this tariff which occafioned a flight modification in the monetary fyftem during the reign of Conftantine, who reduced the weight of the aureus to feventy-two to the pound, and gave to this new coin the name of *folidus* in Latin and *nomifma* in Greek. This piece remained in circulation fo long as the Empire lafted, maintaining its full weight; and when current at a later period in Weftern Europe, it received the name of bezant or byzant. Conftantine added two frefh filver coins to the currency, the *miliarenfis*, and its half, the *filiqua*, twelve of the former being equal in value to the folidus. Except fome flight modifications in the copper money made by Anaftafius and by Bafil I., no further important changes remain to be mentioned.

<small>The Solidus.</small>

The obverfe of the Imperial coinage had for its type the head or buft of the Emperor, the Emprefs, or the Caefar, and occafionally that of a near relative, fuch as the Emperor's mother or fifter. The type varied with the period. In Pagan times the head or buft was laureate, *i.e.* bound with a wreath, or radiate, *i.e.* wearing a radiated crown, fometimes bare, but rarely helmeted; in the Chriftian and Byzantine period it is ufually adorned with a diadem or a crefted helmet. The portraits, too, may be divided into two claffes,

<small>Imperial Types.</small>

realistic and conventional. The early Caesars, and their successors to Gallienus, fall under the first class, and the remaining Emperors, including the Christian and Byzantine, under the second. The types of the reverse are commonly mythological (divinities), allegorical (personifications), historical (events connected with the history and traditions of Rome), and architectural (the principal public

SESTERTIUS OF VESPASIAN.

buildings, especially those at Rome). On the coins of Vespasian and Titus is recorded the conquest of Judaea, figured as a woman seated weeping beneath a palm-tree, near which stands her conqueror, or else the ferocious Simon, who headed the revolt and only survived to adorn the triumph of his enemies. On the large brass of Titus is to be seen a representation of the Flavian Amphitheatre, begun by his father and completed by himself, standing between the Meta Sudans and the Domus Aurea, with its many storeys or arcades, and its vast interior filled with spectators witnessing the magnificent dedication festival of a hundred days. The coins of Trajan record his conquest of Dacia, Armenia, Mesopotamia, and his descent down the Euphrates and the Tigris to the Indian Ocean, the only Roman general who accomplished this feat. There are representations of the Forum, the most memorable of all Trajan's works; the Circus Maximus, which he embellished with the obelisk of Augustus; and the Aqua Trajana, by which he turned a portion of the pure and limpid Aqua Martia into the Aventine quarter of the city. The coins of Hadrian, besides bearing allegorical representations of divinities, countries, and cities, are of special interest as illustrating his extensive journeys into every Roman province, from Britain to the far East.

Such is the succession of types till the reign of Gallienus, when their interest flags, and for the most part we meet with badly executed representations of mythological personages.

The coins of the Christian Emperors differ much in their character. At first the types are generally allegorical; and though free from Pagan intention are not without Pagan influence, as may be seen in the types of Victory inscribing the Emperor's *vota* on a shield, or two Victories holding a wreath, or the seated figures of Rome and Constantinople. Though the coins of Constantine the Great are of a somewhat Christian character, yet purely Christian types are at first unusual. After a while, however, Victory no longer holds a wreath, but stands grasping a cross, and in place of representations of some mythological personage we find the monogram of Christ formed of X and P. In the purely Byzantine period all the Pagan

Christian Types.

influence difappears, and Chriftian types prevail, the moft common being that of the Holy Crofs raifed high on fteps.

Iconographic Types. The coins of the later Emperors of the Eaft are fpecially interefting for their iconographic types. Reprefentations of a large number of facred figures are to be found upon them, and thefe reprefentations are far fuperior in execution, and, therefore, of much greater value for the ftudy of Chriftian iconography than any to be found on the mediaeval coins of Weftern Europe. The figures of Chrift and the Virgin offer a variety of different attitudes. The former is moft frequently feated, holding in one hand the gofpels and with the other giving the Greek benediction. The Virgin is frequently feated; fometimes fhe holds in her arms the infant Saviour, fometimes fhe crowns the Emperor who ftands befide her, often with both hands raifed in the attitude of prayer. In one very interefting type fhe ftands amidft the walls of Conftantinople. A number of Saints are alfo reprefented, among which may be cited St. George, St. Michael, St. Demetrius, St. Theodore, and (St.) Conftantine the Great; alfo in one famous inftance we fee depicted the worfhip of the Magi.

Infcriptions. The infcriptions on the coins of the Pagan emperors are either defcriptive, giving the Emperor's name and the date, partly on the obverfe, and partly on the reverfe; or elfe they are of a dedicatory nature, adding to the name of the Emperor a reference to the type. From Titus to Severus Alexander the chronological character of the inscription is maintained, giving the current consulship of the Emperor, or his laſt conſulſhip, and the year of his tribuneſhip; but in the latter half of the third century we meet with the Emperor's name alone on the obverſe, and a dedicatory inſcription on the reverſe. Very little change occurs under the early Chriſtian Emperors, except that the legend on the reverſe loſes its mythological character, and it is ſome time before the gradual transformation of the Roman State into the Eaſtern Empire is traceable in the coinage. Anaſtaſius was the firſt who uſed Greek letters to indicate the value of the coins; yet although under Juſtinian I. the Greek language was much uſed by the people, it is not till the reign of Heraclius that the Greek legend EN TOYTΩ NIKA is found upon the coins. In the eighth century the Greek titles of *Baſileus* and *Deſpotes* make their firſt appearance in the place of *Auguſtus*, and under the Baſilian dynaſty Greek inſcriptions occupy the field of the reverſe of both ſilver and copper coins; but the reverſe of the ſolidus retains its Latin form till the latter part of the eleventh century, when it is found for the laſt time on the coins of Michael VII., A.D. 1078. Alexius I. was the firſt Emperor who adopted entirely Greek legends for his coins, and after his acceſſion Latin never appears again on the coinage of the Roman Empire, which now loſes all trace of its Weſtern origin, and becomes purely Byzantine. The moſt remarkable change in the coinage of the late Byzantine period was the introduction of concave pieces, *scyphati nummi*. This form was introduced as early as the close of the tenth century, but did not become the prevailing type of the gold, silver, and copper coinages till the end of the eleventh.

Local Mints.

When the Roman Empire came under the sway of Augustus, the Roman monetary system was imposed as the official standard in financial business throughout the Empire, and no mint was allowed to exist without the imperial licence. This permission was, however, conceded to many Greek cities, which for the most part struck only copper coins; a few issued silver, but the only local mint of which gold coins are known is that of Caesarea in Cappadocia. These coins are usually designated Greek Imperial.[1] Pure silver coins do not appear to have been issued to any great extent; and, if we except the large silver pieces struck in the provinces of Asia, and usually called medallions, the local currencies in this metal may be said to have ended with the reign of Nero, when the abundance of copper money placed the silver at a premium, and gradually drove it out of circulation.

The copper coinage of the Provinces had for the type of the obverse the head of the Emperor, etc., and for the reverse some mythological or historical subject: the inscriptions were always in Greek. In the second century the issues of this copper money increased very rapidly; but as the Roman denarius became more and more debased, and the local mints could no longer make a profit by issuing coins on any local standard, one city after

---

[1] See Chapter II., page 40.

the other gradually ceased to exercise the right of coining, and by the end of the reign of Gallienus almost the only provincial mint of importance remaining was that of Alexandria, which continued to issue its coins till the reign of Diocletian. This mint was able to hold out longer than the others, because it adopted the same tactics as the imperial mint at Rome: as the denarius became more and more debased, Alexandria, to keep pace, lowered the standard of all her coins, and the silver became potin, and the potin, copper. Alexandrian Coinage.

Apart from these mints there existed from time to time others, which issued gold and silver coins after the Roman types and standard. It is probable that these coins were of the same nature as the *nummi castrenses* of the time of the Republic, their issue being superintended by the military or civil governors of the provinces. One of these mints was established at Antioch in the time of Vespasian and continued through the succeeding reigns to Gallienus. Its coins, the aureus and denarius, are of a peculiarly rude fabric. The denarius was also struck at Ephesus during the reigns of Vespasian and Domitian. In the western part of the Empire Spain struck coins of the Roman standard and types in considerable numbers from the reign of Augustus to that of Titus, and in Gaul we find a large number of aurei issued during the same period. The coinages of Clodius Macer in Africa, of Clodius Albinus in Gaul, of Pacatianus, Regalianus, and Dryantilla at Siscia, and similar issues, must be considered as exceptional and as having no legitimate authorisation.

When the base silver State coinage had driven the Greek Imperial copper coins out of circulation, Gallienus established local mints throughout the whole Empire, which struck money after the Roman types and standard. The number of these mints was further increased by Diocletian, and they continued to exercise their rights till the extinction of the Roman rule in the West and afterwards in the East. At first there was no indication on the coin that it was struck out of Rome; but Diocletian placed on all the coins, both of Rome and elsewhere, a monogram or initial letter of the city whence they were issued.

Medallions and Tickets.

Besides coins proper, there are certain pieces in metal which resemble money in appearance, but which were never meant to pass as currency. These are the medallions, which correspond to medals of the present time, and the tickets, which served as passes to the public entertainments, etc.

The types of the medallions resemble those of the copper sestertius, having on one side the portrait of an imperial personage, and on the other some mythological, dedicatory, historical, or architectural subject, which more often than in the case of the coinage has some special reference to the imperial family. The size of the medallion is usually somewhat larger than that of the sestertius, and it is easily distinguished from the coins by the absence of the letters s.c., by its finer workmanship, and by being in high relief. These pieces were struck in gold, silver, and especially copper. The silver and copper medallions were apparently first issued in the reign of Domitian; but the first gold specimen extant is of the reign of Diocletian, after whose time gold and silver medallions are more general than those of copper. The finest pieces were issued by Antoninus Pius, Marcus Aurelius, and Commodus; but the quality of the work was fairly maintained at a later period, when the coinage had much deteriorated in style and character. Even during the reigns of Constantine the Great and his successors, the execution of the medallions is throughout much superior to that of the current coins. It is probable that these pieces were all struck as honorary rewards or memorials, and were presented by the Emperor to his troops or to those about the court. It has been supposed that they were intended to be placed on the standards, because some are provided with deep outer rims, but this seems doubtful, as in all representations of standards on the column of Trajan and other buildings it may be seen that the medallions, with which they are adorned, have the bust of the Emperor facing, whereas on existing pieces it is always in profile.

Of the tickets the most important are the *contorniates*, so called because they have the edge slightly turned over. These pieces are of copper, of the size of the sestertius, but somewhat thinner, and they have for types on one side some mythological, agonistic, or historical subject, relating to the public games or to the contests which took place for the honours of the amphitheatre, the circus, the stadium, or the odeum; and on the other side, a head or bust, imperial or regal, or of some philosopher, author, or poet. The question of the object of these pieces, and the time when they were struck, has provoked much discussion, but these two points seem now to have been fairly settled. It appears that they were made for presentation to the victors at the public games and contests, who used them as a kind of check, on the presentation of which at some appointed place and time they were awarded the allotted prizes; and, judging from the fabric, their issue appears to have begun in the reign of Constantine the Great, and to have been continued to about that of Anthemius, A.D. 464-472, that is, for a space of about 150 years.

Medallic Art.

In the massive and rude forms of the early coinage of Rome, bold in relief, and not without some knowledge of the laws of perspective, we see illustrated the stern, hard character of the Roman, whose entire attention was given either to universal conquest abroad or to agricultural pursuits at home. Art to him possessed no charm; he was devoid of elegance and taste, and even the nobles prided themselves on their natural deficiency in matters of art, which they considered unworthy of a warlike and free people. This feeling, at the end of the second century B.C., became somewhat softened by the presence in Rome of the vast spoils of Greece, consisting chiefly of statues and paintings; and if the people still despised the practical cultivation of the arts, they were in general delighted with the beauty, or perhaps the novelty, of thefe acquifitions. This increafing tafte for art may be traced in the types of the coins, which during the Republic acquire a pictorial character. If compared artiftically with the earlier period, this may be called progreffive.

With the Auguftan age came a vifible change, and Greek artifts were encouraged to visit Rome, not only to adorn the temples of the gods, but alfo to embellifh the villas of the rich, into many of which numerous original works from Greece, Afia, and Egypt had already found their way. As the tafte increafed, and it was impoffible to furnifh all with original Greek works, there arofe a great demand for copies of the moft famous and beft-known objects. Inftances of thefe copies may be feen in the Britifh Mufeum in fuch works as the Difcobolus, which is fuppofed to be taken from a bronze figure by Myron; the Townley Venus, which, if not a work of the Macedonian period, may be a copy of one; and the Apollo Citharoedus, probably adapted from fome celebrated original, fince two other nearly fimilar figures exift. Though we cannot claim much originality for the Roman artifts at this period, they are not mere fervile copyifts; by a frequent modification of the original defign they give a ftamp of individuality to their works. What has been faid of fculpture applies alike to medallic art, and the effect of this Greek influence is very marked on the coins of the Auguftan age, and efpecially on thofe of the two Agrippinas, Caligula, and Claudius. The mythological figures which we meet with on thefe coins often ftrike us very forcibly as copies of Greek ftatues. Jupiter feated holding his thunderbolt and fceptre; Minerva leaning on her fpear and fhield ornamented with the ferpent; Spes tripping lightly

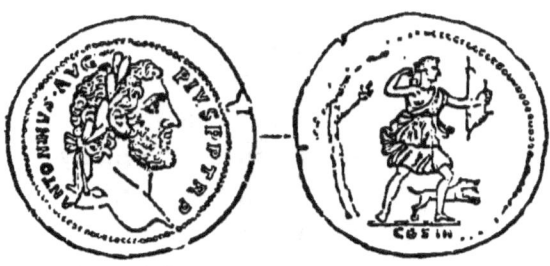

MEDALLION OF ANTONINUS PIUS.

forward, holding a flower and gently raifing her drefs; and Diana rufhing onward in the chafe, her bow in her outftretched hand, and her hound at her heels—are all reprefentations of Greek fubjects. The coins of Nero fhow the perfection which portraiture had attained, the growth of his paffions being traceable in the increafing brutality of his features; whilft the coinages of Trajan, Hadrian, Antoninus Pius, and Aurelius difplay the higheft ftate of Roman medallic art. With the decay of the Empire comes an immediate decline in the workmanfhip of the coinage; from Commodus to Diocletian it was one continued downward courfe. The coins of the early Chriftian Emperors fhow a flight artiftic revival, and when, in later times, the artifts of the Weft poured into Conftantinople, carrying with them all that remained of artiftic life in the ancient world, they imported into the coinage that ftyle of ornament fo peculiarly Byzantine, the traces of which are ftill to be feen in the architecture of the Greek Church both in Europe and Afia.

CHAPTER IV.

THE COINAGE OF CHRISTIAN EUROPE.

NDER this title is included the coinage of all that portion of Europe which was not fubject to the rule of Mohammedan princes, from the fall of the Weftern Empire to our own day. When we confider what vaft fields of fpace and time are covered by this branch of numifmatics, it will be feen to be too large a fubject to be fully dealt with in a fingle chapter. The difficulty is found to be increafed when we take into account how many different interefts the ftudy touches. The mere economift, the hiftorian, the ftudent of the hiftory of art, and the ftudent of Chriftian iconography, might each expect to have his enquiries anfwered were there an entire volume at our difpofal. The only circumftance which makes it poffible to deal with the fubject briefly as a whole is the fortunate tendency which in all ages the different countries of Europe have fhown to bring their coinage into fome fort of common conformity.

Of this tendency we have plenty of examples in our own day, as, for inſtance, the practical uniformity which by the "Monetary Convention of the Latin Nations" was eſtabliſhed in the coinages of Belgium, France, Switzerland, and Italy; in the recently-eſtabliſhed uniformity of coinage throughout the German Empire; and in the inclination which the eſtabliſhers of this coinage have ſhown to model their currency upon that of England. The ſame kind of tendency among contemporary nations is to be detected throughout the numiſmatics of the Middle Ages, and in truth by no means diminiſhes in force the further we retreat toward the beginnings of mediaeval hiſtory; a fact which will ſeem ſtrange to thoſe who are accuſtomed to look upon the Europe of theſe days as a mere collection of heterogeneous atoms, and its hiſtory as nothing better than a "ſcuffling of kites and crows."

It is thus poſſible in ſome degree to ſtudy the numiſmatics of the Middle Ages, and of more modern times, as a whole; and in a very rough way to divide its hiſtory into certain periods, in each of which the moſt ſtriking characteriſtics numiſmatically and the moſt important events can be pointed out, without any attempt to follow in detail the hiſtory of the currency in each land. When in a ſubſequent chapter we come to ſpeak of the Engliſh coinage, a more minute treatment of that ſpecial branch will be poſſible. *Division of the Subject.*

The periods into which I propoſe to divide the numiſmatic hiſtory of Chriſtian Europe are theſe:

PERIOD I. Transition between the Roman and the true mediaeval: let us say, from the deposition of Romulus Augustulus (A.D. 476) to the accession of Charlemagne (A.D. 768).

PERIOD II. From the rise of the new currency which was inaugurated by the house of Heristal, and which attained its full extension under Charles the Great, for all the time during which this currency formed practically the sole coinage of Western Europe.

PERIOD III. From the re-introduction of a gold coinage into Western Europe, which we may date from the striking of the *Fiorino d'oro* in Florence, in 1252, to the full development of Renaissance Art upon coins, about 1450.

PERIOD IV. From this year, 1450, to the end of the Renaissance Era, in 1600.

PERIOD V. That of modern coinage, from A.D. 1600 to our own day.

Special Points of Interest belonging to each Period.

This division of our subject may serve at once to give the student some general notion of the sort of interest which pre-eminently attaches to the numismatics of each period. If he is concerned with the earliest history of the Teutonic invaders of Roman territory, with what may almost be called the *prehistoric* age of mediaeval history, he will be disposed to collect the coins which belong to our first division. The coins of the second period are of great value for the study of the true Middle Ages, not only as illustrations of that history, but for the light which they shed upon the mutual relations of the different nations of

Christendom, upon the economical history of this age, and lastly upon the iconography of this, the dominant, era of mediaeval Catholicism. The coinage of the third period illustrates, among other things, the rise in wealth and importance of the Italian cities, the greater consideration which from this time forward began to attach to the pursuits of wealth and commerce, and a consequent growth of art and of intellectual culture. The coins of the fourth period, beside their deep historical interest for the portraits which they give us of the reigning sovereigns or rulers, are pre-eminent in beauty above those of any other of the five periods, and alone in any way comparable with the money of Ancient Greece. Finally, the fifth period will be most attractive to those whose historical studies have lain altogether in the age to which it belongs.

It is generally found that a monetary change follows some time after a great political revolution. People cannot immediately forego the coinage they are used to, and even when this has no longer a *raison d'être*, it is still continued, or is imitated as nearly as possible. Thus, though from the beginning of the fifth century (A.D. 405) a steady stream of barbarian invasion set into the Roman Empire, from the Visigoths in the south and from the Suevi and Burgundians and their allies in the north (in Gaul), no immediate change in the coinage was the result. The money of the Roman Empire in the West and in the East circulated among these barbarians, and was imitated as closely as possible by them. The new-comers

PERIOD I.
From Augustulus to Charlemagne.

did not even venture to place their names upon the money; but the names of their Kings were sometimes suggested by obscure monograms. The first coin which bears the name of any Teutonic conqueror is a small silver coin which shows the name of Odoacer (A.D. 476-490), and this piece is of great rarity. The Ostrogothic Kings in Italy, after the accession of Athalaric to the end of their rule (A.D. 526-553), and the Vandal Kings in Africa subsequent to Huneric (*i.e.* from A.D. 484-533), placed their names upon coins, but only upon those of the inferior metals. The full rights of a coinage can scarcely be claimed until the sovereign has ventured to issue coins in the highest denomination in use in his territory. These full rights, therefore, belonged, among the people of the Transition Era, only to three of the conquering Teutonic nationalities: (1) to the Visigoths in Spain, (2) to the Franks in Gaul, and (3) to the Lombards in Italy.

The Visigothic coinage begins with Leovigild in 573, and ends with the fall of the Visigothic kingdom before the victorious Arabs at the battle of Guadaleta in 711. The coins are extremely rude, showing (generally) a bust upon one side, on the other either another bust or some form of cross. Three main types run throughout the series, which consists almost exclusively of a coinage in gold.

The Frankish coinage is likewise almost exclusively a gold currency. It begins with Theodebert, the Austrasian (A.D. 534), and, with unimportant

I.—Augustulus to Charlemagne. 79

intervals, continues till the accession of the house of Pepin. At first the pieces were of the size of the Roman *solidus* (*solidus aureus*), but in latter years more generally of the size of the *tremissis*. Below is a specimen of a Frankish tremissis, struck by Chlovis II. (A.D. 638-656), and with the name of his treasurer, St. Eloi. It is noticeable that in this series only a few pieces bear the names of the monarchs, while the rest have simply the names of the towns and the moneyers by whom they were struck.

COIN OF CHLOVIS II.

The Lombardic coinage of North Italy—of the Kings of Milan and Pavia—begins with Cunipert (A.D. 687), and ends with the defeat of Desiderius by Charlemagne, 774, in which year the Frankish king assumed the crown of Lombardy. The coinage is generally of gold, and of the type of

_{Coins of the Lombards.}

COIN OF CUNIPERT (680—702).

the coin of Cunipert represented in the figure, showing on one side the bust of the King (imitated from the Roman money), and on the reverse the figure of St. Michael, legend scs MIHAHIL. This

80   *II.—True Mediaeval Period.*

faint was, we know, especially honoured by the Lombards.¹ Another Lombardic coinage was that of the Dukes of Beneventum, who struck pieces upon the model of the money of the Eastern Emperors.

The figure below represents the earliest papal coin, that struck by Pope Adrian I. after the defeat of Desiderius in A.D. 774.

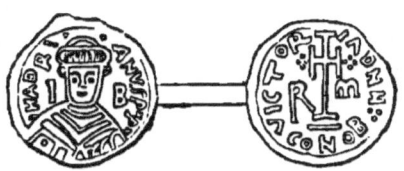

COIN OF POPE ADRIAN I. (772—795).

PERIOD II.
True Mediaeval Period.

The second age is the true Middle Age, or what is sometimes called the Dark Age; for with the beginning of our third period, which it will be seen is nearly that of the last crusade, the first dawn of the Renaissance is discernible. It follows that in the scarcity of printed monuments of this age, the coinage of the period is one deserving of a very attentive study, and of a much more detailed treatment than I am able to bestow upon it.

The coinage inaugurated by the house of Pepin has the peculiarity of being totally unlike any currency which preceded it. The three chief autonomous barbarian coinages which we have enumerated above consisted almost exclusively of gold money; the coinage inaugurated by the

¹ Paul. Diac., *Hist. Lang.*, iv. 47; v. 3, 41.

Carlovingian dynasty was almost exclusively of silver. Silver from this time forth, until the end of our second period, remained the sole regular medium of exchange; a gold coinage disappeared from Western Europe, and was only represented by such pieces as were imported thither from the east and the south. Such gold coins as were in use were the bezants or *byzantii*, *i.e.*, the gold coins of the Roman Emperors of Constantinople, and (much less frequently) the *maravedis*, or gold coins struck in Spain by the Moorish dynasty of Al-Moravides (El-Murábitín). When Charles extended his Empire to its greatest limits, he introduced almost everywhere in Europe the new silver coinage, which was known as the new denier (*novus denarius*), or possibly in German as *pfenning*.[1] This denarius was the first coinage of Germany. In Italy it generally superseded the Roman denarius, or the coinage of the Lombards.

The usual type of this *New Denarius* was at first (1) simply the name or monogram of the Emperor, and on the reverse the name of the mint or a plain cross; (2) the bust of the Emperor, with a cross on the reverse; or (3) the bust of the Emperor on the obverse, and on the reverse a temple inscribed with the motto XPISTIANA RELIGIO. The pieces engraved on the next page, probably of Charles the Bald, are good examples of the earliest

New Denarius.

---

[1] Our word *penny* (orig. *pending*, *pening*) is equivalent to the Old High German *Phantine*, whence *Pfenning*, *Pfennig*, and is derived from the Anglo-Saxon *pand* (German *Pfand*), a pledge. So Sanders and Skeat; but F. Kluge (*Etym. Wörterb.*, 1883) speaks doubtfully concerning the derivation of Pfennig.

types of denarii. One of the first documents referring to this coin is a capitulary of Pepin the Short (755), making its use compulsory in his dominions. In imitation of the new denarius, the *penny* was introduced into England by Offa, King of Mercia (757-794). The only exceptions to the general use of this denarius in Western Europe were afforded by those towns or princes in Italy which imitated the money of the Byzantine Empire.

CARLOVINGIAN DENARII.

This was the case with some of the earlier Popes, as is shown by the coin of Adrian I., represented on p. 80, which is quite Byzantine in type. Venice, which at first struck denarii of the Carlovingian pattern, after a short time changed this currency for one closely modelled upon the Byzantine pattern, while other neighbouring cities followed her example.

Mediaeval Coins of France. After the accession of the race of Capet to the throne in France, the denarii continued little changed; and not only in the districts over which ruled the early kings of this dynasty, but over the greater part of what is now France. The number of feudal divisions into which the country was split up is shown by the numerous princes' names which appear upon the currency, but they did not cause much variety in the type of the money. The types continued to be various combinations of (1) an inscription over all the face of the coin; (2) a rude bust, sometimes so degraded as to be barely distinguishable; (3) the conventional equal-limbed cross; (4) a changed form of the temple, made to take the appearance of a Gothic arch between two towers. This type in its most altered shape has been sometimes taken for the ground-plan of the fortifications of Tours.

In Germany, the Carlovingian Emperors were succeeded by the Saxon dynasty, which in its turn gave place to that of Franconia. During all this period (A.D. 919–1125), the denarius continued the chief, and almost the sole, coin in use in Germany. Here, however, the variety of types was much greater, though most of these varieties may be shown to have sprung out of the old Carlovingian types. The right of coinage was at this time even more widely extended in Germany than in France; but in the former country the nominal supremacy of the Emperor was generally —though far from universally—acknowledged, and his name was placed upon the coinage. *Of Germany.*

In Italy, most of the towns which possessed the right of a coinage derived it directly from the *Of Italy.*

Emperor: thus Genoa obtained this right from Conrad III.; Venice (at firſt), Piſa, Pavia, Lucca, Milan, are among the cities which ſtruck coins bearing the names of the early German Emperors.

<small>Pfaffen-Pfennige or Bracteates.</small>
The firſt change which took place in the coinage of this our ſecond period aroſe in Germany from the degradation of the currency. This reached ſuch a pitch (eſpecially in the eccleſiaſtical mints) that the ſilver denarius, of which the proper weight was about 24 Engliſh grains, was firſt reduced to a ſmall piece not more than one-third of that weight, and next to a piece ſo thin that it could only be ſtamped upon one ſide. This new money, for ſuch it was in fact, though not in name, aroſe about the time that the dynaſty of Hohenſtaufen obtained the imperial crown, that is to ſay, in the middle of the twelfth century. The pieces were called ſubſequently *Pfaffen-Pfennige* (parſon's pennies), becauſe they were chiefly ſtruck at eccleſiaſtical mints; they are now known to numiſmatiſts as *bracteates*.

Beſide the coinages of France, Germany, Italy, and England, we have alſo briefly to notice thoſe of Scandinavia and of Spain, both of which were inaugurated during the ſecond age of mediaeval numiſmatics.

<small>Arabic Currency in the North.</small>
It is a curious fact that in the north, during the ninth and tenth centuries, we find that a large number of the contemporary Arabic ſilver coins (*dirhems*) were current. It ſeems at firſt ſight extraordinary that they ſhould have travelled ſo far, but leſs ſtrange when we bear in mind the extenſive

Viking expeditions which took place during the fame period. As has been well faid by a recent writer,[1] the Vikings gave a fort of reality to the popular notion that Chriftian Europe was an ifland; for, ftarting on one fide to the weft, they crept down all that coaft of the continent until they reached the Straits of Gibraltar, and thence made their way into the Mediterranean, while on the other fide, mounting the rivers which emptied themfelves into the Baltic—the Viftula or the Dvina—with but a few miles of land-carriage they brought their boats to the Dnieper, and by that route upon the eaftern fide ftole down into the fame Mediterranean. It was in this way that the Vikings came in contact with the Arab merchants, and carried Arab money to the far North. It happened that this filver coin, the dirhem, was in weight juft double that of the denarius current in Europe. Carlovingian denarii, Englifh pennies, and Arab dirhems were alike hoarded by the Norfe pirates. It was not till the end of the tenth century that the Danes and Scandinavians began to make numerous imitations of the contemporary coinage of England. On the acceffion of Canute the Great to the Englifh throne, A.D. 1016, a native currency obtained a firm footing in Denmark.

Between the battle of Guadaleta (A.D. 711) and the union of the crowns of Caftile and Aragon (A.D. 1479), the Chriftian coinage of Spain was reprefented by the coins of thefe two kingdoms, Spain.

---

[1] Steenftrup: *Normannerne*, page 1.

the rest of the peninsula being in the hands of the Arabs or Moors. The coinage of Castile begins with Alfonso VI. (1073-1109); that of Aragon with Sancho Ramirez of Navarre (1063-1094). The money of these countries is a denarius of the same general module as the contemporary denarii of France. The usual types of these coins, as of all the contemporary coinage of Europe, consist of some combination of a profile head and a cross. Some pieces have a bust, facing.

Iconography. The best specimens of Christian iconography contained upon coins are to be found in the series of Byzantine coins. Of these mention has been already made. In Italy we have S. Michael on the coins of the Lombards; S. Peter on the Papal money; S. Mark on that of Venice; and S. John upon the coinage of Florence. The Virgin and Child appear on the copper coins of the Norman Kings of Sicily, and S. Matthew on those of the Norman Dukes of Apulia. The *Sanctus Vultus* or holy icon of Christ, still preserved at Lucca, is represented on the money of that town. Upon the denarii of Germany and the Low Countries the iconographic types are also numerous, but the representation of the persons is very rude. Besides the symbols of the Three Persons of the Trinity—the Hand, the Cross, and the Dove —the second universal, the third comparatively rare—we see representations of numerous saints, each on the money of the town of which he was the special patron. Thus we have S. Lam-

III.—Return to a Gold Currency.

bert for Liège and Maeftricht, S. Servatius for Maesftricht, S. Martin for Utrecht, S. Remachus (Stablo), S. Maurice (Magdeburg), S. Charlemagne (Aix la Chapelle), S. Boniface (Fulda), S. Kilian (Würzburg), S. Stephen (Metz and other places in Lorraine), SS. Simon and Jude (Magdeburg, Goflar), S. Peter (Lorraine, Toul, Cologne, Berg, Trèves, etc.), the Virgin (Lower Lorraine, Huy, Hildefheim, Spier, Augfburg).

On the coins of France facred types and fymbols, excepting the crofs, which is all but univerfal, are lefs frequent during this age. The head of the Virgin occurs upon fome coins. On the money of the Crufaders iconographic types are very common.

Period III. Return to a Gold Currency.

The general revival of a gold coinage in Europe followed, as we have faid, the coining of the *fiorino d'oro* in 1252. But the firft attempt to inftitute a currency in the moft precious metal was made in Apulia by the Norman Dukes of that place. Roger II., who had long made ufe in Sicily of Arabic gold coins of the Fátimy type, at length ftruck gold coins of his own, which having his name and title, DVX APVLIAE, were called *ducats*. Thefe pieces were ftruck about A.D. 1150. After the Hohenftaufen dynafty had fucceeded the Norman Dukes in Apulia and Sicily, Frederick II., befides ftriking fome gold pieces for his Arab fubjects, iffued a very remarkable coinage modelled upon the old Roman folidus and half folidus: on the obverfe the buft of the Emperor in Roman drefs, and on the reverfe an eagle with wings displayed. The legend was (obv.) FRIDERICVS, (rev.) IMP. ROM. CESAR AVG. The next State to follow this example was Florence, which in A.D. 1252 struck the gold florin, bearing on one side the figure of S. John the Baptist, and on the other the lily of the city. The corresponding silver coin bore the rhyming Latin verse,

> "Det tibi florere
> Christus, Florentia, vere."

Owing in part to the great commercial position of the city, in part to the growing want felt

FIORINO D'ORO.

throughout Europe for a gold coinage, the use of the gold florin spread with extraordinary rapidity—

> "La tua città . . . .
> Produce e spande il maladetto fiore
> Ch'a disviate le pecore e gli agni
> Però c'ha fatto lupo del pastore."[1]

So general was the currency obtained by this coin in Europe that we presently find it largely copied by the chief potentates in France and Germany, as, for example, by the Pope John XXII. (at Avignon), the Archbishop of Arles, the Count of Vienne and Dauphiny, the Archduke Albert of Austria, the Count Palatine of the Rhine, the

[1] *Paradiso*, ix. 127-131.

Archbifhop of Mainz, the free town of Lübeck, the Kings of Hungary and Bohemia, and the King of Aragon; while in other places, as France and England, where the firft gold coinage was not fo diftinctly an imitation of the florin, it was obvioufly fuggefted by it.

The town of Italy which rivalled Florence in the extent of its iffues was Venice, which firft ftruck its gold coin, the ducat, about A.D. 1280. The piece was afterwards called *zecchino* (fequin). It bore on one fide a ftanding figure of Chrift, on the other the Doge receiving the ftandard (*gonfalone*) from S. Mark. The motto was of the fame kind as that on the filver florin:

> "Sit tibi, Chrifte, datus,
> quem tu regis, ifte ducatus."

Genoa alfo iffued a large currency in gold, as did the Popes (when they returned to Rome), and the Kings of Naples and Sicily.

The country north of the Alps which firft iffued an extenfive gold coinage was France. This was inaugurated by S. Louis, of whom we have numerous and various types. Of thefe the *agnel*, with the Pafchal Lamb, is the moft important. Louis's gold coins are, however, now fcarce, and it is poffible that the iffue was not large. It became extenfive under Philip the Fair.

Other changes were introduced into the money of Northern Europe at this period. Large denarii, *groffi denarii*, afterwards called *groffi* (gros), and in Englifh *groats*, were coined firft at Prague, afterwards chiefly at Tours. We have already spoken of the so-called *bracteates* of Germany. These at this time became larger, to correspond in appearance with the grossi of France and the Low Countries. The use of gold coins and of groats became general in England during the reign of Edward III.

Fourteenth Century.

We have now arrived at the fourteenth century. The coinage of this period has certain marked characteristics, though the exact types are far too numerous to be even mentioned. The general characteristics of the fourteenth century money are these. In the first place it reflects the artistic, specially architectural, tendencies of the time. The architecture of this period, leaving the simplicity of the earlier Gothic, and approaching the Decorated or Flamboyant style, when more attention is paid to detail, is very well suggested by the coins, where we see the effects of the same minute care and beautiful elaboration. Nothing can in their way be more splendid than the gold deniers of Louis IX. But as time passes on, this elaboration becomes extreme, the crosses lose their simple forms, and take every imaginable variety suggested by the names fleury, fleurt, quernée, avellanée, etc., while the cusps and tressures around the types are not less numerous and varied. The iconographic types are fewer upon the whole, especially in comparison with the number of types in existence at this time; the crosses themselves are rather parts of the structure of the coins than religious symbols, while now for the first time

IV.—The Renaissance Era.

shields and other heraldic devices, such as crests, caps of maintenance, mantlets, etc., become common. The coin below may serve as a sample of the coinage of the early years of the fifteenth century. Anyone who is acquainted with the history of this century, the white dawn, as we may call it, of the Renaissance, will discern in these characteristics of the coinage the signs of the times.

GROS OF THE FIFTEENTH CENTURY.

From the time of the issue of the fiorino d'oro, the initiative in most of the great changes which were wrought in the coinage of Europe belonged to Italy. It is naturally on the coinage of Italy that the first rise of the artistic renaissance is discernible. It is in the fifteenth century that we first have portraits upon coins which are distinctly recognisable, and no longer merely conventional. This century is the age of the greatest Italian medallists, of Pisano, Sperandio, Boldu, Melioli, and the rest; and though these earliest medallists were not themselves makers of coin dies, it was impossible that their art could fail before long to influence the kindred art of the die-engraver. Portraits begin to appear upon the Italian coins about 1450. In the series of Naples we have

Period IV. The Renaissance Era.

Portraits.

during this century money bearing the heads of Ferdinand I. and Frederick of Aragon, and later on of Charles V. and Philip of Spain. The Papal feries is peculiarly rich in portrait coins, which were engraved by fome of the moſt celebrated artiſts of the fifteenth and ſixteenth centuries, as by Francefco Francia and Benvenuto Cellini. The portraits of Alexander VI., Julius II., and Leo X., are efpecially to be noted. Cellini alfo worked for Florence, and we have a fine feries of the Dukes and Grand Dukes of this city, beginning with the Aleſſandro il Moro. In Milan we have coins with the heads of Aleſſandro Sforza, of Galeazzo Maria and the younger Galeazzo, of Bona, the mother of this laſt, and of Ludovico, and again, after the French conqueſt, of Louis XII. and Francis; later ſtill, of Charles V. and Philip. The coins of Mantua, Ferrara, Modena, Bologna, Parma, and Mirandola, are all worth a lengthy ſtudy. Venice and Genoa alone among the great towns of Italy kept their money almoſt unchanged, probably from commercial confiderations, like thofe which prompted Athens to adhere to the archaic form of her tetradrachms.

In France, authentic portraits upon coins firſt appear in the reign of Louis XII., and the beauty of the medallic art in France is well illuſtrated by the money of Francis I. and Henry II., and only one degree lefs fo by that of Charles IX. and Henry IV. The celebrated engravers Dupré and the two Warins worked during the latter part of the feventeenth century. In England, the moſt beautiful portraits are thofe on the coins of

V.—Modern Coinage.

Henry VII. and Henry VIII., though thofe of Mary and Edward VI. are only one degree inferior. The firft Scottifh coins with portraits are thofe of James IV. The German coins show traces of the peculiar development of German art. Thofe of the Emperor Maximilian are the moft fplendid and elaborate. Some of thefe are worthy of the hand of Dürer, to whom they have been attributed—though without much authority. Next to thefe, the feries of Saxony, of Brunfwick, of Brandenburg, and the coins of fome of the German and Swifs towns, are to be noted. Even the remote northern lands, Sweden and Denmark, did not efcape the influence of the age.

We muft not omit to mention that the firft rude coinage of Ruffia begins during this period. The country, however, poffeffed no properly ordered monetary fyftem before the reign of Peter the Great.

The coinage fubfequent to 1600, though it receives more attention from collectors than any other, muft be pronounced, upon all hiftorical grounds, by far the leaft interefting. And for this reafon, if for no other, that our hiftorical documents for this period are fo voluminous that the coins can ferve little purpofe, fave as illuftrations of thefe documents; we cannot hope to gain from them any important light upon the times. Still, it cannot be denied that they have an intereft regarded as illuftrations merely, and fome phafes of this intereft muft be briefly indicated.

And firft, in a general way, the modern coinage

<small>PERIOD V. Modern Coinage.</small>

illustrates well the rise of the commercial spirit of the West, which, taking a fresh start with the discovery of America in the fifteenth century, has since become perhaps the chief determining force of our modern civilization. For now the coinage of all countries becomes as much improved for commercial purposes as it is artistically debased. The introduction of the "mill" in the manufacture of coins, in place of the older device of striking them with a hammer, greatly improved their symmetry and the facility with which the money could be counted, while the use of an indented edge (commonly called "a milled edge") prevented the practice of clipping, which was so frequent in earlier times, and thus tended to keep coins to a just weight, and so greatly to simplify exchange.

Portraits of Sovereigns. In a more particular way the coins of each nation are interesting, as now always, or nearly always, bearing the head of the reigning sovereign of the country. By this means we get a series of historic portraits, which, if not of much artistic excellence, are, on the whole, trustworthy. These are the better from the fact that large silver coins (crowns or thalers) were now generally current in Europe, having been introduced during the preceding epoch. Gustavus Adolphus, Frederick the "Winter King" of Bohemia, and other heroes of the Thirty Years' War; Christina, Queen of Sweden; the "Great Elector" of Brandenburg; Charles XII. and Peter the Great; Louis XIV. and the contemporary Emperors of the House

Coins of Medallic Character.

of Auſtria; Frederick William I. of Pruſſia; Frederick the Great and Maria Thereſa; an excellent ſeries of the Popes; and finally the Engliſh ſovereign, may be cited as the coin-portraits moſt likely to intereſt the hiſtorical ſtudent. The money of the Czar Peter deſerves, indeed, a ſpecial attention, as it is the firſt regularly ordered ſeries of coins iſſued in Ruſſia, and, when compared with the money which preceded it, is a type by itſelf of the improvements which Peter introduced into the condition of the country.

Another feature connected with the large ſilver coins is a certain tendency which we find to make uſe of theſe for medallic purpoſes. This is eſpecially the caſe in Germany. Among the earlieſt examples of this uſe may be cited the Luther celebration medals, iſſued in Saxony on the jubilees of the Reformation held in 1617 and 1630. The lateſt is the *Sieges-Thaler*, ſtruck after the Franco-German War in 1870. The thalers iſſued by Ludwig, King of Bavaria, father of the preſent King, almoſt all of which commemorate either ſome event of his reign or the erection of ſome public building, form the largeſt ſeries of coins of this medallic kind. The *ſchütz-thäler*, iſſued in Germany and Switzerland as rewards to thoſe who had been ſuccefsful in the national or cantonal ſhooting-conteſts, deſerve mention in this place. The Papal coins are alſo frequently commemorative of hiſtorical events or of the erection of public monuments.

Finally, in ſome of the towns of Germany

Medallic Character.

Views of Cities. and Switzerland, the reverses of the coins bear views of these towns, which are sometimes so drawn as to form a very pleasing design. Bâle, Lucerne, Zurich, Augsburg, Cologne, Constance, Danzig, Hamburg, Magdeburg, and Nuremberg, give examples in various degrees of excellence of this style of decoration. Thus, while the coinage of England, as we shall have occasion to remark in the next chapter, toward the end of the seventeenth century loses all artistic merit and originality of design, and ceases to perform any function save that of a medium of exchange, the same fate does not till more than one hundred years later overtake some of the continental issues. The latest coins which can boast of artistic beauty are those of Napoleon I., especially the series struck for Italy, on which the head is finely modelled. Some of the coins struck during the French Revolution are interesting from their containing allusions to contemporary historical events.

Weights and Denominations. The student of European history must be upon his guard against the danger of confounding *money of account* with coined money. As we have said, the *new denarius* of Charlemagne was, from the time of its introduction till the thirteenth century, practically the only piece coined in western continental Europe. The Roman gold coin, the *solidus*, however, continued to be used for some time, and for a much longer period it remained in use as a money of account. The solidus was translated in the Germanic languages by *schilling*, *shilling*, *skilling*. Thus when we read of solidi and

Weights and Denominations.

shillings it does not in the least follow that we are reading of actual coins. The real coins which passed current on the occasion spoken of were very probably simply the denarii, or pennies, but they were reckoned in the shilling or solidus of account which contained (generally) twelve denarii.

Other moneys of account were in reality simply weights, as (1) the *pound*, which was the Roman weight, the *libra*, containing twelve ounces, and in silver reckoned as equal to 240 denarii ; and (2) the German (Teutonic) weight, the *mark*, equal to two-thirds of a pound, *i.e.*, eight ounces and 180 denarii. It need hardly be said that the actual weight of the denarius soon fell below this nominal weight of twenty-four grains. The recollection of the three denominations of *libra, solidus*, and *denarius* is preserved in our abbreviations £ s. d. for pounds, shillings, and pence.

We have already spoken of the *grossus*, or groat. The gold coins in France received a variety of names, of which the most usual and the widest spread was *écu*. In Germany the earliest gold pieces seem to have been called *ducats*, and this name was continued in the subsequent gold coinage of the sixteenth and seventeenth centuries. The weight of the ducat was founded upon the weight of the *fiorino* of Florence and of the *ducat* or *zecchino* of Venice, usually about fifty-four grains, and these equal to about one hundred denarii of the old value. As, however, the silver coins contemporary with these ducats, though nominally denarii, were exceedingly debased, the relative value of the gold was very much higher.

One other coin-name of wide extension is the *thaler*, or dollar. The origin of this name lies in the Joachimsthal near the Harz Mountains, the mines of which furnished the silver from which these large pieces were first struck.

CHAPTER V.

COINAGE OF THE BRITISH ISLANDS.

N the laft chapter a brief fketch was given of the general numifmatic hiftory of Europe in Chriftian times. In the prefent chapter we confine our attention altogether to the coinage of our own iflands; not, however, from Chriftian times only, but from the earlieft period in which a coinage was known here. During the greater part of this fketch it will be neceffary to keep in mind the character of the currency in the other lands of Europe, for the monetary hiftory of the Middle Ages—we might add the political hiftory alfo—can only be properly ftudied as a whole. The different epochs into which the hiftory of the coinage of Europe has been divided will therefore ferve us again in the prefent cafe. Our firft period, however, precedes any of thefe epochs, for here we have to do with a currency in ufe in Britain before the introduction of Chriftianity.

The circumftances attending the firft introduc-

The Coin-age of the Britons. tion of a coinage into these islands require some explanation. For the remote causes of this event we have to go back as far as to the times of Philip of Macedon, and to the acquisition by him of the gold mines of Crenides (Philippi). The result of this acquisition was, as is well known, to set in circulation an extensive gold currency, the first which had been widely prevalent in the Greek world. The gold staters of Philip obtained an extensive circulation beyond the limits of Greece—a much wider circulation than could have been obtained by any silver currency. Through the Greek colony of Massalia (Marseilles), they came into the hands of the Gauls. Massalia was, we know, the chief trading centre for the western lands, and for the barbarian nations of Northern Europe. It was not long after the death of Philip that Pytheas, the great "commercial traveller" of Marseilles, made his voyages to Britain and the coasts of Germany, as far as the mouth of the Elbe, or even, some think, the Baltic. We may readily believe that Marseilles was then in some relation with Northern Europe through Gaul; and it would seem that at this time the Gauls began to appreciate the use of a coinage, and to make one for themselves. The pieces thus manufactured were simply imitations of the gold stater of Philip. That coin bore on the obverse a beardless head laureate, generally taken to be the head of Apollo, but by some the head of young Heracles, or of Ares. On the reverse is a two-horse chariot (*biga*). The Gaulish coins were copies of this piece, gradually becoming more rude as time went on, and about the middle of the second century B.C., the southern coast of Britain adopted from Gaul the same habit. The earliest British coins were thus of gold, and though immediately only copies of the Gaulish money, they were in a remote degree copies of the staters of Philip of Macedon. The copies have, in nearly every case, departed so widely from the original, that, were it not that the Gaulish money affords us examples of an intermediate type, we should have

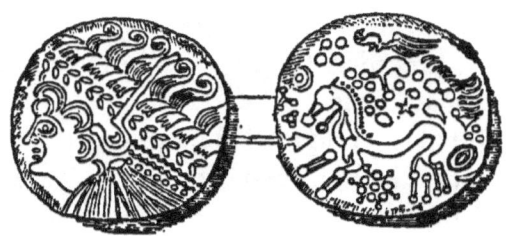

BRITISH GOLD COIN.

great difficulty in recognising the relationship of the British to the Macedonian coin. This is the history of the introduction of a coinage into the British Isles.

The earliest coins of Britain were exclusively of gold, and were devoid of inscription; any sign which has the appearance of a letter being in reality only a part of the barbarous copy of the Greek coin, and without meaning in itself. About the time of Caesar's invasion, however, the coins begin to carry inscriptions upon them—the name of some chief or tribe, the former being in most cafes unknown to hiftory fave from his coins. One or two hiftorical names do occur—as Commius, poffibly the King of the Atrebates, who may be fuppofed to have fled into England ; and certainly Cunobelinus, King of the Trinobantes, the Cymbeline of Shakefpeare. After the Roman conqueft of Gaul, the native currency there was exchanged for the imperial coinage, and the change foon affected the coinage of Britain, which from about the Chriftian era began to make coins upon the Roman pattern. This fact is fymbolical of the Romanifing influence in the fouthern diftricts, which in this country, and in fo many others, preceded the actual fubjugation of the land by Roman arms.

Roman Mints. After the complete Roman conqueft the native currency ceafed. Roman mints were not eftablifhed in Britain until the time of Caraufius (A.D. 287-293), who was Emperor in Britain only. Caraufius' mints were Londinium and Camulodunum (Colchefter). Between the time of Allectus and that of Conftantine the Great no money was coined in Britain. The latter Emperor did not ufe a mint at Colchefter, and ftruck at London only. The laft imperial coins ftruck in Britain were thofe of Magnus Maximus (died A.D. 388).

Coinage of the Saxons. From this period till after the beginning of the feventh century there is an almoft total want of numifmatic documents. There can be no queftion that the Britons continued to ufe the later Roman coins, efpecially thofe of Conftantine and his immediate fucceffors, which feem to have been ſtruck in large numbers. Such coins as came into the hands of the Saxon invaders would probably be cheriſhed rather as ornaments than for any other purpoſe. This would at any rate be the caſe with the gold coins. We find that Roman gold coins were very extenſively uſed as ornaments by the northern nations during the Viking age, and that they were imitated in thoſe peculiar diſc-like ornaments known as bracteates.[1] In the ſame way we find an imitation of a gold coin of Honorius engraved with Saxon runes. But gold belonged rather to the chiefs than to the great body of the people, and for the uſe of theſe laſt a regular coinage of ſilver appeared ſoon after the beginning of the ſeventh century.

The earlieſt Saxon coins, like the earlieſt Britiſh, are anonymous, the only trace of letters upon moſt of them being nothing more than a blundered imitation of the coin-legend which the engraver was endeavouring to copy; and for this reaſon it is impoſſible accurately to determine their date. Theſe early Saxon coins are generally known to numiſmatiſts as *ſceattas*, and it ſeems probable that at one time they were diſtinguiſhed by that name. But *ſceat* properly ſignifies only treaſure,[2] and it is not likely that the word was at firſt used to denote any ſpecial denomination of coin.

The Sceat.

The anonymous ſceattas, hardly poſſeſſing an

---

[1] Theſe bracteates are not to be confuſed with the German ſilver bracteates ſpoken of in the laſt chapter. Theſe were of gold, were made in the Scandinavian countries, and uſed as ornaments, not as coins.

[2] Primarily, *treaſure;* ſecondarily, *tax*.

historic, or, in the strict sense, a numismatic interest, have suffered too much neglect at the hands of collectors. For they are, in some respects, the most curious and noteworthy coins which have been issued since the Christian era. In no other series of coins do we find among so small a number of individual pieces so great a variety of designs. The only series of coins which can in this respect be compared with the sceattas is that of the electrum pieces struck in Asia Minor in the fifth and fourth centuries B.C. The larger number of actual pieces among the sceattas are indeed copied from Roman coins; many also from Merovingian silver pieces. But among those which remain there are a great number of designs which seem perfectly original, and which far outnumber the *types* taken from any other source. Of these apparently original and native works of art we may count between thirty and forty distinct designs; and as they are probably earlier than most of the extant remains of Saxon or Irish architecture, and earlier than most of the Saxon and Irish manuscripts, the interest which belongs to these pieces is very great. It is impossible to describe these designs here; a great number consist of some fantastic bird, or animal, or serpent, similar to the animals which appear in such profusion in the Saxon manuscripts, and at a later period in architecture.

It is evident that the Germanic peoples had a special partiality for a coinage in silver; and this may have dated back to quite early days, when

The Penny.

the old confular denarii (*ferrati, bigatique*[1]) were current among them. Mommfen tells us that when the filver coinage of Rome was debafed, the old pieces of pure metal were almoft abforbed for the purpofe of exchange with the barbarian nations of the North. We find further evidence of this partiality in the fact that the filver fceattas were current in England before the grand reform made by the introduction of the new denarius into Europe,[2] and in the fact that this very reform was due to the moft Teutonic (laft Romanifed) fection of the Frank nationality. When, therefore, the great reform was brought about on the Continent, of which we have fpoken in the preceding chapter, the effect was lefs felt in England than in any other land; it refulted merely in the exchange of the fceat for the filver penny, the former ftanding probably to the latter in the proportionate value of 12 to 20 ($=\frac{3}{5}$), though according to fome documents they were in the proportion of 24 to 25.

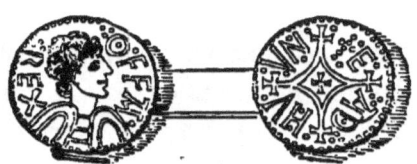

PENNY OF OFFA.

The penny, introduced about 760, differed from the fceat in appearance. The latter was fmall and thick, the penny much broader but thin. The

[1] Tacitus, *Germ.*, c. 5.
[2] See Chapter IV., p. 81.

pennies of Offa are remarkable for the beauty and variety of their defigns and an artiftic excellence which was never recovered in after years. The ufual type of the penny confifts of, on one fide, a buft, a degraded form of the buft on Roman coins, and on the reverfe a crofs; but a very large number of coins have no buft, and the crofs is by no means an invariable concomitant. The legend gives the name of the King as OFFA REX, AELFRED REX, or with the title more fully given, OFFA REX MERCIORUM. On the reverfe appears the name of the moneyer, that is to fay, the actual maker of the coin; at firft the name fimply, as EADMUUN, IBBA, later on with the addition of MONETA (for *monetarius*), and later ftill with the name of the town at which the piece has been ftruck, as GODMAN ON[1] LUND. Town names begin to appear on coins in the reign of Egberht, King of Weffex. They are not infrequent on the pennies of Aelfred, and univerfal from the time of Aethelred the Unready.

It is to be noticed that the treafure plundered from England by the Vikings feems firft to have given to the Northern people the notion of iffuing a currency. Rude imitations of Saxon money are frequently difcovered in the Weftern Ifles of Scotland, and were doubtlefs iffued by order or for the behoof of the Danifh or Norwegian Kings of thofe parts. In the fame way we find that the Norfe Kings in Ireland iffued a coinage in imitation of that of Aethelred II. Moft of the early coins of Norway are likewife copied from the coins of this King. When the Danifh dynafty of Cnut

[1] Probably for [M]ON[ETARIUS].

(Gormsſon) ſupplanted the Engliſh line of Kings, it made no change in the coinage of this country, though it was inſtrumental in introducing an improved coinage into Denmark.

Nor, again, did the Norman conqueſt make any immediate change in the Engliſh currency. The penny long remained the ſole Engliſh coin. The variety of towns at which money was ſtruck, of moneyers employed for this work, and of types made uſe of by them, reach their maximum in the reign of Edward the Confeſſor; but thoſe of William I. and William II. (for the coins of theſe two Kings cannot with certainty be diſtinguiſhed) are little leſs numerous. After the reign of William II., however, all theſe begin ſteadily to decline, until we find, in the reign of Henry II., only two different types, and the latter of the two extending, without even a change in the name of the King, into the reign of Henry III. This ſimplification in the appearance of the penny correſponds with a certain amount of centralization in the regulation of its iſſues. It would ſeem that down to the middle of the reign of Henry II. each ſeparate moneyer was reſponſible for the purity of his coins, but that ſhortly after this date a general overſeer was appointed, who was reſponſible to the King's Government.

Norman Coinage.

In this approach to uniformity the general types which ſurvive are thoſe which have on the obverſe the head or buſt of the King facing, and on the reverſe ſome kind of croſs. At the beginning of the reign of Henry II. the latter is a croſs *patée* cantoned with crofflets. This changes to a fhort crofs voided (that is, having each limb made of two parallel lines, very convenient for cutting the coin into halfpence and farthings), and that again changes to a longer crofs voided. But in the reign of Edward I. the forms of both obverfe and reverfe become abfolutely ftereotyped. And this ftereotyping of the coin into one fingle pattern is the firft very important change in the penny which took place fince its introduction. The ftereotyped form henceforward until the reign of Henry VII. is as follows: *obverfe*, the King's head (fometimes with flight traces of buft), crowned, facing; *reverfe*, a long crofs *patée* with three pellets in each angle. In this reign, too, the names of moneyers ceafe to be placed upon coins. Robert de Hadleye is the laft moneyer whofe name appears. Finally we have to notice that Edward I. re-introduced a coinage of halfpence, unknown fince Saxon times, and firft ftruck the groat and the farthing. The groats were not in general circulation till the reign of Edward III.

Groat, Halfpenny, Farthing.

We have many documents fhowing that in making thefe changes of coinage Edward I. alfo reformed the conftitution of the mint in many particulars. His pennies obtained a wide circulation not only in this country but on the Continent, where they prefently (much as the *fiorino* did) gave rife to imitations. The clofeft copies are to be feen in the money of the various ftates of the Low Countries, as the Dukedom of Brabant, the Counties of Flanders, Hainault, etc. Other imitations are to be found in the denarii of the

Emperors of Germany and the Kings of Aragon. The English money never followed the rapid course of degradation which was the lot of the continental coinages; wherefore thefe English pennies (alfo called *efterlings*, *fterlings*, a word of doubtful origin) were of quite a different ftandard from the continental denarii. The English penny did, indeed, continually diminifh in fize, fo that before the type introduced by Edward I. was radically changed (in the reign of Henry VII.), the penny had fhrunk to not more than half of its original dimenfions. But this degradation was flow compared to that which was undergone by the continental coins.

We have now for a moment to retrace our fteps to the latter part of the reign of Henry III. In the preceding chapter we fpoke of the re-introduction of a gold currency into Weftern Europe. Only a few years after the firft iffue of the *fiorino d'oro*, namely, in 1257, we find the firft record in the annals of the English coinage of the iffue of a gold currency. In this year Henry III. ftruck a piece called a gold penny. It reprefented on one fide the King enthroned, on the other bore a crofs voided cantoned with rofes; and was at firft valued at twenty pence, afterwards at twenty-fix. The innovation was premature, and the coin being unpopular had foon to be withdrawn from circulation. It was not till nearly ninety years afterwards that a regular gold coinage was fet on foot.

In 1343 or 1344 Edward III. iffued this new gold coinage. It at firft confifted of pieces

Introduction of a Gold Coinage.

Florins.　called *florins*, half and quarter florins. The obverſe types of theſe three orders of coins were—(1), the monarch enthroned between two leopards; (2), a ſingle leopard bearing the Engliſh coat; (3), a helmet and cap of maintenance with ſmall leopard as creſt; a croſs formed the reverſe type in every caſe. Theſe pieces were rated too high, and were almoſt immediately withdrawn from circulation; after which were iſſued coins of a new type and denomination, *nobles*,

Nobles.　half-nobles, and quarter-nobles.

NOBLE OF EDWARD III.

The nobles and half-nobles were the ſame in type; on the obverſe they ſhowed the King ſtanding in a ſhip; the quarter-noble contained a ſhield merely on the obverſe. The type of the noble is perhaps commemorative of the naval victory off Sluys. The legend on the noble was IHS [JESUS] AVTEM TRANSIENS PER MEDIVM ILLORVM IBAT (S. Luke iv. 30), a legend which long continued on the Engliſh money, and which has given riſe to a good deal of abſurd ſpeculation. The legend was a charm againſt thieves, but poſſibly bears ſome further reference to the victory commemorated by the type. The noble was made equal to half a mark (a money of account), or 80 pence English; in weight it was exactly that of the modern English sovereign, 120 grains. As it was of very pure gold, and perhaps the finest coin then current in Europe, it was, like the penny of Edward I., a good deal imitated abroad (always, we may be sure, to the advantage of the imitator), and laws were constantly being enacted, without much success, to hinder its exportation.

Before we leave the reign of Edward III. we must cast one glance at a class of coins which now began to assume considerable dimensions, namely, the *Anglo-French* money, or coins struck for the English possessions in France. These naturally followed French types and denominations. As early as the reign of Henry II. we have deniers struck for Aquitaine; Richard I. struck for Aquitaine, Poitou, and Normandy; Edward I. coined for Aquitaine and Bordeaux. But under Edward III. and the Black Prince (Governor of Guienne) quite a large issue of Anglo-French coins, both in gold and silver, appeared. The gold coins of Edward III. were the *guiennois* (standing figure in armour), *leopard*, *chaise* (King enthroned), and *mouton* (Paschal Lamb), and in silver the *hardi* (half-figure holding sword), *double-hardi*, *gros*, *demi-gros*, *denier*, *demi-denier* (also apparently called *ardit* [*sic*]). Edward Prince of Wales struck guiennois, leopard, chaise, demi-chaise, hardi (d'or), and *pavillon* (prince under a canopy), and in silver money the same as his father. Edward III. began,

<small>Anglo-French Coinage.</small>

too, the issue of Calais silver groats, which (as Calais was really henceforth an English town) can scarcely be counted among the Anglo-French coinage. In every respect, this coin, as well as the Calais half-groat, penny, etc., exactly corresponded to the English money. In order to end the subject we may add that Richard II. struck gold and silver hardis and demi-hardis as well as deniers and half-deniers. Henry V. struck in gold moutons and demi-moutons, and possibly *salutes* (the angel saluting Mary), and gros. Henry VI. struck salutes, *angelots*, and *francs*, and in silver grand and petit *blancs*. He also continued an extensive issue of Calais money. With Henry VI. the Anglo-French coinage really comes to an end.

Edward IV. introduced some important changes into the gold coinage. He seems to have struck a few nobles of the old type; but he very soon made an alteration in the type of the noble by substituting on the reverse a sun for the older cross, and on the obverse, placing a rose upon the side of the ship, in the form of which last some other changes were introduced. From the rose on the obverse the coins came to be called *rose nobles*, and owing to changes in the relative values of gold and silver they were now worth 10s. (120 pence), instead of 6s. 8d. (80 pence) as before. To supply a coin of the old value of half a mark, a new gold piece was struck, called at first the angel-noble, but soon simply the *angel*. On one side it represented a ship, bearing (instead of the King) a cross; on the other was S. Michael

Rose Noble.

Angel.

The Coinage of Scotland. 113

overcoming Satan. The motto was PER CRVCEM TVAM SALVA NOS XPE (CHRISTE) REDEMPTOR.

> They have in England
> A coin that bears the figure of an angel
> Stamped in gold, but that's insculped upon:
> But here an angel in a golden bed
> Lies all within.[1]

Shakespeare is much given to playing upon this word,[2] and we find frequent allusions of the same kind in other writers, his contemporaries.

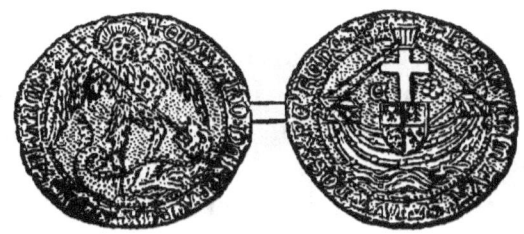

ANGEL OF EDWARD IV.

We have spoken of some coins probably struck by the Norsemen in the western isles. The regular coinage of Scotland does not begin before 1124 (David I.), when an issue of pennies (or *sterlings*, as they were generally called in Scotland) began. Even yet we find that offences were more frequently punished by fines of cattle than of money. At first the money of Scotland copied very closely the contemporary currency of England. Thus the pennies of David resemble those of Henry I.; the next coinage, that of William the Lion, grandson of David (1165-1214) resembles the money of

Scottish Coinage.

Sterling.

---

[1] *Merchant of Venice*, ii. 7.
[2] Cf. *Merry Wives of Windsor*, i. 3; *King John*, ii. 1.

Henry II.; the pennies of Alexander II. have short and long voided crosses, like those of Henry III., and the coins of Alexander III. are like those of Edward I. This King, like Edward, added halfpennies and farthings to the currency of pennies. But both the moneyers and the places of mintage are far less numerous in Scotland than in England. We count no more than sixteen of the latter. The coinage of John Baliol and of Robert Bruce followed the type of Alexander III. The mint-records for these reigns are lost: they begin again in the reign of David II. This King issued nobles after the pattern of Edward III.'s nobles. He also struck groats and half-groats, pennies, halfpennies, and farthings.

All this time it will be seen that, despite the war between the two countries, English influence was paramount in determining the character of the Scottish coinage. There was present a certain French influence as well, which may be detected in minor marks upon the coins (fleurs-de-lis, and such like), and which was exercised also in a very unhappy direction towards a degradation of the currency. Scotland followed the continental fashion in this respect, and the commercial relations of the two bordering countries are marked by a perpetual chorus of complaint on the part of England of the debased character of the Scottish money. Thus in 1372 we find both Scottish gold and silver forbidden in England, and as if the prohibition had been relaxed, it is repeated in 1387. In 1390 Scottish money is admitted at half its nominal value; in 1393 it is forbidden again, save as bullion, and in 1401 there is a decree of Parliament to the same effect.

In the reign of Robert II. Scotland took a new departure by coining some gold pieces of an original type (no longer borrowed from England), viz., the *Lion* and *St. Andrew*. The first had the shield of Scotland with rampant lion, the second the figure of St. Andrew with a shield on the reverse. In the reign of Robert III. we note a further sign of continental influence in the introduction of *billon* (base metal) coins. James I. struck the *demy* (Obverse, arms in lozenge; Reverse, cross in tressure) and *half-demy*; James II. struck demies, St. Andrews, and half St. Andrews. James III. introduced two new types of gold coins, viz., the *rider* (knight on horseback) and the *unicorn*, which shows a unicorn supporting the Scottish shield. The same King issued several denominations of billon coins, as *placks, half-placks,* farthings.

<small>Lion.
St. Andrew</small>

<small>Demy.</small>

<small>Rider.
Unicorn.</small>

<small>Plack.</small>

Hoards of English coins of the ninth century have been found in Ireland, and were doubtless taken there by the Norsemen settled in the land. The actual coinage of these Norse Kings, however, does not begin till the end of the tenth century. It copies almost invariably a peculiar type of the coinage of Aethelred II. (978-1016), having on one side a bust uncrowned, and on the other a long voided cross. After that we have no Irish coinage until subsequent to the conquest of a portion of the country by Henry II. Henry made

<small>The Coinage of Ireland.</small>

his fon John governor of the ifland, and John ftruck in his own name pennies, half-pennies, and farthings, having on the obverfe a head (fuppofed to be that of John the Baptift) and on the reverfe a crofs. During his own reign John coined pennies having the King's buft in a triangle on one fide; on the other the fun and moon in a triangle. Henry III.'s Irifh pennies are like his Englifh long crofs type, fave that the King's head is again furrounded by a triangle. This diftinction once more ferves to feparate, in point of type, Edward I.'s Irifh from his Englifh coins, the reverfe types of the two being the fame. John ftruck at Dublin and Limerick, Henry III. at Dublin, and Edward I. at Dublin, Cork, and Waterford. One or two Irifh pennies of Henry V. or VI. have been fpoken of, but there was no extenfive coinage for Ireland between the reigns of Edward I. and Edward IV. The Irifh coins of Edward IV. were very numerous, and confifted of double-groats, groats, half-groats, pennies, and (in billon) halfpennies and farthings. The types of thefe coins are varied; fome are but flight divergences from the correfponding Englifh coins; others have for reverfe a fun in place of the ufual crofs; others again have a fingle crown on obverfe, on the reverfe a long crofs; and another feries has three crowns, with the Englifh fhield for reverfe. The mints are Dublin, Cork, Drogheda, Limerick, Trim, Waterford, and Wexford. No gold coins were ever ftruck for Ireland.

Hen. VII.   We have thought it beft to difpofe of the

Henry VII.

Middle Age coinage of all Great Britain and Ireland before we come to speak of any currency struck in more modern days. We have thus carried our enquiries down to the accession of Henry VII. The division which has been thus made in our subject is not, indeed, an equal division in respect of time nor even of recorded historical events; but it is obviously the most suitable which could be found. It corresponds generally with the line of demarcation separating modern from mediaeval history, and with what we may call the installation of the Renaissance. The line is always more or less shadowy and indefinite, but nowhere is it less so than in England. The Wars of the Roses were the final act in the drama of mediaeval English history. When these ended in the Battle of Bosworth the new era definitely began.

We have seen[1] that this age of the Renaissance was for the whole of Europe, so far as the coins were concerned, notable chiefly as being the era of portraiture. Portraits begin on English coins with Henry VII. Up to his nineteenth year this King continued the older forms of silver currency, but in 1504 he made a complete change. He coined shillings in addition to the groats, half-groats, pennies, etc., which had up to that time been current; and on all the larger pieces, in place of the conventional bust facing which had prevailed since the days of Edward I., he placed a profile

<small>Shilling.</small>

---

[1] Chapter IV., pp. 91-95.

bust which had not been seen on coins since the days of Stephen.[1] The bust appears upon all coins of higher denomination than the penny. A new type was invented for the latter coin, the full-length figure of the monarch enthroned. The portrait of Henry VII. is a work of the highest art in its own kind. Nothing superior to it has appeared since, nor anything nearly equal to it except upon some of the coins of Henry VIII. and Edward VI. The artistic merit of these pieces is so considerable that on that account alone they are worthy of peculiar study. It has been well pointed out by archaeologists that one interest belonging to the study of Greek coins lies in the fact that they are tokens of the artistic work of many places of which no other such monuments remain. The same may almost be said of the coinage of England during the Renaissance. In the great artistic movement of those days, England seems at first sight to take no part. While Italy, France, and Germany had each its own schools of artists, and each its separate character of design, the conspicuous monuments made in England were the work of foreigners; they were the sculptures of Torrigiano or the paintings of Holbein. But as smaller monuments the contemporary coins are an evidence of native talent,

Art.

---

[1] It is worth noticing that Henry VII. was the first King subsequent to Henry III. who used a numeral upon his coins. Some of his shillings read HENRIC VII., others HENRIC SEPTIM. James IV. in the same way introduced (for the first time on Scottish coins) the word QUART. after his name.

The Sovereign. 119

for moſt of the engravers to the mint during theſe reigns bear genuinely Engliſh names.¹

Next to the evidence of art-culture which the coins afford, comes the evidence of greater wealth, of larger trade and manufacture, and of an increaſed demand for a medium of exchange. When Henry VII. aſcended the throne, although the country had juſt been ſuffering from a bitter and prolonged civil war, the great maſs of the community was far from having been impoveriſhed thereby. It was during all this period ſteadily acquiring wealth, and the wealth of the country, as a whole, was upon the increaſe.² The careful reign of Henry VII. foſtered this increaſe. It need not ſurpriſe us, therefore, to find an addition made to the coinage of the previous reigns.

Increaſe of Wealth.

SOVEREIGN OF HENRY VII.

Henry VII. ſtruck the principal gold coins which were current in former reigns; that is to say,

---

¹ Nicholas Flynte, John Sharpe, and —— Demaire, are the names of the engravers during the reigns of Henry VII. and Henry VIII., as given by Ruding; the third may, likely enough, be a French name.

² Rogers' *Hiſt. of Prices*, vol. iv., Intr., v. 22.

the ryal, or rose-noble (now worth ten shillings), the angel, and the angelet. In addition to these pieces he struck for the first time the pound sovereign, or double ryal, worth twenty shillings, a large gold coin representing the King enthroned, and on the reverse a double rose charged with the English shield. The piece measured more than one-and-a-half inches, and weighed two hundred and forty grains; that is to say, twice as much as the present sovereign. It was without question the finest gold coin then current in Europe. It does not appear, however, to have been issued in large quantities.

<small>Sovereign.</small>

As we follow the history of coinage under the Tudors, we see the currency gradually increasing in quantity and in the variety of its denominations. Henry VIII. did not indeed make any decided step in this direction, and in one respect, presently to be noticed, he made a conspicuous retrogression. Nevertheless he struck some two-sovereign pieces, and he largely increased the number of sovereigns. At first this coin followed the type instituted by Henry VII., but later on a second type was introduced, having the King seated on a throne upon one side, and on the other the English shield supported by a lion and a griffin. Henry coined half-sovereigns of the same type. He coined crowns or quarter-sovereigns and half-crowns in gold, having on one side the English shield, and on the other the Tudor rose. He likewise struck rose-nobles or ryals, angels, and angelets of the types formerly in use. The

<small>Hen. VIII.</small>

<small>Crown.</small>

older nobles had given place to the ryals which, at firſt meant to be current for ſix-and-eightpence like their predeceſſors, had at once riſen to be worth ten ſhillings. Henry VIII. now iſſued a new ſeries of nobles at the leſſer value. They were called George nobles, from having on the obverſe the figure of St. George on horſeback ſlaying the dragon. In ſilver Henry ſtruck pieces of the ſame denomination as thoſe of his father—namely, ſhillings, groats, half-groats, pennies, halfpennies, and farthings. The earlier groats ſhowed a profile buſt like the groats of Henry VII., but in 1543 for this was ſubſtituted a buſt facing or turned three-quarters towards the ſpectator, and the ſhillings of Henry VIII., which were firſt coined at this date, were of the ſame pattern. [margin: George Noble.]

It has been noticed how in the continental coinage heraldic devices begin during the fourteenth century to take the place of the ſimpler croſſes which generally decorate the mediaeval coins. Owing to the ſtereotyped character of the Engliſh coinage between Edward I. and Henry VII., the ſame change could not be ſo early diſcovered here. But it is very noticeable in the currency of the Tudor dynaſty. From the time of Henry VII. the Engliſh ſhield (quartering France) is rarely abſent from the coins. It is laid over the croſs on the reverſe, which in many caſes it almoſt completely hides from view. A great number of the heraldic devices, with which we are ſo familiar in the chapel and tomb of Henry VII. in Weſtminſter Abbey, are introduced upon his coins or those of his immediate successors, as the lion, the griffin, the double rose, the portcullis. The last device was derived from the Beaufort family (the legitimated children of John of Gaunt and Catherine Swynford), from which Henry could claim descent.

Wolsey's Groat.

One coin of Henry VIII. has a special historical interest. It is the groat struck at York by Cardinal Wolsey when Archbishop of York. On the piece he placed his cardinal's hat; and as this act was accounted illegal, and even treasonous, it was included in the bill of indictment against him:

> That out of mere ambition you have caused
> Your holy hat to be stamped on the king's coin.[1]

In the actual articles of indictment he is only blamed for, "of his pompous and presumptuous mind," stamping the hat upon the *groats* struck at York, as if the offence lay especially in the issuing of such large pieces with the insignia of his office. Several prelates before his time had placed their own initials and some symbol of their dignity upon the pennies of York, Durham, etc. It may, however, have been considered part of the offence for which, as a whole, Wolsey was held to have incurred the penalties of a *praemunire*; namely, the endeavour to exalt unduly the position of his holy office, and to spread an impression among the people that his legateship gave him a power independent of the power of the Crown. The groats and half-groats struck by Cardinal Wolsey

[1] *Henry VIII.*, iii. 2.

have, beneath the shield on the reverse, a cardinal's hat, and on either side of the shield the letters T. W.

Edward VI. still further increased the gold coinage, especially the coinage of sovereigns. He struck triple, double, and single sovereigns. The latter at first followed the type of Henry VII., and the earlier sovereigns of Henry VIII., and Edward's double sovereign was of that type also. Other pieces showed the king with shorter robes, and of this type was the triple sovereign. Later Edward adopted a new design—the half-length figure of the King to right, crowned, and holding the sword and orb. On the reverse was a shield. The half-sovereign was either of this type, or else presented only the bust of the King, with head either crowned or bare, and the reverse as before. In silver Edward VI. coined for the first time crowns, half-crowns, and sixpences. The first two denominations represented the King riding to right, and the English shield on the reverse. The shillings and sixpences contained a bust crowned, either in profile to right or facing. The coins of this reign are the first of English coins which bear a date. *Edw. VI.* *Sixpence* *Date.*

Mary coined sovereigns of the earliest (Hen. VII.'s) type, the ryal of the old type—only that the figure in the ship is the Queen—as well as angels and angelets. Her groats, half-groats, and pennies were all of the same type, having a crowned bust of the Queen to right upon the obverse, and on the reverse a shield. After her marriage with Philip, Mary struck half-crowns and shillings. *Mary.*

The former have the buſt of the King and Queen upon the two ſides of the piece, while the latter have the two together, facing one another, "amorous, fond, and billing," on the obverſe, and on the reverſe a ſhield.

<small>Elizabeth.</small>

The number of coin denominations reaches its maximum in the reign of Elizabeth, from whoſe mints were iſſued no leſs than twenty diſtinct kinds of coin; that is to ſay, in gold, the ſovereign, ryal, half-ſovereign, quarter-ſovereign, half-quarter-ſovereign, angel, half-angel, quarter-angel; in ſilver, the crown, half-crown, ſhilling, <small>Three-penny, Two-penny, Three-half-pence, etc.</small> ſixpence, groat, threepenny, half-groat (or two-penny), three-halfpenny-piece, penny, three-farthings, half-penny, farthing. Fortunately the varieties of type were much leſs numerous. It is enough to ſay that, of the firſt iſſue, the ſovereign, the ryal, and the angel did not materially differ from the correſponding coins of Mary, and that the ſovereign of the ſecond iſſue, with all its diviſions, ſhowed ſimply a crowned buſt to left, with hair flowing behind; on the other ſide, the ſhield, as before. The ſilver crown and half-crown had a crowned profile buſt to the left holding a ſceptre; and all the other denominations of ſilver coins had a crowned profile buſt without the ſceptre. The ſixpence and its diviſions were diſtinguiſhed by a roſe placed at the back of the head.

Another ſeries of coins ſtruck by Elizabeth deſerves particular mention. By virtue of a commiſſion, dated January 11th, 1600, or 1601, a coinage was ordered, "unknown to the Engliſh mint, either before or since her time, for it was by law exportable, and intended for the use of the East India Company." This is, in fact, the first appearance of a colonial coinage for England. This coinage consisted of silver pieces, the size of the Spanish coins of eight, four, and two ryals. The coins had on one side the royal arms, on the other a portcullis. The reasons which induced the Queen to take this step were sound and statesmanlike. The East India Company had applied for leave to export Spanish dollars, representing that these coins alone were familiarly known, and therefore readily accepted, in the East. The Queen determined to issue a currency which was genuinely English, in order "that her name and effigies might be hereafter respected by the Asiatics, and she be known as great a Prince as the King of Spain."

All the facts which we have here summarised witness to the growth of fiscality throughout the prosperous reigns of the Tudor dynasty. With this growth a number of economic questions came to the front, which long continued to tax the sagacity of statesmen. We are too ready to congratulate ourselves on our supposed superiority over our ancestors in the art of statecraft. But there can be no question that in one respect we stand in a position of immense advantage over them—in respect, that is, to our mastery of the most important laws of economy and finance. There can be nothing more melancholy than to follow the enactments of successive reigns concerning the supply of bullion, and to note the radically false conception which the laws show touching the nature of wealth. Thus, in the reign of Henry VII., an Act was passed forbidding "any person dwelling in the realm to pay to any alien for merchandise, or other thing, any piece of gold coined in *that or any other realm,*" etc. And the same kind of enactments follow one another with wearisome iteration. A still more important example of the ignorance of economic laws was shown in the liberties which the Government took with the purity and weight of the currency.

In earlier times, though men were no better instructed in economic science, a certain healthy moral instinct had long kept the rulers from degrading the title of the coins they issued. Men's instinct had taught them that such an act was fraudulent and unworthy, though in many cases, especially among the petty Princes (and still more especially the Prince Prelates) of Germany, this instinct had not been very efficient. Philip the Fair, of France, was one of the first who persistently debased his coinage, and Dante's scornful description of Philip—

> Lì si vedrà lo duol che sopra Senna
> Induce, falseggiando la moneta,
> Quei che morrà di colpo di cotenna[1]—

shows in what way his acts were regarded by healthy minds. But at the age at which we are

[1] *Paradiso,* xix. 118.

now arrived, no traditional laws of morality could hold their force unquestioned. Why, it was said, seeing that a pound or a shilling gains its value through the royal sanction, may not the same sanction and the same value be given to a piece of much lower metallic value, and thus the Government be the gainer, and yet the subjects not the losers? From the time of Philip the Fair the degradation of the coinage had proceeded rapidly in France and in most other European countries, including Scotland; but the purity of the English money had been hitherto unassailed. Henry VIII. was the first of English monarchs who debased the sterling fineness of the coin. Some of his shillings and groats contained only one-third silver to two-thirds copper. Some of his gold coins consisted of about five-sixths of gold to one-sixth of silver. This evil continued through the two successive reigns, and was finally reformed by Elizabeth. Even Elizabeth, however, did not do her work completely, as, instead of withdrawing the base coins completely from circulation, she passed them over St. George's Channel for the use of her subjects in Ireland. It is a curious fact, and one which reflects credit upon the Queen and her advisers, that her reform of the coinage, wise, and indeed necessary as it was for the welfare of her subjects, was by no means forced upon the Queen by public opinion, but was on many sides viewed with great dislike. The opposite state of things would, of course, confer some slight and temporary advantages upon the producer, while the chief sufferers would be, as Elizabeth's proclamation said, "All poor people that lived of their hand-labour, as well artificers in cities and towns as labourers in husbandry, or men that took dayetall wages, either by land, by sea, or by fresh waters, and all mean gentlemen that lived upon pensions and stipends, foldes and wages."

Another reason why the old state of things was favoured by some was that it would tend to bring into circulation a large number of pieces of low denomination. So soon as men had come to an understanding that a penny and a halfpenny were each not worth more than half their nominal values, a large number of what really were half-pennies and farthings would be found to be in circulation, and the making of small purchases would be greatly facilitated. There is no doubt that these facilities were very much desired by the poor, and the want of a lower currency was much felt. Up to this time no regular copper coinage had been introduced. The place of it was first supplied by the issue of tokens by private persons. These appear first to have been of lead. Erasmus speaks of the *plumbei Angliae*, apparently referring to leaden tokens in the reign of Henry VII. In the reign of Elizabeth there was a very extensive issue of private tokens in lead, tin, latten, and leather. At length proposals were made for the issue of a copper coinage—proposals not then carried into effect, though some patterns were struck.

To bring this subject to a close, we may add

that in James I.'s reign the ufe of copper tokens was fully recognifed, but that the monopoly of ftriking them was conferred upon certain individuals, at firft upon Lord Harrington. The fame cuftom was continued in the reign of Charles I., but in the abolition of privilege, which refulted from the Civil War, the monopoly lapfed, and the refult was an iffue of copper tokens by the principal tradesmen of almoft all the towns of England. Thus arofe the *feventeenth century tokens*, which are much prized by their collectors, and which are often of confiderable value to the local hiftorian. In 1672 an authorized copper coinage of halfpennies and farthings was undertaken, and in confequence the iffue of copper tokens, though it did not immediately ceafe, fell gradually into difufe. It revived again for a fhort time at the end of the laft century, and the early years of this; that is to fay, from 1787 to 1795, and again from 1811 to 1815, owing to a fcarcity in the copper money of the realm.

In order to difmifs the hiftory of copper coinage, we have advanced far beyond the period with which we had been dealing. Before we again return to it—that is, to the Englifh coinage immediately fubfequent to the death of Elizabeth —we will take one glance at the Scottifh coinage during the intervening period between the acceffion of James IV., already fpoken of, and that of James I.

The coinage of Scotland during this period *Scotland.* follows the fame general lines as the Englifh currency, but in many respects it likewise shows clear traces of French influence. Such influence is most apparent in matters belonging to art. We have said that the first coins with portraits are some groats of James IV. These pieces are noticeable from the fact that the type of bust does not resemble the type on any English contemporary coin. It is a three-quarter face to left. James V. at first struck groats nearly resembling those of Henry VII.'s later coinage; that is to say, having a crowned bust to right. The most artistically beautiful among the Scottish coins belong to this reign and the early part of the succeeding one—the reign of Mary. Few coins are more beautiful than the bonnet-piece of James V., a gold coin in weight $88\frac{1}{2}$ grains, midway between the English half-sovereign and the angel, and having on the obverse the bust of the King wearing a square cap or bonnet, or than the ryal of the early years of Mary's reign. The same influences which were at work bringing about an immense extension of the English coinage, are traceable, though in a less degree, between the reigns of James IV. and James VI. A large number of gold coins was issued during these reigns. James IV. struck *St. Andrews*, *riders*, and *unicorns*, with the divisions of these pieces; James V., *écus* and *bonnet-pieces*; Mary, écus or crowns, *twenty-shilling pieces*, *lions*, *ryals*, and *ducats*, with the divisions of most of these coins. The same Queen struck silver ryals, a much larger coin than had been issued by any of her predecessors. Her other silver coins were the

[margin: Bonnet Pieces.]

two-third and third ryal, and the teftoon and half-teftoon.

We have faid that the Scottifh monarchs went far beyond the Englifh both in degrading the title and in debafing the material of their money. No profeffedly *billon* coins were ever iffued from the Englifh mint: the Scottifh had long eftablifhed a currency in this bafe metal ftanding between filver and copper.[1] Moreover, the Scottifh penny had long fallen in value far below that of the Englifh penny. The Kings of Scotland from time to time made efforts to eftablifh a currency which fhould be exchangeable with that of the neighbouring country, and we find orders taken for the making of certain fpecial denominations of money defigned to ferve this end. In 1483, for example, it was ordered that a gold coin fhould be ftruck of the finenefs and weight of the Englifh rofe noble, and groats of the value of the Englifh groat. The firft of thefe defigns was never carried into effect, but in 1489 a groat of the defired ftandard was coined. We find that it was equal to fourteen-pence Scottifh, fo that the Scottifh penny was between a quarter and a third of the Englifh coin. When James VI. came to the Englifh throne, however, the Scottifh penny had funk to be one-twelfth of the Englifh.

James I. of England and VI. of Scotland had to James I.

[1] Among thefe billon pieces the *bawbee* (corrupted from *bas pièce*, in Scottifh French) was the longeft remembered, and is the moft worthy of notice. The name is expreffive of the influences under which the bafe money was introduced into Scotland.

maintain a double currency. In fact, the coinages of the two realms were not brought into entire uniformity until the reign of Anne, when the complete union was effected. For Scotland James struck in gold the *twenty-pound piece*, the ducat, the lion noble, the thistle noble, and the rider, before his accession to the English throne; and in silver, the *sword dollar*, the *thistle dollar*, and the *noble*, with the divisional parts of most of these coins, as well as pieces of two, four, five, eight, ten, sixteen, twenty, thirty, and forty shillings, and several billon pieces. After his accession his peculiarly Scottish coins were the sword and sceptre piece, and the thistle mark.

The English coins of James were the sovereign, and the double or rose ryal. These were during his reign generally current for thirty shillings. The type of the ryal was that of the sovereigns of Henry VII. The half of this was the spur ryal, which at first followed the old type of the rose nobles or ryals, but afterwards showed on one side a lion supporting the English shield (quartering Scotland and France), on the reverse the spur, or sun as on the rose nobles. The angel showed some variety of type from that of the previous reign. But the most distinctive coin of James I., and that which superseded all the others, was the *unite* or *broad*, a piece of twenty shillings, and designed to pass current in both countries. The type was at first a half figure holding sword and orb; subsequently a bust, either crowned or laureate. This last type prevailed, and earned for the piece the

Unite.

name *laurel*, while the motto FACIAM EOS IN GENTEM UNAM was the origin of its older name. The laurel wreath had never appeared upon the head of any previous Englifh monarch upon his coins. As it is commonly worn by the Roman Emperors on their money, it was moft likely adopted by James with the object of proclaiming his imperial rank as King of England, Scotland, and Ireland; for we find that he alfo, for the firft time, adopted the title Imperator upon fome of his medals.

It is noticeable that in the reign of James I. we for the firft time have the values of the coins given upon them. His thirty, fifteen, ten, and five-fhilling pieces in gold, and his fhillings, fixpences, half-groats and pennies, are marked with numerals expreffing their value. The cuftom was continued in the reign of Charles I., and during the Commonwealth. {Value.}

The variety of coin denominations reaches, as has been faid, its maximum under Elizabeth. From the time of the introduction of the unite this number begins rapidly to decline; fo that in the reign of Charles I. it almoft reached the fame fimplicity which it now has. A comparifon might, in truth, be inftituted between the refpective coinages of the Tudor and the Stuart dynafties and their refpective literatures. The greateft artiftic excellence belongs to the coinage (as to the literature) of the firft era, while that of the fecond era ftands next to it, and fuperior to anything which was fubfequently produced. In the fecond clafs we {Number of Denominations.}

find a marked tendency toward fimplicity and adaptability to the ordinary needs of life.

Thus the filver coinage of the Stuarts is practically the fame as that which now exifts, with the exception that James I. did not ftrike the fmaller pieces, and that Charles I., in the midft of the Civil War, ftruck fome large coins which were never afterwards reproduced. The crowns and half-crowns of James I. reprefent the King on horfeback, the fhillings the crowned buft of the King, the ordinary fhield (now without any appearance of a crofs) forming the reverfe in each cafe.

Charles I. Charles I.'s ufual gold coinage is the unite, half-unite, and crown. Thefe pieces have the King's buft on the obverfe, and on the reverfe a fhield. His filver coins of higher denominations were like thofe of his father, and the lower denominations follow the type of the fhilling. After the outbreak of the Civil War, Charles adopted for the reverfe of his coins, both in gold and filver, what is called the Declaration type, namely the legend RELIG. PROT. LEG. ANG. LIBER. PARL. (The Proteftant Religion, the Laws of England, and the Liberty of Parliament), written in two lines acrofs the field of the reverfe. Of this type he ftruck fome pieces of three pounds, as well as large filver coins worth twenty and ten fhillings, made out of the plate which was brought by his adherents to the royal mints.

Charles I. eftablifhed mints at a great number of towns during the Civil War. Altogether we

Oxford Crown.

have coins struck during his reign at the following places: Aberystwith, Bristol, Chester, Cork, Dublin, Edinburgh, Exeter, London, Oxford, Shrewsbury, Weymouth, Worcester, York. Beside the regular coinage, there was during the Civil War a large issue of *siege-pieces* struck in towns or castles which were in a state of siege. These are of Beeston Castle, Carlisle, Colchester, Newark, Pontefract, and Scarborough. Some of the Pontefract pieces may count as the earliest coins struck in the name of Charles II. The castle still held out after the death of Charles I. Accordingly the governor placed upon the siege-pieces the legend CAROLUS SECUNDUS, or CAROL. II., etc., and on the other side POST MORTEM PATRIS PRO FILIO.

Various Mints.

Siege Pieces.

In artistic merit the coinage of Charles I. is

OXFORD CROWN OF CHARLES I.

only inferior to that of the earlier Tudor sovereigns. This King, whose taste in art is well known, employed upon his money several engravers of distinguished merit. Among these were Thomas Rawlins and Nicholas Briot. The latter had firſt been engaged at the French mint, and while there had invented ſeveral improved methods of ſtriking coins; but finding no appreciation of his talents, he came to England, and was at once employed by Charles. Rawlins was for a long time engraver at the Tower mint, and on the outbreak of the Civil War he removed with the mint to Oxford. While there he executed the famous *Oxford Crown*. The coin, though it does not differ materially from the crowns of Charles I. of the Declaration type, ſhows, behind the figure of the King on horſeback, a view of the city of Oxford, in which the fortifications and ſome of the chief buildings, notably Magdalen tower, are very clearly pourtrayed.

Commonwealth.

The Commonwealth employed as their engraver the famous medalliſt, Thomas Simon, whoſe medallic portraits, made in conjunction with his brother Abraham, are among the fineſt art products of that age. The extreme ſimplicity of the types upon the coins did not, however, give Simon room for any great diſplay of artiſtic talent. The coin bore upon one ſide a ſhield charged with St. George's croſs (England), on the other ſide two ſhields, one with St. George's croſs, and the other with the harp of Ireland. Preſumably the figure of the ſaint would have been conſidered more idolatrous than his emblem preſented in the baldeſt form. It is remarkable, too, that during the Commonwealth was adopted for the firſt, and alſo unhappily for the laſt time, the ſenſible device of having the legends both on obverſe and reverſe in Engliſh inſtead of Latin. On the obverſe was ſimply THE COMMONWEALTH OF ENGLAND, on the reverſe the motto GOD WITH US. In 1656, when Cromwell had been raiſed to the rank of Lord Protector of the Commonwealth, he entruſted to Thomas Simon the taſk of preparing dies for a new coinage, which had on one ſide the profile buſt of the Protector, on the other the ſhield of England, Scotland, and Ireland, and as an eſcutcheon of pretence that of Cromwell himſelf. The motto was appropriate and expreſſive, PAX QUAERITUR BELLO; and the whole piece was one of the fineſt of Thomas Simon's works.

All this time the coinage had been wonderfully ſimplifying its character. We have ſeen that James VI. definitely ſettled the ſilver currency upon the baſis (ſo far as the number of pieces is concerned) which it has ſince reſted upon. In the time of the Commonwealth there were, in reality, only two regularly current gold coins—the broad and half-broad. During the reign of Charles II. further changes were made, which had the effect of definitely ſettling the denominations of coins down to the middle of the reign of George III. So that all that is really worth record in the hiſtory of Engliſh money comes to an end in the courſe of the reign of Charles II.

After his reſtoration Charles II. continued for ſome little time to employ the engraver of the Commonwealth, Thomas Simon, and this artiſt executed the sovereigns and shillings of the first years of the reign, which are the most beautiful of Charles II.'s coins, in truth the last really beautiful coins which were issued from English mints. Simon was superseded by the engraver Blondeau, who had produced some patterns for Commonwealth coins, and Blondeau was succeeded by the Roettiers. Simon, in order to obtain his recall, executed his famous *petition crown*, in which the King is besought to compare the likeness upon that piece with any that was issued by the Dutch engraver to the Royal Mint. And in truth there can be no question that this pattern is in delicacy of treatment superior to any other English coin.

In the same year the twenty-shilling pieces began to be called guineas, from the fact that most of them were made from gold brought from Guinea by the African Company. The pieces actually made of this gold were stamped with an elephant below the bust, but the name which properly belonged to them was transferred to all, and by accident the value of the piece increased from twenty to twenty-one shillings. The earliest coinage of Charles had consisted of twenty and ten-shilling pieces and crowns: but in 1662 this issue was exchanged for a coinage of pieces made by the mill, which were five guineas, two guineas, guineas, and half-guineas. This currency became henceforth stereotyped, so that from the reign of Charles II. to that of George II. inclusive, the English coinage consisted of five guineas, two guineas, guineas, half-guineas, in gold; of crowns, half-crowns, fhillings, fixpences, groats, three-pennies, two-pennies, and pennies, in filver. The last four denominations were only ftruck for iffue as Maundy money. The copper coinage during thefe reigns was much lefs fixed. It generally confifted of halfpennies or farthings. Five-guinea and two-guinea pieces were not coined after the reign of George II., and in the courfe of the reign of George III. a twenty-fhilling piece was once more introduced, bearing the older name of fovereign.

The only coins ftruck fubfequent to the reign of Charles II. which are of intereft to the hiftorian are thofe iffued in Ireland, by the authority of James II., after his abdication of the Englifh crown.

The King began firft, in order to meet his preffing neceffities, to ftrike bronze (or gun-metal) fixpences. Subfequently he iffued fhillings, half-crowns, and crowns in the fame metal. The value of thefe pieces was of courfe a purely ficti-tious one, the real worth of a crown being no more than a penny, and the lofs to the nation when the money was recalled by William III., and paid for at its actual value, was very great, It was found that the total iffue amounted nomi-nally to £22,489, of which the actual value was £642.

The filver coins of Anne, made from the treafure feized in the Vigo Bay expedition, and in confequence marked with the word VIGO; the coinage of George I., marked with the letters s s c, because struck from silver furnished by the South Sea Company; and that of George II., with the word LIMA, because made from treasure which had come from thence, are worthy of a passing notice.

The copper coinage of Queen Anne consisted of a limited number of farthings struck in the year 1714. Several patterns for farthings were likewise made in this and the preceding year. They would scarcely claim mention here, but that through some unexplained cause a ridiculous notion has gained currency that these pieces are of immense value. Their real value is from 10s. to £1, if in fine condition.

CHAPTER VI.

EARLY ORIENTAL COINS.

HE art of coinage was, as has been already pointed out, of Oriental invention. The first coins seem to have been issued at about the same time, the seventh century B.C., by the Lydians in the west of Asia, and by the Chinese in the extreme east. When the Persians under Cyrus conquered Lydia they adopted the useful art of coinage; but chose a simpler system than the Lydian. If we exclude money issued by Greek cities under Persian rule and by Persian satraps on the occasion of some military expedition, there were in use in the length and breadth of the Persian Empire but two classes of coins—the gold *darics* and the silver *sigli*, or *shekels*. The daric bore on one side as type a figure of the King shooting with the bow; on the other side a mere punch-mark or incuse: it weighed rather more than a sovereign, and was of almost pure gold. The shekel was of nearly the same size, and stamped with the same type; but was

_{Persia.}

_{Darics and Sigli.}

only two-thirds as heavy; in fact, almoſt exactly of the weight of a ſhilling. Twenty ſhekels were equivalent to a daric. It is intereſting to find the equivalents of pounds and ſhillings circulating throughout Weſtern Aſia at a period ſo early.

Until the Perſian Empire fell, darics and ſigli were probably the only officially recogniſed currency between the Halys in Aſia Minor and the borders of China. Other coins were, however, ſtruck in ſome places. The Greek cities of the coaſt were not allowed to iſſue gold coin; but the Perſian rulers did not interfere with their autonomous iſſues of ſilver and copper money, which bore types appropriate to the ſtriking cities. And ſome of the ſatraps of the Perſian King were allowed, more eſpecially on the occaſion of military expeditions, to iſſue ſilver coins, the types of which curiouſly combine Perſian and Greek mythology, one of them, for inſtance, preſenting on one ſide the figure of Hormuzd, on the other that of Zeus. And there were certain ſtates which enjoyed, among other privileges of partial autonomy, the right of ſtriking coins. Such was the Lycian league, conſiſting of moſt of the cities of Lycia, all of which impreſſed on one ſide of their money a circular three-membered ſymbol, which moſt writers conſider to be of ſolar meaning. And ſuch were ſome of the kingdoms of Cyprus which were ſaved by the intervening ſea from complete ſubſerviency to the Perſian Empire, and the coins of which bear Greek legends written in the curious Cyprian character, of cuneiform appearance.

It is a curious fact that coinage in Phoenicia, one of the most commercial of ancient countries, should have been late in origin, and apparently not very plentiful. There are, in fact, no coins of earlier period than the third century which we can with certainty attribute to the great cities of Tyre and Sidon. Some modern writers, however, consider that many of the coins generally classed under Persia—notably those bearing the types of a chariot, a galley, and an owl respectively—were issued by those cities in the fifth and fourth centuries B.C. But it is certain, in any case, that the Phoenicians were far behind the Greeks in the art of moneying. *Phoenicia.*

With the invasion of Persia by Alexander the Great came a great change; and all the ancient landmarks of Asiatic government and order were swept away. During the life of Alexander the Great the coins bearing his name and his types circulated throughout Asia; and after his death the same range of currency was attained by the money of the early Seleucid Kings of Syria— Seleucus I., Antiochus I., and Antiochus II., who virtually succeeded to the dominions of the Persian Kings, and tried in many respects to carry on their policy. Of these monarchs we possess a splendid series of coins, beginning with Seleucus, the general of Alexander, and going down to Tigranes. Their features are thoroughly familiar to us, and by the help of their portraits we can *Successors of Alexander.*

judge more satisfactorily of their appearance in history as recorded by Justin and Appian. At first their rule extended from the Aegean Sea to the great desert of Gobi; and their coins were issued by numberless mints throughout Asia, and copied by the barbarous tribes of the Chinese and Indian frontiers.

In the reign of Antiochus II., however, the Syro-Greek kingdom began to fall to pieces; and with its decay Oriental coinage, as opposed to Greek, may properly be said to commence. About B.C. 250 the Greek satraps of the wealthy provinces of Bactria and India became independent; and the Parthian Arsaces raised the standard of a successful revolt on the southern shores of the Caspian. In the next century smaller kingdoms arose in Arabia, Armenia, and Mesopotamia; and the Jewish people wrested their independence from the hands of Antiochus Epiphanes. In the far East rude tribes of Sacae and Huns from the borders of China swept down on the eastern provinces of the Persian Empire, and founded dynasties which seem, however, to have soon passed away.

I shall not speak of Asia Minor on the west, for that district was dominated by Greek and Roman influences; nor of China on the east; each of these regions is treated of elsewhere in this volume. The vast space between these two extremes may be divided into three regions: (1) Armenia, Syria, and the country to the west of the Tigris and the Caspian; (2) Central Asia;

Beginning of Oriental Coinage. 145

(3) India and Afghaniſtan. We will ſpeak in turn of the coins of the two former regions, during the whole period which elapſed between the break-up of the Syro-Greek kingdom and the conquering ſpread of Iſlam—that is to ſay, from the third century before, until the eighth century after, the Chriſtian era. India is reſerved for a ſeparate chapter.

The earlieſt coins which we poſſeſs which belong diſtinctively to Central Aſia are thoſe recently diſcovered in Bokhara, bearing the name of Andragoras, who muſt have been a revolted Greek ſatrap of Parthia or Media. Central Asia.

In the courſe of the ſecond century the Parthians, under their great King Mithradates, occupied all Mid-Aſia, or rather gained a ſort of lordſhip over it, and defended it for centuries from the attacks of the Greeks and Romans on the one ſide, and of the Huns on the other. The Parthian ſilver coins conſiſt of two diſtinct claſſes—regal and civic. The regal coins are of ſilver, of the weight of an Attic drachm, 60-65 grains, and bear during the whole of Parthian hiſtory uniform types—the head of the ruling King on one ſide, and on the other the firſt King, Arſaces, ſeated, holding a bow. The civic coins were iſſued by the ſemi-Greek cities of Perſia and Meſopotamia. They are four times as heavy, and preſent a greater variety of type. Subſidiary copper pieces accompany each ſeries. Parthians.

As the Parthians were conſtantly at war with the Syro-Greek kingdom ſo long as it laſted, it may at first surprise us to find that the legends of the Parthian coins, except in the case of a few of the latest, are in Greek. The date of them is indicated by the increasing complexity of these legends as time goes on. All the successors of the first Arsaces keep his name as their dynastic title, just as all the Kings of Egypt are styled Ptolemy, and the Roman Emperors Augustus; but they add to this dynastic name a constantly increasing number of epithets. In fact, the number of these epithets which are to be found on a coin is usually the readiest means of assigning its date. The earliest pieces bear only the legend Ἀρσάκου or βασιλέως Ἀρσάκου; but already the second King Tiridates assumes the title of Great King, βασιλεὺς μέγας; his successors add a variety of epithets, θεοπάτωρ, ἐπιφανής, εὐεργέτης, and the like, until, under Orodes the Great, we reach the formula βασιλέως μεγάλου Ἀρσάκου εὐεργέτου δικαίου ἐπιφανοῦς φιλέλληνος, which remains usual until the end of the dynasty. The last-mentioned title, Philhellen, is interesting, and records the fact that, at all events after the fall of the Syro-Greek kingdom, the Parthian Kings were anxious to secure to themselves the goodwill of the semi-Greek population which dwelt in many of the large towns under their rule.

The title of "Great King" was not in the style of the Parthian monarchs a mere parade or an unmeaning phrase. It signified that he was master of a number of under-kings or satraps, who ruled under his authority the various districts of Central Asia, and in comparison with whom he might well be called great. Some of the rulers adopt the alternative title, "King of Kings," which has much the same meaning. The coins supply us with full and trustworthy information as to the dress and armour of those Parthian horsemen who more than once spread the terror of their name as far as Rome.

The great cities of Mesopotamia, such as Charax and Seleucia on the Tigris, in all probability issued the large coins already mentioned. The type of these is more varied. Before

AN EARLY PARTHIAN KING.

the time of Orodes it is like that of the regal money; but after that time it usually represents the Parthian King seated, receiving a wreath either from the goddess Nike (Victory), or from Pallas, or more often from a City personified in a female deity who holds a cornucopiae. The head of a personified City appears on the copper pieces which go with the civic coins. Both silver and copper bear a date, the year in which the coin was struck according to the Seleucid era, which begins in B.C. 312; sometimes even the month of that year. We thus gain most valuable means of checking the dates of the events of Parthian history, at all events of the acceſſion and depoſition of the Kings. Once in the ſeries we have a portrait of a woman, Muſa, an Italian girl preſented by Auguſtus to Phraates IV., who made ſo good a uſe of her talents that ſhe perſuaded the King to declare her ſon Phraataces his heir, and reigned in conjunction with that ſon until he loſt his life in a revolt. She wears a jewelled head-dreſs, and is clad in Oriental ſplendour.

The diſtrict of Perſia proper ſeems to have enjoyed partial independence in Parthian times; and we may feel juſtified in aſſigning to this diſtrict a long ſeries of ſmall ſilver coins which are uſually called ſub-Parthian; bearing on one ſide the head of a king, on the other uſually a fire-altar, and inſcriptions in Pehlvi characters, which have as yet been very imperfectly read.

Saſſanian Dynaſty. About A.D. 220 the princes of Perſia revolted againſt their Parthian maſters, and ſucceeded in wreſting from them the ſupremacy of Aſia. A great Perſian dynaſty then aroſe, beginning with Artaxerxes or Ardeſhir the Saſſanian, and ruled the Eaſt until the riſe of Mohammadaniſm. The coins of the Saſſanian Kings preſent a great contraſt to thoſe of the Parthians. Their execution is far neater and more maſterly, and they ſhow in all reſpects a reaction of the more manly tribes of Southern Aſia alike againſt the debaſed Helleniſm which had invaded the cities of Weſtern Perſia, and againſt the barbarous Parthian hordes, who ſeem to have paſſed out of hiſtory with their overthrow, leaving scarcely a trace on the art, the religion, or the customs of Asia.

The great bulk of the Sassanian issues is in silver, and consists of flat, well-wrought pieces, of the weight of an Attic drachm, 67 grains. There are also gold coins weighing 110-115 grains, rather heavier than the contemporary solidi of Rome, and a few copper pieces. Gold and silver coins are of similar legends and devices, and throughout the whole of Persian rule preserve an almost unchanged character. On the obverse is universally the head of the King. The various monarchs have different styles of crown and coiffure, sometimes of a very extravagant character, the hair being rolled into huge balls and

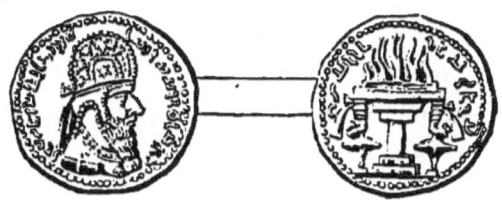

ARTAXERXES I.

tufts. On his earliest coins, Artaxerxes' head is closely copied from that of Mithradates I., the greatest of the Parthian monarchs, whom the Persian King seems thus to claim as prototype and model. Around the King's head on all the Persian coins is his name and his titles in Pehlvi letters. Artaxerxes is termed the worshipper of Ormazd, the divine King of Kings of Iran. Later monarchs vary the formula; on the money of some of the latest, the mint where the coin was issued and the year of the reign are written in Pehlvi characters in the field of the reverse. The reverse type of all Sassanian coins is the same, the fire-altar, the symbol of the worship of Ormazd, usually guarded by soldiers, or approached by the King in humble adoration.

Western Asia.

Between Armenia on the north and Arabia on the south, coins were issued during Parthian times by a number of small states which maintained a precarious autonomy against the Romans on the one hand, and the Parthians on the other. Most of them disappear before the revived force of the empire of the Sassanians.

Armenia.

Armenia was, until the time of the Parthian Mithradates (B.C. 160), the seat of several small dynasties. We hear of Arsames, a king of Arsamosata, who received the Syrian prince Antiochus Hierax when he fled from his brother Seleucus; and of one Xerxes, who ruled in the same district, and resisted the arms of Antiochus IV. Both of these rulers have left us coins of Greek fashion, but bearing on the obverse a head of the King in peaked Armenian tiara. But Mithradates, if we may trust the history of Moses of Khoren, overran Armenia, and set on the throne his brother Vagharshag or Valarsaces, who was the first of a line of Arsacid Kings of Armenia, under whom the country reached a higher pitch of prosperity than ever before or since. We possess coins of several of these Kings—of Tigranes, who became King of Syria and son-in-law of Mithradates of Pontus, and whose numerous silver coins struck at Antioch bear as type the Genius or Fortune of that city seated on a rock; of Artaxias, who was crowned by Germanicus; and of Artavasdes, who was for a brief period maintained by the arms of Augustus. We also have a long series of coins in copper issued by the Kings of Osroene or Edessa, whose dynastic names were Abgarus and Mannus, and who flourished during the first three centuries of the Christian era, living in independence by no means complete, for the one side of their coin is generally occupied by the effigy of a Roman emperor.

The Arab tribes to the east of Palestine at <small>Nabathea.</small> some periods enjoyed independence under kings of their own. We have a series of coins of the first century B.C. struck by the Nabathean Kings Malchus and Aretas, partly at Antioch, partly at Petra. The inscriptions and types of these coins are in earlier times Greek, and one of the Kings who bore the name Aretas calls himself Philhellen; but later the legends are written in local alphabet and dialect, and the portraits assume more of a native aspect. The short-lived Palmy- <small>Palmyra.</small> rene Empire, founded by Odenathus and Zenobia, and put down by Aurelian, has also left numismatic traces of its existence in money quite identical in fabric, weight, and types, with the contemporary coins issued by Roman emperors at Alexandria. Some of the effigies of Zenobia on these coins may, however, be considered fairly good portraits for the time.

Further south, in Arabia, we find at least two <small>Arabia</small>

tribes who iffued abundance of coin before the birth of Mohammad. The Himyarites circulated great quantities of imitations of the Athenian coins of various periods, and at a later age of the money of Auguftus. Types of their own they feem not to have ufed, but they imprefsed on their imitations of civilized coins an infcription which identifies them as Himyarite. The people of Characene, a fmall diftrict on the Perfian Gulf, began in the fecond century B.C. a feries of tetradrachms of Greek ftyle, the general appearance and types of which are copied from the coins of contemporary Greek Kings of Syria and Bactria. The names of a feries of thefe monarchs, Tiraeus, Attambelus, and fo forth, together with their order of fucceffion, are preferved to us by coins.

One of the moft curious facts noticeable in the coins of Arabia is the frequency with which the heads of queens occupy the obverfes, in conjunction with thofe of their hufbands and fons. This peculiarity illuftrates the hiftorical fact, known from other fources, that before the days of Mohammad women not unfrequently ruled among the Arabian tribes, either alone or conjointly with fome male relative. The abundance of the known money of this country, and the purity of the metal of which it is compofed, fhow that while the Ptolemies ruled in Egypt, a brifk trade went on between Arabia and the countries to the eaft and weft of it. But for art the Arabs feem never to have had a tafte. They merely copied the coins which paffed current moſt freely in their neighbourhood.

Moſt people will take a greater intereſt in the coins of Judaea, although none of theſe are very ancient, nor are they artiſtically pleaſing. It would ſeem that, until the middle of the ſecond century B.C., the Jews either weighed out gold and ſilver for the price of goods, or elſe uſed the money uſually current in Syria, that of Perſia, Phoenicia, Athens, and the Seleucidae. Simon the Maccabee

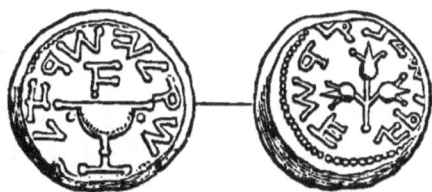

EARLY JEWISH SHEKEL.

HALF SHEKEL.

was the firſt to iſſue the Jewiſh ſhekel as a coin, and we learn from the Book of Maccabees that the privilege of ſtriking was expreſſly granted him by King Antiochus VII. of Syria. We poſſeſs ſhekels of years 1-5 of the deliverance of Zion; the types are a chalice and a triple flower.

The kings who ſucceeded Simon, down to Antigonus, confined themſelves to the iſſue of copper money, with Hebrew legends and with types calculated not to shock the susceptible feelings of their people, to whom the representation of a living thing was abominable—such types as a lily, a palm, a star, or an anchor. When the Herodian family came in, several violations of this rule appear. For example, we find objects of heathen cultus, such as a tripod and a caduceus; and money was even struck in Judaea bearing the effigies of men, sometimes of the reigning Roman Emperor, sometimes even of the Jewish King. Both the Agrippas are guilty of this violation of principle. The Roman Procurators of Judaea also issued coin with Greek legends, and carefully dated, so that we can distinguish the money issued during the eventful years of the rise of Christianity at Jerusalem.

Both of the desperate but unsuccessful revolts

SIMON BAR COCHAB.

of the Jews against their Roman masters—that in the reign of Vespasian under Simon and Eleazar, and that in the reign of Hadrian under Bar Cochab—have left a deep impression on the Jewish coin. In both periods the issue of shekels was resumed, and Roman denarii were freely restruck by the revolted leaders with their own types and names. With thefe coins the Jewifh money comes to an end. Jerusalem became a Roman colony under the name of Aelia Capitolina, and all money iffued in that region bears witnefs in its types only to the defeat and flavery of the Hebrews.

CHAPTER VII.

MOHAMMADAN COINS.

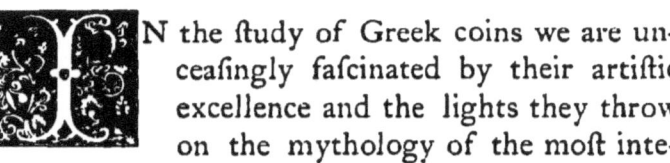N the ſtudy of Greek coins we are unceaſingly faſcinated by their artiſtic excellence and the lights they throw on the mythology of the moſt intereſting people of antiquity. Roman and mediaeval coins have their importance in ſhowing us the ſource of our monetary ſyſtem, and poſſeſs an added charm in the many hiſtorical aſſociations they awake, though they ſeldom increaſe our actual knowledge of hiſtory. Engliſh coins we ſtudy becauſe we are Engliſhmen, and like to know what our anceſtors bartered their ſouls for. None of theſe attractions belong to Mohammadan coins. Art we ſhould ſcarcely look for, ſince we all know that the Bleſſed Prophet declared that "every painter is in hell-fire," and ſtraitly forbade the making of "ſtatues" (by which he probably meant idols) and images of living things, on pain of the artiſt's being compelled to put a ſoul into his creation on the Day of Judgment. Hence

true believers have always been very cautious of reprefenting human or even animal forms as an aid to decoration, and we fhall find that it is only when barbarous Tartars or heretical Perfians enter the field that figures of living things appear in the art of Mohammadan countries, and then very rarely upon their coins. The Eaftern draughtsman, being debarred from the moft fruitful of artiftic materials, took refuge in the elaboration of thofe beautiful arabefque defigns and geometrical patterns which are characteriftic of fo-called Arabian work, and even turned the natural grace of the Arabic writing to account as an element in decoration. Thus, on coins, as in mofques, we find the Kufic character ufed as a thing of beauty, and difpofed to the beft advantage, where a European artift would have relegated the letters to an obfcure corner, and devoted all his fpace to the head or other figure that occupied the face of the coin. It was a matter of neceffity rather than of choice, but it had a good effect in developing the graceful and elfewhere little cultivated art of calligraphy.

Calligraphy

Nor muft we expect any very interefting metrological data to be derived from Mohammadan coins. Their metrology, fo far as it is known, is borrowed—like moft other fo-called Arabian things, whether philofophical, artiftic, literary, or even religious—from the more cultivated nations the Muflims conquered, and the fcience ftill refts in deep obfcurity, chiefly becaufe no one, except my indefatigable friend M. Sauvaire,[1] has had the patience to work so dreary a vein. Historical associations it were vain to call up at the sight of a Muslim coin, since the great majority of even well-educated and reading folk are profoundly ignorant of everything oriental, except what is Biblical or Japanese. There are, perhaps, three or four Mohammadan celebrities known by name to a fair proportion of ordinary readers. "The good Haroun Al-Raschid" owes his popularity to the *Arabian Nights* and Lord Tennyson, and coins bearing his name, together with that of the ill-fated Vizir Jaafar, of which there are many examples in the British Museum and every other large collection, might touch a chord of remembrance; while a piece issued by the famous Saladin, though in itself uninteresting, carries upon its surface a long train of Crusading associations for the historical student. The currency of the great fighting Sultans of Turkey, the Amuraths and Mahomets, the Selims and Solimans—to adopt the barbarous kakography of Western writers—has its memories, and so have the large gold pieces, with their uncompromising declaration of faith, issued by "Bobadil" and the other heroes of the dying kingdom of the Moors in Spain. To a very few the solitary piece of gold struck by the Mamlûk Queen, Shejer ed-Durr (which, being interpreted, means Tree of Pearls), may

Historical Associations.

Coin of a Mamlûk Queen.

---

[1] *Matériaux pour servir á l'Histoire de la Numismatique et de la Métrologie Musalmanes;* and several profound papers in the *Journal of the Royal Asiatic Society.*

recall the fact that it was this apparently fascinating but not quite irreproachable lady who first made the pilgrimage to Mekka in the palanquin or mahmal, which has ever since been a notable feature of the departure of the pilgrims from Cairo, and which, being inextricably confused with the Holy Carpet, severely exercised the British conscience during the triumphal ceremonies that followed hard upon the battle of Tell-el-Kebîr.

The coin in question is a good example of the rich genealogical material to be extracted from an Arabic half-guinea. On one side, in the margin, is the profession of faith, testifying that "there is no God but God, and that Mohammad is His Prophet,"—a formula which appears on the majority of Mohammadan coins, often accompanied by other expressions of religious orthodoxy, and by sentences from the Korân. This very marginal inscription goes on to tell, in the words of the Korân, how God "sent Mohammad with the guidance and religion of truth, so that he might make it triumph over all other creeds." Encircled by these pious words, the field shows a long string of titles, all belonging to Queen Shejer ed-Durr, from which a sort of outline of her life may be constructed. In the first place she is called El-Mufta'fimîyeh, which means that she was once a slave-girl of the 'Abbâsy Khalif El-Mufta'fim. Her next title is Es-Sâlihîyeh, showing that she was transferred from the Khalif's harîm to that of Es-Sâlih, the grand-nephew of Saladin, who had

Genealogical data.

succeeded to the kingship of Egypt after the deaths of his grand-uncle, grandfather (the scarcely less famous "Saphadin" El-'Adil), and father. Further, this coin gives her the title of "Queen of the Muslims," and " Mother of El-Manfûr Khalîl," a son who, we know from the historians, died in infancy. On the other side are the name and titles of the reigning 'Abbâsy Khalif El-Mufta'fim, the Queen's former husband, round which is arranged a marginal infcription which records how, "in the name of God, the compaffionate, the merciful," the coin was ftruck at Cairo in the year of the Hijreh 648, *i.e.*, A.D. 1250.

Crusade of St. Louis.

This year was a very critical one for the Mohammadan fupremacy in Egypt. In 1249 Es-Sâlih had died, and the French army of the last Crufade, under St. Louis, was in occupation of Damietta, and already advancing upon the capital. In this pofition of affairs, the Slave-queen undertook the government. She concealed the death of her hufband, and fubdued the panic which the Frank invafion was exciting. Then the tide of fortune changed; the Bahry Mamlûks, under the command of Beybars of the lion-creft, won a complete victory over the French at Manfûrah; St. Louis and his army were made prifoners of war; and, on the death of the heir to the throne, Shejer ed-Durr was proclaimed Queen of Egypt. For two months and a half fhe reigned alone, and then, on the remonftrance of the Khalif, firft of her three hufbands, at the impropriety of a woman exercising royal power, she associated the Emir Eybek and another nominal colleague with her in the sovereignty. But from the first moment she took the reins of government into her hands till the day of her death, she was sovereign mistress of Egypt, let who would enjoy the name of Sultan. She made Eybek Sultan, and married him; but she retained the absolute authority she had held before, and when her colleague showed symptoms of independence, and seemed inclined to enlarge the circle of his affections, she had him murdered in his bath, under her own eyes. Three days afterwards " Tree of Pearls" herself was beaten to death with wooden bath-clogs by the slaves of a divorced wife of the murdered man.

The unique coin described above must have been issued during these two stirring months of female autocracy, of which it is the only numismatic evidence we possess, in corroboration of the statements of the historians, which it confirms in the most minute particulars, in every detail of the long string of titles attached to the Queen's name; and it derives a peculiar interest from having been struck at the very moment when St. Louis received his final discomfiture at the hands of the infidels, and by the very Queen whose treasury was enriched by a million gold byfants, which formed the ransom of the King of France.

In the wealth of information afforded by this coin we see the real value of Mohammadan numismatics. The coins of the Muslim East do not so much recall history as make it. The student is

Wealth of Historical Information.

constantly meeting with a perfectly unknown King or even dynasty, which fills up a gap in the annals of the East. A Mohammadan coin generally gives not only the date and place of issue, and the name of the ruler who caused it to be struck, but frequently the names of his father and grandfather, his heir-apparent, his liege-lord, and other valuable genealogical data and aids to the due understanding of the inter-relations of different dynasties; while the religious formulae employed will enable us to tell the sect to which the ruler who issued the coin belonged, at least so far as the broad distinctions of Islam are concerned. If the complete series of coins issued by every Muslim state were preserved, we should be able to tabulate with the utmost nicety the entire line of Kings and their principal vassals that have ruled in every part of the Mohammadan Empire since the eighth century, and to draw with tolerable accuracy the boundaries of their territories at every period. Minting was ever one of the most cherished rights of sovereignty: the privileges of "Khutbeh and Sikkeh," that is, of being prayed for in the Friday prayers in the Mosque and of inscribing his name upon the currency, were the first things the new King thought about on ascending the throne. We may be confident that the right was exercised at the earliest possible opportunity, and that a prince who occupied the kingly office for but a few weeks was sure to celebrate his royalty on a coin. Shejer ed-Durr is a case in point, for the coin above described must have been struck in her brief reign of two months.

Numismatic Evidence. 163

It is this monetary vanity of Eaſtern princes that makes their coinage ſo valuable to the hiſtorian, and indeed compels him to regard numiſmatic evidence as the fureſt teſtimony he can obtain. Of courſe it may be urged that the facts thus derived from a ſtudy of coins are not worth having; they may be abſolutely true, but they relate to perſons and countries concerning which nobody feels any poſſible intereſt, and even of theſe they tell only ſuch meagre items as dates and chief towns, the very things we are now carefully expunging from our ſchool-books! It is eaſy to reply that, like every currency, that of the Mohammadan Eaſt really ſupplies important evidence concerning the economic ſtate of the country by its quality and rate of exchange. But we join iſſue on the main queſtion, and venture to aſſert that no ſcrap of poſitive hiſtorical fact is really uſeleſs, or may not at ſome time be turned to important ends. The Mohammadan coinage, more than any other, abounds in hiſtorical data, and when the as yet unwritten hiſtory of the Eaſt during the Middle Ages comes to be told, the author will find no ſurer check upon the native annaliſts than the coins.

If the hiſtory of the Mohammadan Eaſt were compriſed in the annals of a few great dynaſties, the value of the coins would not be ſo conſiderable, for we ſhould only learn perhaps ſome freſh dates or confirmation of dates already known, and the mints would only be the capitals and large towns

Value of Numismatic Evidence.

of well-known provinces. But Mohammadan hiftory is made up of the ftruggles for fupremacy of hundreds of petty houfes, and thoufands of petty dynafts, of whofe very exiftence we should often be wholly ignorant but for their coins. Thefe petty dynafts ftruck their money at towns of which next to nothing is often known, and thus the coinage is frequently our only means of eftablifhing the pofition of the fmaller towns of the mediaeval Eaft. Sometimes thefe fmall towns preferve the names of cities famous in antiquity, but whofe fite, fave for this numifmatic evidence,

GOLD COIN OF 'ABD-EL-MELIK, KHALIF OF DAMASCUS, A.D. 696.

was uncertain. Thus geographically as well as hiftorically Mohammadan coins have a high value.

Origin of the Coinage.

It took the Arabs half a century to difcover the need of a feparate coinage of their own. At firft they were content to borrow their gold and copper currency from the Byzantine Empire, which they had driven out of Syria, and their filver coins from the Saffanian Kings of Perfia, whom they had overthrown at the battles of Kadifia and Nehavend. The Byzantine gold ferved them till the feventy-fixth year of the Flight, when a new, but theologically unfound and confequently evanefcent, type was invented, bearing the effigy of the reigning Khalif inftead of that of Heraclius, and Arabic inftead of

Greek inscriptions. So, too, the Saffanian silver pieces were left unaltered, save for the addition of a governor's name in Pehlvi letters. The Khalif 'Aly or one of his lieutenants seems to have attempted to inaugurate a purely Muslim coinage, exactly resembling that which was afterwards adopted; but only one example of this issue is known to exist, in the Paris collection, together with three other silver coins struck at Damascus and Merv between A.H. 60 and 70, of a precisely similar type. These four coins are clearly early and ephemeral attempts at the intro-

REFORMED GOLD COIN OF 'ABD-EL-MELIK, A.D. 696.

duction of a distinctive Mohammadan coinage, and their recent discovery in no way upsets the received Muslim tradition that it was the Khalif 'Abd-El-Melik who, in the year of the Flight 76 (or, on the evidence of the coins themselves, 77), inaugurated the regular Muslim coinage, which was thenceforward issued from all the mints of the empire so long as the dynasty endured, and which gave its general character to the whole currency of the kingdoms of Islam. The copper coinage founded on the Byzantine passed through more and earlier phases than the gold and silver, but it always held so insignificant a place in the Muslim

'Abd-El Melik.

currency that we can afford to difregard it in the prefent brief outline.

Religious Infcriptions.

Specimens of 'Abd-El-Melik's reformed coinage are here engraved. The gold and filver both bear the fame formulae of faith: on the obverfe, in the area, "There is no god but God alone, He hath no partner;" around which is arranged a marginal infcription, "Mohammad is the apoftle of God, who fent him with the guidance and religion of truth, that he might

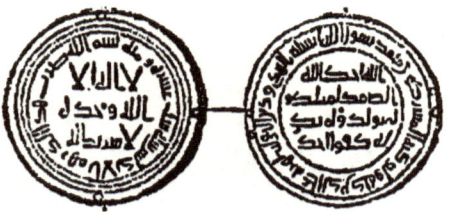

SILVER COIN OF THE KHALIFATE.
Struck in Andalusia, A.D. 734.

make it triumph over all other religions in fpite of the idolaters," the gold stopping at "other religions." This infcription occurs on the reverfe of the filver inftead of the obverfe, while the date infcription which is found on the reverfe of the gold, appears on the obverfe of the filver. The reverfe area declares that "God is One, God is the Eternal: He begetteth not, nor is begotten;" here the gold ends, but the filver continues, "and there is none like unto Him." The margin of the gold runs, "In the name of God: this Dînâr was ftruck in the year feven and feventy;" the filver fubftituting "Dirhem" for Dînâr, and inferting the place of iffue immediately after the word Dirhem, *e.g.*, "El-Andalus [*i.e.* Andalufia] in the year 116." The mint is not given on the early gold coins, probably because they were uniformly ſtruck at the Khalif's capital, Damaſcus. The contemporary copper coinage generally offers portions of the ſame formulae, with often the addition of the name of the governor of the province in which the coin was iſſued.

Theſe original dînârs (a name formed from the Roman denarius) and dirhems (drachma) of the Khalifs of Damaſcus formed the model of all Muſlim coinages for many centuries; and their reſpective weights—65 and 43 grains—ſerved as the ſtandard of all ſubſequent iſſues up to comparatively recent times. The fineneſs was about ·979 gold in the dînârs, and ·960 to ·970 ſilver in the dirhems. The Mohammadan coinage was generally very pure. The 'Abbâſy dînârs retained the fineneſs of ·979 for many centuries, and the ſame proportion of gold was obſerved in the iſſues of the Fâtimy Khalifs, the Almohades, and ſometimes of the Almoravides, but the laſt usually employed a lower *titre*. At firſt ten dirhems went to the dînâr, but the relation varied from age to age. Weight and Fineness.

The dynaſty of Umawy or "Ommiade" Khalifs, to which 'Abd-El-Melik belonged, continued to iſſue their dînârs and dirhems without any change until their overthrow at the hands of the 'Abbâſis in the year of the Flight 132, and even then one of the family fled to Spain, and there continued both the Umawy line and coinage in the Khalifate Coinage of the Khalifate.

of Cordova, which lasted three centuries. The 'Abbâsy Khalifs, on succeeding to the eastern dominions of the Umawis, retained in all essential respects the coinage of their predecessors, substituting, however, for the formula of the reverse area, the words, "Mohammad is the apostle of God," thus repeating the beginning of the marginal inscription. They also inserted the name of the mint-city on the gold, as well as on the silver. Soon, moreover, the strict puritanism of the early Khalifs, which did not permit them to place their own names on the currency, gave way to the natural vanity of the ruler, and the names and titles of the 'Abbâsy Khalifs were regularly inserted beneath the reverse area inscription, often accompanied by the names of their heir-apparent and grand-vizir. Thus, for some 250 years the universal coinage of the Muslim Empire was of one simple and uniform type.

Dynastic Coinage. But with the sudden and general upspringing of small independent, or only nominally dependent, dynasties in the fourth century of the Hijreh, the tenth of our era, Muslim coins acquire their highest value. The history of the Khalifs has been carefully recorded, and their coins, though they confirm and sometimes give additional precision to the statements of the historians, do not greatly enlarge our knowledge. But when the Sâmânis in Transoxiana and Khorasan, the Saffâris in Seistan, the Buweyhis in various provinces of Persia, the Hamdânis in Syria (all adopting a predominantly silver coinage), and the Beny Tûlûn and Ikhſhîdis in Egypt (who coined almoſt excluſively gold), and the Idrîſis (ſilver) and Beny-l-Aghlab (chiefly gold) in North Africa, began to ſtrike coins after the model of thoſe of the Khalifate, but abounding in names of local dynaſts, the hiſtorical value of the coinage riſes. Theſe dynaſtic coins always retain the name of the reigning Khalif in the place of honour, and this conjunction of names of Khalif and dynaſt will often ſupply the required chronological data, in the abſence or the obliteration of a definite year.

With the advent of the Seljuk Turks, who ſubdued the greater part of Perſia, Syria, and Aſia Minor, in the fifth century of the Hijreh, the coins acquire a ſpecial importance in deciding the difficult queſtion of the territorial diviſions of the various Seljuk lines; and the numerous dynaſties of Atâbegs or generals of the Seljuk armies, which ſprang up as ſoon as the central power grew weak, poſſeſs a numiſmatic intereſt in their general adoption of Byzantine types on their large copper pieces. On coins of the Urtukis, for example, a petty dynaſty of ſome cruſading fame that ruled a few fortreſses in Meſopotamia, we meet with not only the figures of Byzantine Emperors, but thoſe of Chriſt and the Virgin, with mangled inſcriptions of Chriſtian import. Figures of a ſimilar character alſo appear on the coinage of the Ayyûbis (Saladin's Kurdiſh houſe), and that of the Beny Zengy of Môſil and Syria, together with the earlieſt known repreſentation of the two-headed eagle, which has ſince ob-

Christian Figures.

tained high favour in Europe. But this divergence from the eſtabliſhed theory of Iſlam was only a temporary and exceptional phaſe, due to the irruption of foreign barbarians. The contemporary dynaſties of Africa—the Fâtimy Khalifs of Egypt,

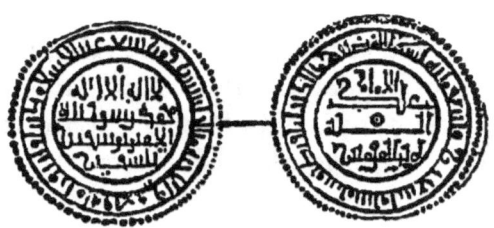

"MARAVEDI:" GOLD COIN OF ALMORAVIDES.
Struck at Cordova, A.D. 1103.

"MILLARES:" SILVER COIN OF ALMOHADES, MOROCCO.
Thirteenth and fourteenth centuries.

and the Almoravides and other Berber dynaſties of North Africa and Spain—adhered ſtrictly to the orthodox tradition which forbade the repreſentation of living things, and this was all the more noteworthy inaſmuch as moſt of theſe African dynaſties belonged to heretical ſects. Specimens of theſe Weſtern coinages are ſhown in the engravings, in which the "maravedi" and "millares" of mediaeval chronicles may be recogniſed. The ſquare ſhape is peculiar to North-Weſt Africa and Spain.

Maravedi and Millares.

Mongol Coinage.

In the ſeventh century of the Flight—our thirteenth—the Muſlim world was almoſt wholly in the poffeffion of foreigners. The Mongols had overrun the Eaftern provinces, which had not yet recovered from the inroad of the Turks, and henceforward the monotonous (chiefly filver) currency, and irregular ftandards, of the various Mongol houfes, fuch as the Ilkhâns of Perfia, the Jagatay family in Bokhâra, the different branches of the

SILVER COIN OF HOSEYN, SHAH OF PERSIA.
Struck at Isfahân, A.D. 1709.

Houfe of Timur (Tamerlane), the Khâns of Kipchak, of the Krim, etc., weary the ftudent; till the fine iffues of the Shahs of Perfia and the Kings and Emperors of Dehli reftore fomething like order and beauty to the chaos that, numifmatically as well as historically—the two generally go together—succeeded the terrible swoop of Chinguiz Khan. Even here, however, there are points of interest; and the long series of coins of the Khanates of the Caspian throw a valuable light upon the early history of the Russian States under the Mohammadan supremacy.

Mamlûks of Egypt.

Meanwhile the Mamlûks, in their two lines—Turkish and Circassian—held sway over the provinces of Egypt and Syria, and left many a noble monument of art and culture behind them. Their (predominantly gold) coinage, however, in spite of the representation of Beybar's lion, and some forms of ornament which are interesting to compare with the contemporary architecture, is poor and debased.

Berber Dynasties.

Several Berber dynasties had established themselves since the eleventh century in the Barbary States, and continued for half a millennium to issue their large gold pieces, resembling the coin engraved opposite. One of these, the line of Sherîfs of Morocco, endures to the present day, but the Ottoman Turks extinguished the others in the sixteenth century. This clan of Turks rose into power about the same time as the Mongols and Mamlûks. From one of ten petty dynasties that fattened upon the decay of the Seljuk kingdom of Anatolia, they became by the end of the fourteenth century rulers of all Asia Minor and a slice of Europe, and the middle of the sixteenth saw them possessed of an empire that stretched from Hungary to the Caspian, and from Baghdad to Algiers. The Ottoman currency at first con-

fifted of fmall filver and copper pieces, bearing no
very obvious relation, either in weight or ftyle, to
the old Seljuk or the older Khalif's coinage, and
for a long time they were content to ufe foreign
gold. Mohammad II., the conqueror of Conftantinople, was the firft to ftrike gold coins, upon the
model of the Venetian fequins, but of courfe with
Arabic infcriptions. Various gold fequins or
"altuns," fmall filver "akchehs," and copper
"manghirs" conftituted the Turkifh currency up
to the beginning of our feventeenth century. A
double ftandard of fequins and a perfectly new

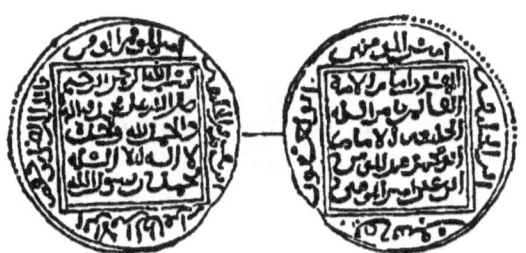

GOLD COIN OF ALMOHADES, MOROCCO. Fourteenth Century.

filver coinage, bafed upon the Dutch dollar, with
numerous fubdivifions and multiples, was then
introduced, and was ever after the fubject of count-
lefs modifications and degradations, until, after
an unfuccefsful attempt at reform by the great
Mahmûd II., the modern Turkifh feries, approxi-
mating the monetary fyftems of Europe, was inaugurated by Sultan 'Abd-El-Mejîd, and is hence
known as the Mejîdîyeh. A fimilar feries, bearing
the Sultan's but not the Viceroy's names, was and
is in ufe in Egypt, and a third feries, on a different
bafis, in Tunis. The Turkifh coinage as a whole

is important in its relations with the Mediterranean currencies, and it has a certain bearing upon the hiſtory of trade in the Middle Ages. It has alſo a value in determining the limits of the Turkiſh Empire at different periods, as the number of mints is very conſiderable.

The true value of Mohammadan coins lies, as has been ſaid, in their hiſtorical data. What is really wanted is a *Corpus* of Mohammadan Numiſmatics, which ſhould preſent, in well-arranged tables and indexes, the reſults of the coin-evidence of all the collections of Europe, and ſhould place them at the ſervice of hiſtorical ſtudents without compelling them to learn a difficult language and a ſtill more difficult palaeography. There is little that is intereſting in Mohammadan coins apart from their aid to hiſtory, and if their actual contributions to hiſtorical knowledge were once ſummarized and tabulated, few but inveterate collectors would want to ſtudy them. I write after finiſhing the eighth volume of my *Catalogue of Oriental Coins in the Britiſh Muſeum*, which has been going on for the laſt ten years, and deſcribes over ſix thouſand coins iſſued by a hundred ſeparate dynaſties, ſome of which conſiſt of thirty or forty Kings; and I have no heſitation in ſaying that Oriental numiſmatics is a ſcience which is intereſting mainly in its reſults. Thoſe reſults, however, are of the very firſt importance to the hiſtorian, and in this reſpect Mohammadan coins may challenge compariſon with any other ſeries without fear of being found wanting.

CHAPTER VIII.

COINS OF INDIA.

THE first section of this chapter deals with the coinage of India from its commencement to the Mohammadan Conquest; the second section treats of the coins of the foreign dynasties of Islam who ruled in Northern India.

The earliest coinage of India is, like the earliest works of Indian art which have come down to us, purely Greek. To trace the gradual absorption of Greek language and art by those of the older inhabitants is a possible and very interesting employment. One of the most important and interesting of all numismatic series is that of the coins issued on the borders of the Oxus and the Indus in the ages succeeding the revolt of the Eastern provinces of the Syro-Greek Empire in the reign of Antiochus II., about B.C. 250. The earliest rulers of the revolted regions were Diodotus and Euthydemus, followed in the second century by Antimachus, Eucratides, Menander, and a bewilder- Greek Kings ing crowd of kings with Greek names, whofe coins have reached us to teftify, in the abfence of all hiftorical record, to their wealth and fplendour, their Greek language and religion, their fkill in art and the wide extenfion of their conquefts. The number of thefe rulers is fo great that we muft give up the hypothefis that they fucceeded one another in a fingle royal line; rather would it appear that they belonged to a number of different, probably rival, dynafties, who reigned in different

ANTIMACHUS, INDIAN KING. About B.C. 150.

parts of Afghaniftan, the Panjâb, and the Indus valley. Of all thefe powerful monarchs there is fcarcely a trace in hiftory; their cities, their palaces, their civilization, have entirely perifhed; their coins alone furvive. Hence, while in the cafe of Greece and Rome coins are aids to hiftory, in India they contain all the hiftory we can hope to recover. And by degrees, as the number of our coins increafes, fo that we can form wide generalizations, and as the fpots where the pieces of different forts are found are more fcrupuloufly recorded, we may hope to be able to form an idea of the hiftory of Greek India. At prefent we are far from being in fo fortunate a condition; all that I fhall now attempt is to gather from the coins a few general indications.

The coins prove that Greek rule in India went on fpreading eaft and fouth during the fecond century. Greek Kings ruled even at the mouth of the Indus, and as far as the Ganges. And their civilization, or at leaft that of their courts and armies, was thoroughly Greek; the legends of their coins are at firft purely Hellenic; and well-executed figures of Zeus, Pallas, Pofeidon, Herakles, the Diofcuri, and other Greek deities prove that they brought with them the religion of their anceftors. Probably there was a conftantly fetting ftream of Greek mercenaries towards thefe remote lands, who formed military colonies in them, and peopled dominant cities which occupied in India the fame pofition which the Greek cities of Ptolemais and Alexandria held in Egypt, and the Greek cities of Seleucia, Ragae, etc., in Parthia.

In the beginning of the fecond century the Parthian Empire was driven like a wedge between Greek-fpeaking countries and the Graecized cities of the Cabul valley, cutting off intercourse between the two; and the Indo-Greek cities began at once to languifh, and their inhabitants to become more and more barbarized. We can trace the whole procefs on coins. Eucratides and his fucceffor Heliocles introduce the cuftom of adding on the reverfe of the coin a tranflation in Indian of the Greek legend of the obverfe. And under fome of the Kings we find traces of the barbarization of Greek divinities, as when on a coin of Telephus we find ſtrange outlandiſh figures of Helios and Selene, when on a coin of Hippoſtratus

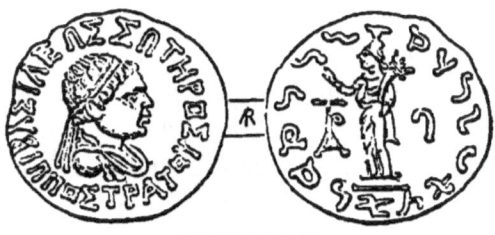

HIPPOSTRATUS.

we find a barbarous imitation of the Greek Genius of a city, or when on coins of Amyntas we find a divinity wearing a Phrygian cap from which flames or rays iſſue.

Hermaeus, who may have reigned late in the firſt century B.C., was the laſt of the Greek Kings of Cabul. During his life came the deluge: hoſts of Sacae, Yu-chi, and other nomad tribes from the borders of China ſwarmed down upon the devoted Greek kingdoms of the Eaſt and completely overwhelmed them. But theſe barbarians adopted,

HERAUS, KING OF THE SACAE.

like the Parthians, ſomething of the civilization of thoſe they conquered. The coins of Maues, Azes, and others of their Kings bear Greek inscriptions, and the figures of Greek divinities, and conform in most respects to Greek usage, so that but for the barbarous character of the names of these Kings we might have supposed them to be of Greek descent.

The powerful and wealthy Scythian Kings who ruled in North-western India in the second century of our era—Kadphises, Kanerkes, and Ooerkes—have left us a wonderful abundance of remarkable coins, which are sometimes found in India together with the aurei of contemporary Roman Emperors in the stupas or mounds which they erected over the relics of Kings or Buddhist saints. These Kings did not use issues of silver, like their Greek and Scythian predecessors, but of gold. On one side of their coins is an effigy of the reigning monarch, and an inscription in barbarized Greek, giving his name and titles. On the other side is the figure of some deity accompanied by his name in Greek letters; and the number and variety of these types are enormous. We have figures of the Greek Sarapis and Herakles, of the Persian Mithras and Nanaia, of the Indian Siva and Parvati, and even of Buddha, who appears on the coins in the attitude of a preacher. The Pantheon of these barbarians must have been of the most eclectic character, though we know from their inscriptions and other remains that they considered themselves Buddhists.

As early as the first issues of the Indo-Greek Kings, or scarcely later, are the first coins of native fabric. These are what are termed "punched coins." They are small squares cut out of a thin plate of silver, and impreſſed with devices by means, not of a die, but of a mere punch. The figures which they bear are very various, Buddhiſt emblems, archaic patterns, aſtrological devices, each probably the ſpecial mark of ſome mint, and authorizing the circulation of the piece ſo ſtamped in ſome particular diſtrict or city.

The punched coins circulated extenſively in Central India. And at the ſame time there paſſed in Weſtern India a great quantity of imitations of the coins of Greek and Scythian Kings. The coins of the dynaſty of Kanerkes, in particular, were copied through a ſeries of centuries, art and metal alike gradually deteriorating until in place of gold we have copper, and in place of the forms of kings and deities mere ſhapeleſs blotches.

The Sunga Kings of Magadha, who reigned in the ſecond century before our aera, have left us a few coins which are valuable becauſe of their early date. There were, however, in Northern India, before the time of Mahmud of Ghazny, notably three lines of native rulers who iſſued coins of creditable ſtyle, and impreſſed with legible Sanſkrit legends. Firſt of theſe we may name the Gupta Kings of Kanauj. Theſe wealthy and powerful monarchs, who ſeem to have been ſupreme throughout the whole of Northern India, iſſued money of almoſt pure Indian ſtyle, which bears types ſometimes taken from Indian religious cult, as when Parvati is depicted ſeated on a peacock; or alluſion is made to the Aſvamedha, the Indian

Guptas.

horse-sacrifice. The gold pieces of the Gupta Kings may be ranged beside those of the powerful Scythic Kings, as illustrative of the conflict of two civilizations, the native and the foreign.

In the district of Sauraſtran, or Gujarat, there began, about the first century of our aera, the issue of silver coins by the Sah dynasty. These pieces are copied from those of Menander and other Greek Kings, but yet have something distinctively Hindu about them. The heads which they bear on their obverse are portraits of a succession of native Rajahs; on the reverse, in the midst of a rather long Sanskrit legend, is a Buddhist emblem, usually one which is interpreted as representing a sacred hill erected over some relic. Their fabric is remarkably clear and neat, and they look as if the race to whom they belonged was by no means backward in civilization and commerce. And it is notable that the land of Gujarat is that which would be the natural *entrepôt* of trade between the marts of India on the one hand, and those of Rome and Egypt on the other. The Sah Kings were succeeded by a dynasty of Guptas, who issued coins of quite similar kind. ·

Sah Kings.

Very well known to Indian collectors are the coins which show on one side a bull, on the other a horseman bearing a spear, and which are called "bull and horseman" coins. They are of silver, and the commonest class bear in Sanskrit letters the names of certain Rajput Kings who ruled in Cabul shortly before the invasion of India by Mahmud of Ghazny. The work of these is neither

Brahman Kings of Cabul.

purely Greek nor entirely Indian, but reminds us rather of some of the issues of Byzantium.

These are, perhaps, the most important classes of native coins of early time; but there are many other groups. For instance, we have whole series of coins issued by the Kings of Kashmir and of Ceylon; and in the mist which hides early Indian history we can make out vaguely the forms of kings and dynasties which fast succeeded one another, or carried on war and commerce side by side. The majority of these rulers issued coin; and by slow degrees the few workers who have given attention to Indian numismatics are beginning to identify and arrange the multitudinous coins struck by them, a process which may in time bring us valuable evidence as to the divisions and the history of early India. But as yet comparatively little has been ascertained, and still less published; and our readers would only be fatigued by a list of dynasties as to which we have no information, and rulers whose names survive only on the money which they issued, or in some bare dynastic list.

The Mohammadan coinage of India possesses the same merits and defects that have already been assigned to Mohammadan coins in general. We must not, as a rule, expect to see the triumphs of the engraver's art upon the face of the Indian currency. Inscriptions, and nothing but inscriptions, form the chief interest of the Indian coins of the Muslim period; and to these inscriptions belongs the principal value of the study of such pieces. There is alſo the intereſt attaching to metrological peculiarities, which cannot be touched upon here, but of which the curious reader may obtain a thorough knowledge by an inſpection of the works of Prinſep and Thomas. But even the latter, *facile princeps* among living Indian numiſmatiſts, devoted as he is to the intricate queſtions connected with the weights and ſtandards of India, is ready to allow to the inſcriptions the chief place among the characteriſtics of the coinage. The value of the illuſtration that theſe inſcriptions afford, as applied to mediaeval Indian annals, is greatly enhanced, he ſays, " by the exaggerated importance attached by the Muſlims themſelves to that department of the conventional regal functions, involved in the right to coin. Among theſe peoples, the recitation of the public prayer in the name of the aſpirant to the throne, aſſociated with the iſſue of money bearing his ſuperſcription, was unheſitatingly received as the overt act of acceſſion. Unqueſtionably, in the ſtate of civilization here obtaining, the production and facile diſperſion of a new royal device was ſingularly well adapted to make manifeſt to the comprehenſion of all claſſes the immediate change in the ſupreme ruling power. In places where men did not print, theſe ſtamped moneys, obtruding into every bazaar, conſtituted the moſt effective manifeſtoes and proclamations human ingenuity could have deviſed: readily multiplied, they were individually the eaſieſt and moſt naturally tranſported of all official documents; the verieſt fakîr in his ſemi-nude coſtume might carry the oftenfible proof of a new dynafty into regions where even the name of the kingdom itfelf was unknown. In fhort, there was but little limit to the range of thefe Eaftern heralds; the numifmatic Garter King-at-Arms was recognised wherever Afiatic nations accepted the gold, and interpreters could be found to defignate the Caefar whofe 'epigraph' figured on its furface. So alfo on the occafion of a new conqueft: the reigning Sultân's titles were oftentatioufly paraded on the local money, ordinarily in the language and alphabet of the indigenous races, to fecure the more effective announcement that they themfelves had paffed under the fway of an alien fuzerain. Equally, on the other hand, does any modification of, or departure from, the rule of a comprehenfive iffue of coin imply an imperfection relative or pofitive in the acquifition of fupreme power."[1]

Copper Currency. The firft important fact to be noted about the Mohammadan coinage of India is that while the gold and filver were generally more or lefs adaptations, affimilated to ancient Indian ftandards, of the dînâr and dirhem which prevailed over the whole empire of Iflam, the copper currency retained as a rule its Indian character, and preferved thofe local characteriftics which it poffeffed before the invafion of the Muflims. In other words, the coins moft in requeft were left in the form which was beft underftood by the people who ufed them, while the lefs frequent gold and filver, the Court currency, received the imprefs

[1] *Chronicles of the Pathan Kings of Dehli*, p. 2.

of the ruling religion. So we find the conquering Mahmûd of Ghazny, the firſt Muſlim to ſnatch any part of India, iſſuing copper coins with Hindu characters ſuch as the people of the Panjâb would underſtand, and with the image of the Bull Nandy, ſacred to Hindus, but repugnant to Mohammadans, while his ſilver coins retain all the puritanical plainneſs that belongs to orthodox Iſlam. Mahmûd's ſucceſſors, the dynaſty of Ghaznawis or "Ghaznevides," who eſtabliſhed themſelves at Lahore, continued to mingle this native coinage with their imported formulas of faith. The ſucceeding dynaſties adopted the ſame principle, and admitted the Bull and the Chohan or Cabul horſeman to a place beſide the profeſſion of faith in one God; and we may ſtate as a general fact that the common copper, or more frequently billon, currency of India, under Mohammadan rule, remained Indian and local, and retained the old ſymbols and characters of Hinduſtan.

The moſt important Mohammadan dynaſties of India were the ſo-called Patans of Dehli, with the ſubordinate but often independent line at Bengal, who reigned over most of Northern India from the end of the twelfth to the middle of the ſixteenth century of our era; and the Moguls, who were the ſucceſſors of the famous Timur or Tamerlane, and following the Patans extended their ſway over a ſtill wider area, from the middle of the ſixteenth century to the well-remembered days when England ſet an Empreſs in the place of the

Muslim Dynasties.

great Mogul. Thefe two great houfes really fill up the chronology of Mohammadan numifmatics in Hinduftan, but by no means exhauft the geography. The number of fmaller dynafties, native or Muflim, who ftruck coins either in their own characters, or, more rarely, the Arabic ftyle, is legion. Among the more important of thefe may be mentioned the Bahmany Kings, who ruled the greater part of the Dekhan, from Kulbarga, (which they re-chriftened Ahfanabad, or the "Moft Beautiful City,") from the fourteenth to the fixteenth century; the Kings of Jaunpûr, Mewâr, Malwah, and Gujarat, who fprung into independence on the weakening of the central power in the fourteenth century, and generally lafted till the great annexations of the Mogul Emperors Baber and Akbar in the fixteenth.

Patans.

The Patans and Moguls, however, may be felected as the Mohammadan coins of India *par excellence*. The Patans introduced a gold and filver coinage of fingular purity and equal weight in either metal (about 174 grains), with often identical infcriptions, called the Tankah, which the Moguls afterwards converted into the gold mohr and filver rupee, which are fo familiar to readers of Indian hiftory. The infcriptions of the Patans are in Arabic, as a rule of flight pretenfions to calligraphic excellence, but clear and folid, and prefenting the ufual ftatiftics of the name of fovereign, of mint, and date, with fometimes a reference to the *fainéant* 'Abbâfy Khalifs who had been fet up in Egypt by the

Mamlûks on the destruction of the Khalifate at Baghdad by Hulagu Khán. Beyond some curious posthumous issues and this homage to a decrepit Khalifate, there is little that is particularly interesting to any but metrologists and professed numismatists in the Patan coinage. One sovereign, however, possessed a genius for innovation, and his coinage presents not a few features of interest. This was Mohammad ibn Taghlak (A.D. 1324-51), a prince whose character abounds in astonishing contrasts. "Generous to profusion, an accomplished scholar, abstinent, a firm defender of his faith, and the most experienced general of his day," he was yet possessed by a ferocious spirit that knew no mercy or regard for human life, and cursed with " a perversion of intellect which induced him to allow despotism to run into insane fury at any sign of opposition to his will."[1] It was his fate at first to gather the empire together more firmly and with wider boundaries than ever; and then, by the eccentricity or madness of his rule, to sow the seeds of that general disintegration which barely waited for his death before it displayed its independence in every part of the empire. Among the signs of Mohammad ibn Taghlak's eccentricity is his coinage. It testifies to his taste, inasmuch as it is infinitely better engraved than any of the issues of his predecessors; and it bears witness to his passion for novelty, since it affords illustrations of several monetary reforms, all of which collapsed

Mohammad ibn Taghlak.

[1] E. Thomas: *Chronicles*, p. 202.

almoſt as ſoon as they were inſtituted. Firſt Mohammad ibn Taghlak reſolved to alter the ſtandard Tankah, which had hitherto been of the uniform weight of 174 grs. for both gold and ſilver, and to raiſe the gold to 200 grs., and lower the ſilver to 140; but he failed to make his new ſtandards acceptable to his ſubjects, and in three or four years the old Tankah had to be reſtored. His next attempt was a much bolder flight. He had apparently heard of the fiduciary paper currency which Khubilai Khán had ſucceſsfully introduced into the Celeſtial Empire, and which had been imitated, with very different reſults, in Perſia, and he reſolved to try the effects of a forced currency in his own dominions. No fraud was apparently contemplated, for the Dehli treaſury was overflowing, and when the experiment failed, the forced pieces were bought in at the mint at the nominal value, without any ſcrutiny for clipping or counterfeiting. This forced currency was of braſs and copper, and was engraved with words meant to compel their acceptance, ſuch as "He who obeys the Sultan, verily he obeys God," and an inſcription ſtating it to be the equivalent of the ſilver Tankah; but no threats, even of ſo abſolute a deſpot as the Patan King, could commend theſe pieces to the people, and in leſs than three years they were abandoned.

Moguls of Dehli. The Mogul coins have inſcriptions mainly in Perſian, and are alſo remarkable not only for occaſional eccentricity of ſhape, ſuch as the ornate oblongs which Akbar iſſued, but for the reprefentation of figures. The zodiacal rupees and mohrs of Jehangîr are well known, with the figns of the Zodiac engraved in bold relief; but the same Emperor even went fo far as to engrave a portrait of himfelf in the act of raifing the forbidden winecup to his lips. As a rule, however, the Mogul coinage contents itfelf with the ufual notices of names, titles, mints, and dates, and felicitous references to the monarchs' happy and

GOLD MOHR OF JEHANGÎR.

aufpicious reigns. Such was the infcription of the Sikkeh rupee which (on a principle of frequent application at Dehli, when a king of doubtful authority fought to fupport himfelf upon the monetary credit of fome predeceffor) was retained by the Eaft India Company till 1835, long after the Sovereign to whom it applied had gone to his Paradife: "Defender of the Mohammadan religion, mirror of the grace of God, the Emperor Shah Alam ftruck this coin to be current throughout the feven climes. Struck at Murfhidâbâd in the year 19 of his fortunate reign."

Sikkeh Rupee.

CHAPTER IX.

CHINA AND JAPAN.

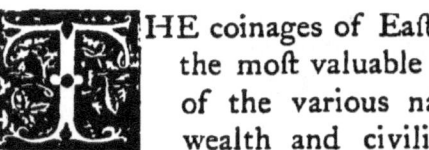HE coinages of Eaſtern Aſia are often the moſt valuable records we poſſeſs of the various nations' progreſs in wealth and civilization. Much of ancient hiſtory is gathered from them, and they are ſometimes the only clue to events for which hiſtorians would otherwiſe have to draw largely on their imaginations. In them we find hiſtorical proofs and materials—records which illuſtrate the political events in the life of great empires—data illuſtrating ſchemes for ſupplying the deficiency of metals, or avoiding the neceſſity of a more extenſive metallic currency. We ſee in China, for inſtance, the continued ſtruggle of the primitive ſyſtem of barter with the ſyſtem of fiduciary money required by the enlargement of the population and the development of exchange; and we ſee, alſo, in the application of economical principles very different from thoſe of Europe, the various attempts made by the Government to detain the

people in a mediocrity of material life (not the *aurea mediocritas* of the poet), where an abfence of wants and defires keeps them within the range of their ideal of happinefs.

Thefe confiderations, interefting to the economift and hiftorian, are not the only elements of value in the ftudy of the coinage, befides the bare ftatements of facts and dates which form the fkeleton of hiftory. The illuftrations and ornamentations of the medals, charms, and tokens exemplify the fuperftitions, the habits and cuftoms of the people, and make fome amends for the chief defect of the coinage of the Far Eaft, the lack of artiftic excellence.

The civilized clans who bore the generic name of Bak or "flourifhing," and travelling eaftwards brought to China all the elements of a culture indirectly derived from the old focus of Babylonia, had not been taught in their previous home, weft of the Hindu-kufh, any other currency than that of weighing metals. Their earlieft traditions do not point to any other; the development of barter and the ufe of cowries arofe from neceffity, and intercourfe with the indigenous tribes of their new country. The fucceffion of the words employed to denote the various fubftitutes of the as yet undifcovered money is in itfelf fuggeftive of what took place in former times. The expreffion ufed by later hiftorians when fpeaking of the early pfeudo-money is *pit*, a character meaning "wealth, riches." We muft underftand from the traditions that in the time of the Great Hot Bak-ket (Ur-

CHINA.

Bagafh of Babylonian tradition), money was *metal*, and that afterwards, from the time of Nak Khunte (Nai Hwang-ti, ? B.C. 2250) and his Chinefe fucceffors, it became any exchangeable merchandife. For the people of Shang and of Ts'i, pieces of filk or hempen-cloth were money; later on, in the feudal ftates of Ts'i and that of Kiu, knives (*tao*) were ufed as currency. During the three dynafties of Yao, Hia, and Shang (B.C. 2100-1080), gold, filver, and copper were employed, befides cloth, tortoife-fhell, and cowries.

Shell Currency.

The ufe of fhells as a medium of exchange by the ancient Chinefe is a matter of peculiar intereft in its antiquity, and its connection with the once widely extended cowry-fhell currency. We find it mentioned at its very outfet among the newly arrived Chinefe, in their earlieft book, the *Yh-King*, where, as an equivalent of "riches," we read "100,000 dead fhell-fifhes." The tortoife-fhell currency is alfo mentioned in the fame canonical book. Shell-currency began under the Hia dynafty (2000-1550 B.C.), when they had relations with the aborigines of the fouth and fouth-eaft of their newly conquered dominion. To what extent it was carried previoufly to their time we know not, but we have literary evidence that, with the fuperior culture which they had brought with them, they foon gave to fhell-currency a development correfponding to their higher wealth and requirements.

Traces of the ufe of fhells as a medium of exchange have remained cryftallized in the written and spoken languages; the ideogram *pei* "shell" has the meaning of wealth and riches, and has been added as a silent determinative to many characters of the same class of meaning: goods, property, selling, prices, cheap, dear, stores, etc.; but it is worth noticing that the use of *pei* in this secondary meaning does not appear in the earliest characters of the language. In the wonderful *Geographical Survey* which goes by the name of Yü the Great, and might be as old as the eighteenth century B.C., the people of the islands along the coasts of Yang-tcheu had to bring cowries as tribute. Yang-tcheu was the southeast division of the Chinese dominion, or rather of the regions upon which they eventually extended their suzerainty; its southern borders were ill-defined, but it included the modern provinces of Tcheh-Kiang, Fuh-Kien, etc. It was from the islands of that part of China that the cowries exhibited at the International Fisheries Exhibition of South Kensington, 1883, were sent.

Cowries were not the only shells used; that of the tortoise of various species and sizes was used for the greater values, which would have required too many cowries; and a survival of the old custom has remained in the language, where the expression *knei-hwo*, or tortoise-shell money, is used elegantly to denote a coin. Several sorts of Cypraea were employed, one of which, the "purple shell," two or three inches long, was formerly found on the shores of the prefecture of Teng-tchen, north of the Shantung peninsula.

The celebrated claffic of the Mountains and Seas (*Shan Haï King*), of which the firft thirteen books have reached their bulk by an innumerable feries of incorporated additions fince the time of the Shang dynafty, twelfth century, down to the fourth century B.C., indicates the ftreams and waters where the precious and variegated fhells could be found; *i.e.*, mainly in the fouth-eaft and weft. And the *Pen-tfao* claffic, for which an earlier origin is claimed, ftates that the cowries (*pei-tze* or *pei-tch'i*) live in the Eaftern Sea; that is, fouth-eaft of the Shantung peninfula.

All thefe fhells, excepting the fmall ones, were current in pairs, and it is this practice which is alluded to in the following third ftanza of an ode of the *Book of Poetry*, commonly attributed to the tenth century B.C.:

> "Luxuriantly grows the after-southernwood,
> In the midft of that great height,
> We fee our noble lord
> And he gives us a hundred pairs of Cypraea fhells."

Mas She, the well-known editor of the *Book of Poetry* in the fecond century B.C., commenting upon the fhell-currency, fpeaks of *tze-pei*, or purple Cypraea, but only as ranking after the fea-tortoife-fhell, meafuring 1 foot 6 inches, which in his time could be obtained but in Kiu-tchin and Riao-tchi (Cochin-China and Annam), where they were ufed to make pots, bafins, and other valuable objects. We learn by this ftatement that the ufe as currency of larger fhells than the Cypraea moneta had not extended outfide China. But as to China proper, the great scholar we have just quoted could hardly speak from personal experience, as the shell-currency no more existed officially in his time. Big shells were still appreciated and sought for as an object of luxury, and remained thus long afterwards. We find recorded in the *Han Annals*, that the Emperor Wen, in 179 B.C., having presented the King of Southern Yueh with a hundred robes, the latter, with other presents, returned five hundred of purple Cypraeae. The shell-currency was, however, fading away. It had received a great blow a long while previously from Hwei Wen, the Prince of Ts'ing, who in his second year, *i.e.* 335 B.C., recognising the difficulties of finding a proper supply of shells and cowries, and the rapidly increasing demand for a convenient currency, altogether suppressed it. The inland position of Ts'ing, far away from the sources of supply, combined with the fact that metallic coins of various shapes and sizes had begun to be recognised as a more practicable medium of exchange in the other states of the Chinese agglomeration, were the two main reasons which led this ancestor of the founder of the Chinese Empire to abolish the cumbrous system of shell-currency and to adopt the more perfect system of metallic coins, already put in practice by private persons in several of the neighbouring states. He issued then the round copper coin, with a central square hole, and the legend *pan-liang* ($=\frac{1}{2}$ ounce), indicating its value, which was afterwards imitated by the rulers of the Han dynasty, and is, in fact, the

Earliest Metal Coinage.

direct and uninterrupted anceftor of the Chinefe coins of the prefent day.

A time-honoured fyftem like the fhell-currency, however, could not difappear without ſtruggling a while in out-of-the-way places, and, among a people of routine like the Chinefe, could not lack fupporters. It is to this confervative tendency that the country was indebted for an attempt to revive the old-fafhioned currency. Wang Mang, the ufurper who ruled in China (A.D. 9-23) between the two great Han dynafties, wanted, indeed, to refcind all the innovations introduced in the country by the eclipfed dynafty. Accordingly he enacted new ftatutes—one of which re-eftablifhed a fhell-currency confifting of five categories, the higher one of tortoife-fhells being divided in ten claffes. How far thefe differed from the old fyftem we are unable to fay for want of proper information; ſtill, it is not unlikely that the difcrepancies were fmall. But the intelligent part of the people, and the traders, objected to the revival of the antiquated fyftem; and, in A.D. 14, Wang Mang had to cancel his former decrees. After his time we hear no more of the cowry-currency in China proper; but we trace its influence in the iffue of fmall copper coins, fhaped, indeed, as a fmall Cypraea, roughly imitated by their ovoidal or pear-like form, and commonly called Dragon's-head coins and Ant-coins, or Antnofe coins. Some have been found of three different fizes, with the refpective legends, *Liang* (for 1 oz.), *pan-liang* (or $\frac{1}{2}$ oz.), and *Koh luh tchu*, "each fix tchus," written in a rather out-of-the-way manner; but certainly, by the ſtyle of writing, iſſued in the laſt centuries before the Chriſtian era, in Tſu, the ſouthernmoſt ſtate of the Chineſe confederation.

The working of mines in China has rarely been left open to private enterpriſe; the authorities ſeem to have been afraid to leave the people free to acquire riches in that way; and as a rule they kept it for themſelves, and exerciſed much care and moderation in its uſe. Strict regulations have always forbidden the extraction of metals beyond limited quantities. Recourſe to the mines could take place in primitive times only in caſes of inundation or other great need. We find in the fragments of a ſtill exiſting work on government and legiſlation, by an able financier, Kwan-tze, who was a prime miniſter of the feudal state of Tai, in 685 B.C., an alluſion to the effect of ſuch floods: "When," he ſays, "from eaſt, weſt, north, and ſouth, all over a ſurface of 7,000 or 8,000 li, all intercourſe with theſe parts was cut off by the inundation, and in conſequence of the length of the way, and the difficulties of reaching them, neither boat nor cart could penetrate thither; the people therefore relied on, and employed according to their meaſures, pearls and gems as the higheſt commodities, then gold, and, as the third and lower claſs, knives and cloth."

Metals in lumps were conſidered, ſince the beginning of the Shang dynaſty, as a ſource of proſperity; they were called *trinon*, "ſpring or

Mines.

fource," and the name lafted till its fubftitution by a quafi-homonym *tſien*, in allufion to the fmall copper implements of hufbandry ufed later as currency. It is from the fame time that the habit of hoarding bullion originated. We read that when the Shang dynafty was overthrown by Wu Wang, the founder of the Tchou dynafty, all the wealth accumulated by the laft King, the fcapegoat of the abufes and miftakes of his whole lineage, in the fplendid palace called the Deer Gallery, was facked and diftributed to the people.

Tchou Dynasty. With the acceffion of the Tchou dynafty (1122 B.C.), a new era opened in the hiftory of Chinefe money. Regulations were eftablifhed to fix the relative value of all the exchangeable commodities. The honour of this inftitution is attributed to the great Duke of Ts'i, who in 1103 B.C. eftablifhed the rules of circulating money for the nine adminiftrative boards of finance, which had been organized previoufly by another famous adminiftrator, the Duke of Tchou. From commentaries of ancient date we underftand that the gold circulated in the fhape of little cubes of one fquare inch weighing a *kin;* the copper in round tongue-like plates was weighed by drachms (*tchu*); the filk cloth, 2 feet 2 inches wide, in rolls of 40 feet length formed a piece. The great man who had fo fuccefsfully introduced order and principles in matters which feem to have been hitherto left to the caprice of individuals or to local and momentary neceffity (and who, by-the-way, was not a Chinefe, but a native of the aboriginal tribes of the East), retired to the Dukedom of Ts'i, where he issued the same regulations as in the Middle Kingdom. We have an insight into the working of the new organization some hundred and fifty years afterwards, from a chapter of the *Shu King*. At the end of the reign of King Muh of Tchou, *i.e.* previous to 947 B.C., enactments were made for the mulcts and fines; to redeem the penalties such as branding, mutilation or death, the culprit was allowed to pay 100, 200, 500 or 1,000 *hwan*. The *hwan* was a ring of copper weighing 6 oz., and this so far corresponds to the round shape enumerated in the Record of Institutes of the great Duke of Ts'i.

The Duke Hwan of Ts'i (the fourteenth successor of the former), who ruled from 685 to 644 B.C., and whose prime minister was the worthy financier Kwan-tze, of whom we have spoken above, in order to make known and accessible to the public the various weights, commissioned the Left Master of the Horses to cast some metal from the mines of the Tchwang mountain. The Duke Hwan was the leader of the feudal princes of the Chinese agglomeration, and he swayed the empire under the nominal suzerainty of King Hwey of Tchou, and his regulations were therefore of a more momentous character than those of any other prince in his dominion. Of the same Duke tradition says that from the bullion cast at his own command he ordered the Inner Great Officer Wang yh to carry 2,000 *tsien* to the state of Tsu, in order to purchafe a living ftag. What was the unit reprefented here by the expreffion *tfien*, is not ftated. Should we truft the word itfelf, it meant a fmall implement of hufbandry in metal, which, being frequently ufed for its weight and intrinfic value, became the current expreffion for money.

Adze Currency.

Indeed, the only obligation of weighing the metal for currency had not prevented the ufe of any object or implement for the purpofe of exchange according to their verified weights; the choice of the tools of conftant and daily ufe among a people exclufively occupied in agricultural purfuits naturally commended itfelf. Small adzes and billhooks above all were prominent by their large number and eafy handling. We can readily conceive how at firft the exchange of fuch tools would be accepted with facility by the people in their tranfactions; they could be either employed for their primeval object if wanted, or exchanged with readinefs in cafe of need. However, there was no limit to the felection of any particular form, while the employ of metal in bare lumps was never difufed. All forts of objects were made ufe of for exchange in early times, and their endlefs variety may be gathered from the following enumeration of ftrangely fhaped moneys of old: " Thofe like a bridge croffwife were commonly mufical-ftone money; thofe fhaped as a comb were commonly padlock money; thofe fhaped as a half-moon were the half-moon money;" the author goes on to mention the fish-scale money and the shell-money. Specimens of these rare shapes rarely appear in numismatic collections, and only in casts, which are always open to some kind of suspicion as to the genuineness of the original used for moulding. We do not know how far the regulations of the great Duke Wang, and those of his later successor, Duke Hwan, limited the variety of shapes; but small implements of husbandry were those which were almost exclusively used for a long period, especially small adzes, chisels, spades, or planes. They are an interesting survival of a peculiar tool of the stone age, hitherto found nowhere else than in South-Eastern Asia. While all the hitherto found implements of this rude stage of industry are limited to a few types which present only slight variations in whatever country they are excavated, the type we are speaking of is an exception. Its name, "shouldered-headed celt," is pretty well descriptive of its shape, which is closely imitated in the bronze implements of China used for currency. The only characteristic of the stone antecedent, which has disappeared because of the thinness of the metal, consists " in the edge being ground down on *one* side like a chisel, instead of on both sides like an axe, as is usually the case." The shouldered-headed celts are generally found in the Malayan peninsula, in the lower part of Burmah, within the provinces of Pegu and Tennasserim; they have been found at Chutiâ Nâgpûr, in Central India; and quite lately at Semrang Sen (south-west of Lake Tanli-Sap), in Cambodia.

Weights and Implements.

Weights and Implements.

Thus we can trace, up to the adminiſtration of Kwan-tze, a twofold development in the hiſtory of Chineſe moneys. Beſides the weights properly ſo-called, whatever may have been the occaſional employ made of them, aroſe the cuſtom of caſting ſmall implements, which for convenience were uſed in exchange, of a regular ſhape and approximate weight; and gradually, as a natural ſequence of that ſyſtem, came the practice of having them inſcribed with the name of the place or city where they were caſt and put in circulation.

Ring Weights.

The ſyſtem of ring-weights, which may, perhaps, be traced to an Egyptian ſource, was continued down to the foundation of the Chineſe Empire, when it was ſlightly modified into the pattern ſtill in uſe in the preſent day. When King Hwei Wan of Ts'in, the future conqueror of the whole of China, wanted to throw over the ſtill ſurviving uſe of cowry currency, in 338 B.C., he ordered ring-weights to be caſt, of which ſpecimens are found. Thoſe hitherto known bear the inſcription of their weight, "weighing 1 oz. 12 drs.," or "1 oz. 14 drs.," or only "12 drs.," differences which are ſuggeſtive of a larger number of varieties at preſent unknown.

Relics of the other ſhapes of metallic currency are ſtill in exiſtence, though not in large numbers, in the European collections. Of the *tch'ang*, or adze or ſpade-pattern, we know by actual ſpecimens that ſome were caſt ſpecially for the purpoſe of currency; for they are too light to have been intended for practical work Some do not bear any infcription whatever, but ufually they are infcribed with the name of the town where they were caft; this cuftom was of courfe of later introduction, when fome tool-fhaped objects were caft in large numbers, without a view to their ufe as implements, or in fmaller fize than was required for induftrial purpofes. Thefe pfeudo-coins were infcribed with the name of the place or city, and they were commonly called flip-weights, or leaf-weights, or helping-weights, flips or leaves. They were not iffued by the governments, but by private individuals. Specimens, with the indication of 2 Kins, 1 Kin, $^1/_2$ Kin, and of proportionated fizes bear the names of the cities of An-yü, Yü, Shan-yang, Liang, etc. Though a private bufinefs, the central government feveral times attempted to modify it. Thus King Tchwang of Tfu, who ruled in his principality from 612 to 589 B.C., vainly endeavoured to create a nominal currency by reducing to the value of units the larger pieces actually worth feveral units; and a fimilar failure attended in 523 B.C. the iffue by King, the ruler of Tchou, of large pieces (hitherto unidentified), intended to fuperfede altogether the fmall ones in circulation, which the King fancied were too light.

During the ages following, which are known as the Period of the Contending States, money was multiplied at a great rate in the Chinefe agglomeration. The confederation of the various ftates, after having lafted feveral centuries, had ceafed to exift, and each of the principalities was fighting for fupremacy over the others; and in some of the states the fight was in fact a struggle for life. After some two centuries of incessant wars, seven stronger states survived, only to be finally subdued and absorbed by the most powerful of them, the western state of Ts'in, the ruler of which established the Chinese Empire in the middle of the third century, and proclaimed himself first Emperor in 221 B.C.

<small>Knife Money of Ts'i.</small> For numismatics, the state of Ts'i during this period of contention is far the most important. The most widely known currency of Ts'i at that time is the *knife-money*, which consisted in a sort of billhooks, some seven inches long, curved, and the handle terminating in a ring. The shape was that of an implement of husbandry in bronze, of which a rude specimen is exhibited in the Chinese Gallery of the South Kensington Museum. The state of Ts'i was one of the most powerful of the Chinese states: it rose in 1122 B.C., and was one of the last which resisted the ever-growing state of Ts'in, as it was not subdued before 224 B.C. It covered what is now a large part of Northern Shantung and Southern Tchih-li, and always exercised an important influence in the empire. We remember that the financial Institutes of the Tchōn dynasty were established by the first Duke of Ts'ï. The population of this region has been conspicuous for its intelligence and boldness; and in the *She-King* the praises of female beauties are all sung for ladies of Ts'i. The merchants of Ts'i, with their enterprising tendencies and the incitement of the sea-trade, always displayed a daring

which proved moſt uſeful to the progreſs of their countrymen. This intereſting feature is revealed to us by their knife-coinage, which gives proof of the extent of their commercial relations. The legends of the knife-coins bear poſitive teſtimony to the aſſociations which exiſted between ſeveral towns of the Ts'i ſtate, among themſelves, as alſo with towns of other ſtates. We do not know by whom theſe iſſues were really made, whether they were caſt by order either of the communities in partnerſhip or otherwiſe, or of aſſociations of

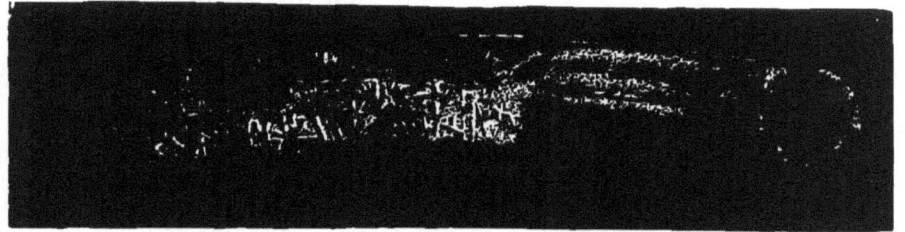

KNIFE MONEY.

traders independent of the communal adminiſtration.

The knife-currency did not outlive the ſubmiſſion of the ſtates of Ts'i and Wei and their abſorption by that of Ts'in, which ſtarted a new currency. It ceaſed to be recogniſed as the ordinary money, and took refuge in out-of-the-way places outſide the borders of China. Though we have no intermediary proof of its continued exiſtence, for lack of information we cannot help connecting with it and conſidering as a ſurvival of the old practice, ſtill exiſting in the preſent century among the Khamti and Sing-Pho tribes on the ſouth-weſt borders of China, of uſing ſmall ſquare iron *dhas* or knives as currency. The very name of theſe *dhas* is obviouſly connected with the Chineſe *tao* or knife-money, and ſpeaks for itſelf.

<small>Leaf Money.</small>

A ſort of deſcendant of the older weights, known as ſlips for weight, or leaf-money, received a greater development than the knife-money. The latter were too large to be the common and popular medium of exchange in a country where the exigencies of life were ſo ſmall and ſo cheap that every man needed 1,000 pieces of money or a little more a year; the equivalent of which in our money of the preſent day ſhould be about eight ſhillings, which was a ſufficient income for a man in China in the third century B.C. In the ſecond half of the fourth century, the King of Tchao (a ſtate to the ſouth of the modern Tchih-li and Shan-ſi provinces) granted to Tchang-y the uſe of ſaddle-money: another name for leaf-money. All the leaf-money of that period may be claſſed in two diviſions, one with ſquare, and the other with pointed feet. They bear on the obverſe the name of the place where they were iſſued, and generally on the reverſe a ſerial figure. The twenty and odd towns whoſe names occur were ſcattered all over the various ſtates, but were moſtly ſituated in the ſtates of Ts'i and Wei. Theſe two ſtates fought to the laſt againſt their abſorption by the powerful ſtate of Ts'in; it is clear that the multiplication of their money during that period of warfare was for the purpoſe of helping and maintaining their ſtruggle. Their rude workmanship, and the simplifications of characters drawn by ignorant hands, exclude any possibility of their being the produce of a state coinage. The signs of the legends are abbreviated so loosely, in defiance of all principles of orthography, and they offer so many variants, that we may be sure that they are the work of private individuals among the people.

The leaf-money did not die out altogether with the foundation of the Chinese Empire; it lingered in obscure corners, and was not extinguished by the state currency issued by the Ts'in dynasty.

Gold Currency.

Of the early gold currency we have very little to say. It could not be in frequent use in a country where life was so cheap, and it was restricted to the purchase of jewels or presents from the princes and wealthy people. Except in the financial arrangements of the Tchöu dynasty as established by the great Duke of Ts'i, we hear only of one historical instance of the use of the 1 inch cube of gold, or *kin*, weighing one pound, which had been made the standard.

In the fourth century B.C. we read of an *yh* of gold, but we know nothing more of it. It was probably a weight of precious metal in the lump. Under the Ts'in dynasty, the *yh* was the unit for gold, and it was then equal to 20 *liang* in weight. When the Han dynasty arose, the Ts'in institutions were revoked, and the old cubic inch of gold or *kin* was again the unit as under the Tchöu dynasty. A specimen of this curious money exists in the Cabinet des Médailles, at Paris, and a great scholar, Ed. Biot, has tried (but in our opinion unsuccessfully) to ascertain by its weight the standard of the ancient Chinese.

STATE COINAGE.

Ts'in Dynasty.

With the Ts'in dynasty appears the first state mintage of the central government, the lineal antecedent of the present coinage. Of the gold currency we have already said the little that can be recorded. The copper money was round, with a square hole in the centre: "round as the sky, square as the earth." The pieces were substantially the same as those of the Tchöu dynasty as far as their regular weight is concerned, and their multiples were in correct proportion to the unit; their weight agreed with that inscribed upon them. They were marked *Pan-liang*, or half-*liang*, equivalent to the eighth part of a *kin* weight. All that were formerly used as mediums of exchange—gems, pearls, tortoise-shell, cowries, silver, tin, etc., etc.—were no longer recognised as equivalent for currency in the official transactions. The purpose of the founder of the empire, Ts'in Shi Hoang-ti, was to effect a thorough assimilation of the various and rather heterogeneous parts of his dominion. His great achievements in this respect were, first, the substitution, for the varieties in the writing which had gradually arisen with the independence of the states, of a uniform style of writing, a sort of ideographical transcription which could be understood everywhere, despite the differences of the vernacular dialects; and, second, his attempts at establishing a State money. The burning of the books, which, indeed, has deprived the world of many ancient records which nowadays would be invaluable treasures, and must therefore be deeply regretted, was nevertheless an act of political wisdom, in order to clear away the impediments by which the ultra-conservatives tried to check his steps. The new Emperor wished to withdraw, out of the reach of the literati and of the people at large, all the accumulated historical traditions, which by the numerous examples there recorded as patterns of conduct, offered too much ground for protesting against the spirit of innovation and progress which characterised his government.

The dynasty founded by this great ruler in 221 B.C. for " ten thousand years," finished in troubles and rebellions against an atrocious and tyrannical policy after only fifteen years, and was soon succeeded by the great *Han* dynasty, which during four centuries, with a slight eclipse of sixteen years, ruled the empire (204 B.C. to 190 A.D.).

The *Hans* considered the money of the Ts'in too heavy and inconvenient, and they authorized the people to cast some *leaf-money;* while the gold coins were again of the weight of a pound, as under the Tchou dynasty. But the small copper pieces became gradually so thin, that indeed they deserved their nickname of elm-leaf money; and they were multiplied to such an extent that they lost their former value, and prices rose enormously. In order to mitigate this evil, the Empress Kao (185 B.C.) issued pieces of 8 *tchus*, equal in value to the half-ounce pieces (*pan-liang*) of the pre-

Han Dynasty.

ceding dynasty; but it was found impossible to withdraw the elm-leaf money from circulation. Eleven years afterwards, the Emperor Wen-Ti, in the fifth year of his reign, tried to meet the difficulty by the issue of pieces having the same legend of *pan-liang* as before, but weighing only 4 *tchus*; and with the intention of rooting out false coining, he let the people cast their own money. The remedy, however, was insufficient, and some uneasiness was felt by the Emperor as to the influence of two feudal and almost independent states which issued their own money at a higher standard than that of the Chinese Empire.

<small>Counterfeiting.</small> The Emperor, in face of the failure of free mintage to check the counterfeiters, was obliged to forbid the people to cast their own money. Ring-Ti (156-140), the successor of Wen-Ti, was accused of having issued false gold coins; so that the people eagerly used the money introduced by the feudal state of Teng. False coiners practised their profession, and severe sentences could not stop the ever-growing evil. Wu-Ti, whose reign of fifty-four years was the most glorious of his dynasty, and whose generals carried the Chinese arms into the heart of Asia, issued, as a palliative measure, a money of real value, bearing the design of 3 *tchus*; but five years later it had to be suppressed again, because it was counterfeited and clipped, and pieces of 5 *tchus*, the standard of the dynasty, were then cast like those introduced by the Empress Kao. But all this was of

no avail againſt the counterfeiters, who iſſued ſuch quantities of debaſed coin, that the genuine money nearly diſappeared in ſome parts of the Empire, where pieces of cloth had to be uſed again as a medium of exchange. To face ſuch an emergency it was decided to aboliſh all the then exiſting pieces which had a nominal value of half an ounce, but which in reality contained only 4 *tchus*, and to make new pieces of a weight of 5 *tchus*, furniſhed all around with a raiſed edge, in order to prevent the coins from being filed.

The third currency iſſued by order of the Emperor Wu-Ti conſiſted of three ſorts of pieces of different ſize and form, made of tin and ſilver melted together, and of a nominal value far beyond the intrinſic. The firſt was round, with the deſign of a dragon, emblem of the Imperial dignity, weighing 8 *liang*, and its value was fixed at 3,000 pieces of money. The ſecond was ſquare, with the deſign of a horſe, weighing 6 *liang*, and worth 500 pieces. The third was oblong, with the deſign of a tortoiſe, weighing 4 *liang*, and worth 300 pieces. The reſult of theſe fiduciary iſſues was very unſatisfactory; and their end was ſad indeed. The very year of their iſſue they could no longer circulate, having been counterfeited on a great ſcale, not only by the people, but alſo by the ſtate officials. No ſpecimens of this fanciful mintage ſeem to be ſtill in exiſtence; and the repreſentations of it which appear in ſome native books of numiſmatics were drawn from the written deſcription, and the falſe ſpecimens which appear

sometimes in collections were made from the drawings, for sale to collectors.

The Shang-lin Mint.

After twenty-three years spent in these unsuccessful essays, the Emperor Wu-Ti was at last convinced that the evil was more deeply rooted than had been hitherto supposed, and that some more adequate measures had become necessary. Accordingly, with these wise views, great changes were made in the monetary management of the empire. Every district and province was not allowed, as formerly, to cast its own money; and a state mint was established in the capital of the empire, under the direction of three members of the Shang-lin, or Academy, which had been created by the same Emperor in 138 B.C. All the metallic currency formerly in use was withdrawn and brought to the Shang-lin mint to be melted and recast; and all money not issued by that mint was considered illegal. The most skilled of the false coiners were engaged as workmen at the mint. The money issued was that of *5-tchu* pieces, which, being very well made, remained the standard, excepting temporary mintages, during seven centuries, or until the issue of the *Kai yuen tung-pao*, the standard coin of the T'ang dynasty, in 622 A.D. These (*5-tchu*) pieces were of the now usual pattern—round, with a square hole in the centre, size 6 of Mionnet's scale, with a small raised edge all around. In consequence of the drastic measures taken by Wu-Ti, the counterfeiters had little chance during the latter part of his reign; and we do not hear of them during the

short rule of his successor Tchao-Ti (86-73 B.C.). However, in the long run, they proved to be stronger than the law of the land. Under the Emperor Suan-Ti (73-48 B.C.), in the years 71 and 60 B.C., it was necessary to make some official variations in the disposition of the design by the addition of a raised edge on both sides of the square central hole. But in the reign of the Emperor Yuen-Ti (48-32 B.C.) the counterfeiting had again reached a dangerous level; the forgers were more than 100,000 in number, and proposals were seriously discussed by the councillors of the Crown to abolish the metallic currency, and substitute in its stead grain, silk, cloth, and tortoise-shell as a medium of exchange; but it was difficult to make a sudden change in money which had been for a long time in circulation. The only means of checking the counterfeiters then was to issue from time to time new alterations, in the shape of additional lines or dots on the 5-*tchu* pieces. We hear no more of changes in the mintage until the usurper Wang Mang, half a century later. From 217 B.C., when the Shang-lin mint began to cast money, till the beginning of the reign of the Emperor Ping-Ti (1 A.D.), the amount of pieces issued was 280,000,000,000. In the time of the Emperor Yuen-Ti (48-32 B.C.) the treasury of the Imperial palace amounted to 4,000,000,000, and the privy purse contained 1,800,000,000 pieces of money.

The most eventful period in the history of Chinese money is that of the eighteen years during

Wang Mang.

which Wang Mang the ufurper ruled the country, firft as Regent, and after as Emperor. He began to cancel the various decrees enacted by the Han dynafty, and reverted again to the money of the Tchou dynafty, the multiple and unit pieces, or, as the Chinefe fay, the mother and child, weighed in proportion to each other. He alfo made again what he fuppofed to have been the pieces of Ring *King* of the Tchou dynafty, and he reintroduced the knife-fhaped money. It is eafy to judge how far thefe revived fhapes were different from the originals when we compare the knife-fhaped money of his iffues to actual fpecimens of the older currency. The fo-called knives of Wang Mang have but the name in common with their originals; they are half as long and much thicker, while the ring at the end of the handle is replaced by the fhape of a thick piece of money with rim and central fquare hole.

Revival of Knife Money.

When the ufurper took actual poffeffion of the Imperial throne (9 A.D.), he was afraid of all that would remind the people of the eclipfed dynafty. As the name of *Lin*, the founder of the dynafty, contained the characters *kin* ("metal"), and *tao* ("knife"), Wang Mang feared that his own knife-money would record the name of its founder (an apprehenfion which later on proved to be well grounded), and he decreed the abolition of the two forts of knives and of the 5-*tchu* pieces. He fubftituted new forts of currency of gold, filver, tortoife-fhell, cowries, and copper. Of the tortoife-fhell and cowries thus revived we have already spoken. The gold piece was, of course, in imitation of the ancient rule of the Tchou dynasty, and was called *kin* (pound), with a value of 10,000 copper pieces. In silver there were two pieces of different values based on a unit called *liu* (= 8 *liang*); their difference consisted only in the quality of the silver, and their value was 1,580 and 1,000 *cash*. As to the shape of this gold and silver money, we know nothing, and no specimen is known to exist.

The copper money received the name of *pu* by a revival of the oldest name used in the state of Ts'i previously to the financial Institutes of the Tchou dynasty, when *pu* (or cloth) was the principal medium of exchange in this region.

In A.D. 23, the usurper Wang Mang was murdered, and the second Han dynasty began to rule. The currency of the country was in frightful disorder; the last issues of Wang Mang were no longer accepted, because they existed only in counterfeit, and the old *5-tchu* pieces were in such small numbers that cloth, silk, metals, and rice were all used as currency, every individual making the most of them. However, Kwang Wu-Ti, the new Emperor, was not able, through the difficulties of the situation, to cast money before 40 A.D., and the pattern then used was that of the *5-tchu* pieces, the standard currency of the Han. The only modification subsequently made was the addition on the reverse of four straight strokes from the corners of the central hole to the outside rim. Some iron *5-tchu* pieces had been cast during the

Revived Han Dynasty

troubles at the end of the laſt reign, two being equivalent to one of copper.

Division of the Empire.

No other currency than the copper *5-tchu* pieces was iſſued till the end of the Han dynaſty (220 A.D.), and the enſuing diviſion for over fifty years of the empire into three kingdoms, Shuh, Wei, and Wu,—except ſmall copper pieces iſſued in 190 A.D. by the laſt Emperor, Hien-Ti, to ſupply the *5-tchu* pieces; for which, as the neceſſary quantity of copper was not available, he ſeized many copper objects and ſtatues, eſpecially thoſe of Fei-lien or Fŏng-pŏh, the God of the Winds, who had incurred his curſe.

Wei.

Four hundred years of monetary troubles and diſorders had not convinced the rulers of the neceſſity of a ſound currency. The King of Wei, in the north, thought that the beſt means of avoiding all theſe difficulties was to ſuppreſs the metallic currency altogether. Accordingly he aboliſhed the *5-tchu* pieces, and ordered the people to uſe as currency only grain and ſilk. It was only opening another door to the counterfeiters, who, inſtead of caſting bad metal, put moiſt grain in the bags, and wove thin and fleecy ſilk, so that after forty years it was neceſſary to return to the metal currency, and pieces of the time-honoured *5-tchu* pattern were caſt again and put in circulation.

Wu.

In the ſtate of Wu, the eaſternmoſt ſtate of the three, matters were ſtill worſe. In 236 A.D. were iſſued large pieces (8 of Mionnet's ſcale), with the legend *Ta tſinen wu pŏh* ("Great money

500 "), and two years afterwards larger ones ($9^1/_2$), *Ta tsinen tang tsien* ("Great money worth 1000"), which were foon counterfeited on a fmaller fcale, fo that it was deemed advifable to difcontinue their mintage, and to melt them for implements. In 256 A.D. was iffued another mintage, the pieces whereof in the ordinary pattern were worth 100 *tsien*, as indicated by their legend, *Tai-ping peh tsien* ("100 *tsien* [or *cash*] of [the period] Tai Ping"), which were of courfe foon imitated in a fmaller fize. This is the firft example of the ufe of the name of the reign or *nien-hao* in the denomination of the money. The cafe is worth noticing, though only fporadic examples are ftill found during the following centuries. Gradually the cuftom became more general, and later on, from the T'ang dynafty up to the prefent day, the iffues are diftinguifhed by the names of the years during which they were caft. Since the Ming dynafty the *nien-hao*, which were generally changed feveral times during one reign, have been made uniform for the full length of a reign, and to a certain extent have become identified with the ruler's own name, which is too facred to be pronounced during his lifetime.

Though the fhape of the currency was pretty well fettled, we ftill find fome eccentricities in the iffues, partly due to the abfence of the neceffary quantity of metal. The Ts'in dynafty (265-317 A.D.), who re-united the empire under one fway, iffued diminutive 5-*tchu* pieces (fize 2 of Mionnet's fcale), and two large iron pieces (fizes 9 and 15), Later Ts'in Dynasty.

worth 100 and 1,000, and so marked from top to bottom *Yh peh* and *Yh tsien* respectively, with *Yung ngan* ("Eternal peace") from right to left, denoting the name of the year (304 A.D.), when they were cast.

The Two Empires.
During a period of one hundred and fifty years, the empire was nominally divided between two Emperors, though in fact it was for a while partitioned into nine different states, in seven of which the rulers had not assumed the Imperial title. Of course, money too was in great disorder, but it is worth noticing that the Tartars, who ruled in the northern part of the Yang-tse Kiang, while the lawful heir of the ancient Chinese had removed to the south, had much more sound views on financial economy than the Chinese themselves, with all their painful and costly experience.

Southern Empire.
In the Southern Empire, under the Sung dynasty (420-477 A.D.), the Emperor Wen-Ti issued, in the year 430, copper pieces with a raised edge, and the design 4 *tchus*, which were equal in value to the old 5-*tchu* pieces; these pieces were hard to counterfeit, but very soon the old frauds began again. Hia Wu Ti's 4-*tchu* coins, with double legends (454-456), and his later 2-*tchu* pieces, were largely imitated, till they received derisive nicknames from the people, who called the thin ones "weed-leaves," and the small ones "goose-eye money."

At the beginning of the Liang dynasty (502-556 A.D.), in consequence of the closing of the state mints in sheer despair, money was so scarce that it was employed only in the capital, Nanking, and its vicinity. In order to put an end to the fraudulent dealings of the money-changers, it was decided to fuperfede the copper money by iron money, and pieces bearing the legends *Ta Kih wu tchu*, *Ta Fuh wu tchu*, *Ta t'ung wu tchu*, in iron were put in circulation. *Ta t'ung* only is a name of year, being that of the years 527, 528. But this was the folution of a difficulty by the creation of a new one. Iron could be got much more eafily than copper, and as the Government itfelf could not refift the temptation of making large profits, in ten years the iron money fell to one-third of its intended value. Iron Money.

When the Tch'en dynafty (557-587 A.D.) arofe, among the confufions caufed by the fall of the Liang, all the iron money was difcarded, and the new princes reverted to the old *5-tchu* pieces, which, in refpect to the ftill circulating "goofe-eye money," had a relative value of 10 to 1.

While all thefe monetary troubles and wild experiments were going on in the Southern Empire, more fober views and found economical principles had guided the Tartar rulers in the north. Indeed, their people, many of whom had fettled in China, were not accuftomed to metallic currency, and continued bartering as formerly, while the Chinefe themfelves ufed the former currency. It is only the feventh ruler of the Topa or Wei dynafty (386-532 A.D.), Hiao Wu-Ti, who directed in 477 A.D. that the falaries of all the ftate officers fhould be reckoned by Northern Empire.

money to be used henceforth in the empire, at the rate of 200 pieces of copper money, being equal to a piece of silk. The new money was inscribed *Tai Ho wu tchu*, or "5-*tchu* of (the period) Tai-ho." Fifty years afterwards false coining had impaired considerably this money, and new ones had to be cast with the legend *Yung ngan wu tchu*, or "5-*tchu* of (the period) Yung ngan" ("Eternal peace").

Sui Dynasty.

Under the Sui dynasty (581-618 A.D.), who ruled again over the whole empire, attempts were made to revive the old standard pieces of 5 *tchus*, and new ones were cast with the new distinctive feature of a broader ring. But the innumerable issues of money which had been made in the preceding centuries in the various states, and which were locally still more or less in circulation, had caused the most hopeless confusion. The old standard was no longer trusted by the people, who were obliged in the North-Western provinces, west of the Hoang-ho river, to use money from the foreign countries of the West with which they had commercial intercourse.

Modern Coinage.

T'ang Dynasty.

With the great T'ang dynasty rises a great change for the better in the metallic currency of China. As we have seen at the end of the last period, the 5-*tchu* pieces, which had been the standard money for more than eight centuries, had fallen into such discredit that it was impossible even to retain the name. An entirely new money was established, bearing the legend *Kai yuen t'ung pao* (or "Current money of the newest beginning "), weighing half as much again as the old 5-*tchu* pieces (*i.e.*, $7^1/_2$-*tchu*), with a fize of 7 on Mionnet's fcale. On the reverfe was a nail-mark, which fince then has fpread all over the Eaft, in Japan as in Corea and Annam. The origin of this curious mark is attributed to this incident: when the Under-Secretary of the Cenfors, Ngeu-yang-fiun, who had himfelf written the characters of the legend, fhowed a model in wax of the new money, the Emprefs Wen-teh in touching it left on the wax the impreffion of her nail.

The new money was so good that it foon fpread all over the empire, and has never been furpaffed. The only reproach was that it was not iffued in sufficient quantities to meet the requirements of the traders. This infufficiency led to feveral abufes. The pieces were counterfeited in a mixture of iron and tin by fkilful forgers, againft whofe cunning the officials were powerlefs. The Emperor tried to abolifh the new money lefs than forty years after its firft iffue, and caufed the ftate-money to be provided with a new legend (*Hien K'ing t'ung pao*); but it was foon found impoffible to go on with the new meafure, which therefore was withdrawn. The only practicable means was to make terms with the counterfeited money, and to accept it in payment. In 666 A.D. a new money with the legend *K'ien fung* (the year-name) *tung pao*, was iffued, to be accepted at the rate of one new for ten old pieces; but it foon became neceffary to caft again the *Kai yuen* pattern. The current money always circulated by

Limited Issue.

strings of 1,000, and thus the false pieces easily escaped detection. Under the reign of the Empress Wu (684-704 A.D.), therefore, it was forbidden to make payment in pieces strung together; they were to circulate loose, that the copper, tin, and iron pieces might be distinguished at once.

Dearth of Metal.

All the efforts of the Government were of no avail. The issue in 758 A.D. of larger money directed to be the equivalent of 50 and of 10 of the old pieces, was received with contempt by the people, because they had no intrinsic value. The metallic currency was so poor that stones for grinding rice were received as money of an intrinsic value at the rate of 1 to 10 *cash*. The great difficulty to overcome, for the Government, was the scanty supply of copper. Though it had been forbidden to any individual to store up more than a fixed quantity of the precious metal, the amount in circulation had gradually diminished by the melting of the good copper pieces to make vases, implements, and Buddhist figures. In 809 A.D. private persons tried to circulate silver money by working the silver mines of the Wuling Mountains (south of Hunan province), but this was soon prohibited by the Government.

Confiscation of Buddhist Treasures.

At last it was found necessary to regulate the use of the various metals. In 829 A.D. it was ordered that the Buddhist figures and ornaments, instead of being made of copper, should be made of lead, tin, clay, or wood, and the girdle either of gold, silver, Persian brass, or steel blued and

Confiscation of Buddhist Treasures. 223

polished; only for mirrors, gongs, nails, rings, and buttons, copper might be used. This restrictive measure was only the prelude of another of a more sweeping character. By the natural reaction from the extraordinary favour bestowed upon Buddhism during the previous reigns, this religion, from its excessive development and the immoderate pretensions of its devotees, came under the displeasure of the Emperor Wu Tsung, who, in 845 A.D., decreed its suppression. 4,600 monasteries and 40,000 smaller temples were destroyed; 260,500 monks and nuns were compelled to return to lay life; more than 15,000,000 acres of land were seized, and 150,000 female slaves were freed. All the copper statues, mallet-bells, gongs, and clapper-bells were confiscated to the profit of the Government, and melted to cast money of the *Kai-yuen* pattern in about twenty-five mints, of which the name was marked on the reverse of the pieces. This new supply of money was received with great favour, because of the quantity of gold supposed by the people to have been mixed with the copper in the temples.

The continuation of the numismatic records of China is a tedious repetition of all that we have seen thus far. Insufficiency in the supply of copper, and struggles against the counterfeiters, with the additional complications of a double standard caused by the temporary casting of iron money under the Sung dynasty and of the development of the paper money, which, from small beginnings in 806 A.D., attained a paramount importance under

Yuen and Ming Dynasties. the Yuen or Mongol dynasty, which cast very small quantities of copper-money. The Ming dynasty had also a poor mintage. It is only the present dynasty, the *Ta Ts'ing* Mandchu, who issued a regular and efficient mintage. From the time of the Ming dynasty the year-names have been reduced to one for each reign, so that the legend was henceforth the same for the whole mintage of a ruler.

Mandchu Dynasty. Regularity, however, is fairly secured in the issues from the mint of the Board of Finance in the capital, which are the pattern for the provincial mints; but the shrinking of the cool metal, when frequently repeated by the casting from moulds made from pieces and not from the pattern, produces sometimes a sensible difference, which is certainly not disadvantageous to some of the mint-masters. The authorized proportion of the alloys was, till 1722, copper 50, zinc $41^{1}/_{2}$, lead $6^{1}/_{2}$, tin 2; after that time the composition consisted of equal parts of copper and zinc. The obverse bears the name of the reign, read from top to bottom, and the words *tung pao*, or "current-money," from right to left. On the reverse the name of the mint in Chinese, or in Mandchu and Chinese, or in Mandchu only. There has been only one dark period in the present mintage, which for a time sunk to the lowest level during the great Taï-ping rebellion. The supply of the copper mines was stopped, and it was necessary to cast iron money, the worst of its kind that was ever made.

Silver circulates generally caſt in ingots, in ſhape rudely reſembling ſhoes, and for that reaſon called "ſhoe-ſilver." With the exception of two unſucceſsful (becauſe counterfeited) attempts in 1835 and 1856 to caſt ſilver dollars, the Government has never iſſued ſilver money. In Fuhkien province and Formoſa iſland, in 1835, a large iſſue of native dollars was made to pay the troops on that iſland; the legend was, "Pure ſilver for current uſe from the Tchang tchöu commiſſariat, (weight) 7 *mace* 2 *candareens*." At Shanghai, in 1856, the *taels*, or dollars, were of the ſame weight and purity (417·4 grs. troy); and beſides the inſcription in Chineſe and in Mandchu, they had an effigy of the god of longevity on the head, and a tripod on the tail, to authenticate the official origin. Gold, caſt into ingots, alſo circulates by weight.

Private individuals have ſometimes cauſed ſilver to be caſt as money; but they are generally ſatisfied to make, with European appliances, imitations of the Mexican and old Spaniſh dollars which are in currency; theſe, as they paſs from hand to hand, are punched with the ſeal or ſtamp of the owner by way of endorſement; and when the marks are ſo numerous that there is no room left on the coin for more, they are melted.

The Japaneſe records tell us nothing about the means by which barter was carried on previous to the uſe of metals, which do not appear in the Empire of the Riſing Sun before the fifth century A.D. Theſe records claim to go back uninterruptedly to 660 B.C., so that, even admitting that this far-reached date has to be shorn of several centuries, there is still a long lapse of time during which regular means of exchange might have been recorded.

<small>Earliest issues.</small>

In the *Ko-ji-ki*, or "Records of Ancient Matters," lately translated with great learning and industry by Mr. Basil Hall Chamberlain, the first appointment of a treasurer is recorded during the reign of the Emperor Tza-ho Wake, or Ri-chin, who ruled from 400 to 405 A.D., according to the "accepted chronology;" and several, but not all, native numismatists of high standing attribute to his immediate successor, Midzu-ha Wake, or Han-zei, in 408 A.D., the issue of rough silver coins, flat and irregular disks, with a small round central hole bearing several marks of rude stars of six lines, and sometimes undistinguishable strokes, size 9 of Mionnet's scale. *Mu-mon-do-sen*, *i.e.* coins bearing no characters, are more often classified among the *Kitte-sen*, *i.e.* coins issued provisionally in times of disturbances and warfare, and therefore very coarsely made, being generally cut out of a plate of metal instead of cast.

The genuineness of the next coins in date, *i.e.*, copper coins issued in 683 and 690 A.D., has remained comparatively unchallenged. They consist in flat and irregular disks of copper, with a small round central hole; size, 6 of Mionnet's scale; marks, 4 crosses, each in a circle.

The working of metallic mines in Japan began very late—674 for silver, 708 for copper, 749 for gold; and previous to thefe dates the fupply of metal by foreign importations was very limited, and if wanted, it was always eafy to get the copper *cafh* from China. It is only in 708 A.D., after the difcovery of copper mines, that the Japanefe began to caft regularly copper coins, of the fame fhape as had then been common in China for many centuries; viz., round, with a fquare hole in the centre. The Chinefe fyftem of the year-names, in Japanefe *Nengo*, which had been adopted fince 645 A.D., was followed in the legends of the coins. The difcovery and working of copper mines was confidered fo important an event for the country, that the actual *Nengo* was changed into *Wa-do*, *i.e.*, Japanefe copper; and the legend of the coins was *Wa-do-kai-tchin*, which may be rendered " New precious article of the *Wa-do* or Japanefe copper period." The Japanefe recognife the various iffues of their coins by differences in the fhape of a character, or of a ftroke of a character, and fo claffify three iffues of the *Wa-do* coin, all rather roughly caft, and a fourth iffue of a fuperior workmanfhip, imitated from the celebrated Chinefe *Kai-yuen* coin, to which it is like in form, fhape of characters, and general appearance. Fifty-two years afterwards, in A.D. 760, there were fo many forged *Wa-do-kai-tchin* in circulation, that the Government decided to iffue a new coin, which was caft, with the legend *Man-nen-tfu-ho*, or "Current money of ten thoufand years," in four iffues. A filver coin, worth ten of the copper ones, was put in circulation the same year, with the legend *Dai-bei-gen-ho*, "Fundamental money of the great tranquillity."

Ten other copper coins were succeffively iffued in A.D. 765, 796, 818, 835, 848, 859, 870, 890, 907, and 958; gradually decreafing in fize and workmanfhip till 870, and in material afterwards. The legends are often undecipherable, and in the laft coins the metal is largely alloyed with lead; in fome cafes they are made entirely of the latter metal. The execution was carelefs, and the refult was a rather disreputable money. Thefe twelve coins conftitute the antique coins of the country, or, as the Japanefe call them,[1] *Jū-ni-hin* ("The twelve kinds"). After the coinage of the latter coin, in confequence of political troubles, no copper coins whatever were iffued by the Central Government for over 600 years. Mintage in lead had begun as a fecondary currency with the iffue of 835 A.D., and down to 1302 the twelve antique coin patterns circulated in lead or in tin.

During this long interruption in the iffue of copper coins, the Chinefe *cash* fupplied the deficiency. Coins of various dynafties of China formed the currency of Japan, efpecially coins of the Northern Sung, and the Ta-tchung, Hung-Wu, and Yung-loh coins of the Ming; thefe were largely imitated. We cannot be aftonifhed to fee them imitated to a fomewhat large extent. For inftance, the Chinefe Sung coins of Siang-fu (1008 A.D.), Tien-Sheng (1023), Kia-yu (1056),

---

[1] W. Bramfen, *The Coins of Japan*, p. 7.

Ming-yuen (1032), Tcheping (1064), Hi-ming (1068), Yuen-fung (1078), Yüen-yu (1086), Shao-sheng (1094), Yuen-fu (1098), were moulded, and specimens cast and issued in quantities at Mito in the province of Fitatsu. In some cases new patterns were made, such as for the *Yuen-fung* coin with five varieties, two being moulded from the Chinese, and three made anew, which exhibits a finish and excellence of workmanship and bronze casting far superior to its Chinese original. All these issues were made by the private Daïmios in their own estates, and not by the Central Government; the metal was bronze, from the finest quality downwards, and sometimes a very poor alloy, and indeed lead. The *Yung-loh* (A.D. 1403) coin of the Ming was imported in not inconsiderable quantities, and largely imitated, not only from moulds of the coin itself, but also with new patterns. The device was used for gold, silver, white alloy, lead as well as for bronze, of which metal a larger coin was also issued.

With the period *Ten-sho* (1573-1591) commences a new era for Japan generally, as well as for its coins. Gold, silver, and copper coins began from thence to be regularly issued. In 1587 the "Current money of Ten-sho," *i.e.* the coin inscribed with the legend *Ten-sho-tsu-ho*, was first issued. As might be expected after the art of coining had been so neglected for centuries at the capital, this coin is not well made; there seems to have been a very limited number of copper coins cast, while silver coins of the same

Ten-sho Coinage.

design were issued in larger quantity, the consequence being that the former are at present much rarer than the latter. While in the twelve antique coins the characters of the legends were read $\begin{smallmatrix}&&1\\4&&2\\&3&\end{smallmatrix}$ the order was changed into $\begin{smallmatrix}&1\\4&3\\&2\end{smallmatrix}$ in this new issue and the after ones.

The *Bun-roku-tsu-ho*, in copper and in silver, were issued in 1592, and followed in 1606 by the *Kei-tcho-tsu-ho* (four varieties and two sizes), in 1615 by the *Gen-na-tsu-ho*, with a serial of 1 to 30 on the reverse. The *Kwan-ei-tsu-ho*, first issued in 1636, presents an almost endless variety of issues, due to the fact that the coinage was continued for over 225 years, during which the device of the copper and iron coins of the Government remained unchanged, with the exception of a few coins of a higher denomination. All the copper coins issued from *Wa-do* up to the period of *Kwan-ei*, and all the copper and iron coins *Kwan-ei-tsu-ho*, excepting the large-sized issue with wave-like lines on the reverse, are of the value of 1 *mon*. The various issues of different sizes, cast of copper or iron, with or without inscription on the reverse, are classified to the extent of more than 1,000 by the native numismatists.

In 1768 coins of the *Kwan-ei-tsu-ho* pattern were issued in brass and afterwards iron, the reverse being covered with twenty-one wave-like lines; they were to be worth 4 of the ordinary *mon*. The number of the wave-like lines was afterwards reduced to eleven. The last coins of this pattern were caſt ſo late as 1860, in iron, of two ſizes, a larger and a ſmaller one. In 1835 a large, oval, bronze coin, having on the obverſe *Tem-po* above and *tſu-ho* below the ſquare hole, was put in circulation; on the reverſe, above the hole, are the two characters *To-hiaku*, "worth 100," indicating that the value of the coin was 100 *mon*, and under the hole the mark of the mint. There are two varieties, diverſified by the reſpective ſizes of the rim and of the ſquare hole.

Finally, in 1863, was iſſued the laſt regular copper coin, with the legend *Bun-Kiu-ei-ho*, "Everlaſting money of Bun-Kiu (period)," with eleven wave-like lines on the reverſe; worth 4 *mon*, three varieties; alſo caſt in iron. Beſides the iron coins caſt by the central Government and current throughout the country, others were at various times iſſued by the feudal lords (Daïmios) for the excluſive uſe of their own dominions, or by certain chief towns. The moſt peculiar of this claſs, frequently met with in the collections, is ſquare, with rounded corners, inſcribed *Sen-dai tſu-ho*, *Sen-dai* being the name of the dominion where this pattern was caſt in ſeveral iſſues, of which the firſt took place about 1782. Space, however, fails us to ſpeak of the various peculiarities of theſe feudal iſſues; or the iron coins caſt in moulds of Chineſe caſt of a thouſand years earlier; or the token-like pieces iſſued at Mito in 1866-68, with the couplet:

<small>Iron Coinnge.</small>

> May your wealth be as vaſt as the Eaſtern Ocean,
> And your age as great as the Southern Mountains.

Bean Coinage.

Bean Coinage. We can only refer to the silver-copper, or billon coinage, of which the most curious examples are the silver-bean coins, shaped, as their name suggests, in various sizes, from a small pea to a large bean. Beginning in 1601 down to 1859, they are variously stamped; but the marks, which are made rather at random, are generally undecipherable. In 1711, etc., they were marked with the figure of Dai-Koku, the god of wealth, sitting on two rice bales, and holding his lucky hammer in the right hand, while the left grasps a sack of money slung over one shoulder. Each time Dai-Koku gives a blow with his hammer, the wallet he has by him becomes filled with money, rice, and other things, according to what may be desired.

Silver Coinage. In our rapid survey of the minor currency we have mentioned several of the regular issues of silver coins, cast on the same patterns as those in lower metals. By far the largest quantity of silver-money circulated under other shapes, viz., flat, square, oblong, plates, and lumps. Those of the first model were issued only during the last and the present centuries. The well-known small oblong coins in silver are quite modern, except the *T-shu* and *Ni-shu* pieces, issued since 1772. The *Itsi-bu* and *Ni-bu* pieces were issued till 1868; the former since 1846, and the latter since 1818. The *Ni-bu*, of golden appearance, presents an interesting peculiarity, while the other named coins were of silver of the usual fineness; the *Ni-bus* were of silver, with a percentage of gold added, which was brought out on the furface of the piece after the coin was made, by treatment with acids.

Silver in lumps by weight was moſt likely in ufe a long while before the evidence of the native collections and numifmatic records begin. The oldeſt, four inches in length, ſtamped with creſts, ſtars, etc., is afcribed to the period 1570-80. In the official records we hear of an iſſue of the fame kind in 1601. Thofe of 1695 bear all around fragmentary ſtamps of Dai-Koku, the god of wealth. In 1706, 1710, 1711, 1714, 1736, 1820, 1859, large filver lumps of various fizes were in circulation, and bear marks which traditions underſtand to have been ſtamped at thofe dates; the evidence is of a moſt ſhadowy character, and reſts on the mere aſſertion of the native writers.

Large plates of filver of various fizes, and fmaller ones like the gold *Obo-bang* and *Ko-bang*, were alfo iſſued between 1570 and 1580, but the practice feems to have been discontinued. In fome provinces filver was alfo ufed in lumps, from which bits of the required value were cut and weighed.

Previous to the adoption of the European fyſtem in 1870, round gold coins had been very rare indeed. A gold coin of the ordinary ſhape, pattern, and fquare hole in the centre, was iſſued in 760, with the four Chinefe characters *Rai-ſhing-ki-pao* as legend. One of the endlefs feries of the *Kwan-ei-tfu-ho* legend, and another in imitation of the Chinefe *yung-loh*, conſtitute the whole feries

Gold Coinage.

of the inscribed coins. Another well-known round coin is that issued in 1599 by Hide-yosi, better known under his posthumous name of Tai-kan-sama, the powerful general who instituted the high post of *taikun*. This rather small coin bears on one side six stamps, one central of the *Kiri-mon*, and on the other side five stamps of the same, with the minter mark in the centre. The *Kiri-mon*, or crest of the Mikado, is composed of three leaves pointed down with three flowers (one of seven and two of five petals) above, of the *Paulownia Imperialis*; it differs of the *Kiku-mon*, or Imperial badge of Japan, which consists of a conventional pattern of the chrysanthemum with sixteen petals, and must be distinguished from the badge of the Takugawa family, to whom belonged the later *Shôguns*, and which consisted in three mallow leaves within a circle, their points meeting in the centre. In 1727 divisionary pieces, or *itsi-bu*, *ni-shu*, and *is-shu* pieces so-called, were issued round, bearing on the obverse the *Kiri-mon* on the upper left side, with the examiner's stamp, and underneath, on the right hand side, the mark of the value; on the reverse are the mint stamp and the name of the year. The *ni-shu* and *is-shu* pieces have on the reverse the name of the particular kind of gold of which it is coined. By far the commonest shape of the gold coins issued since the sixteenth century to twenty years ago was that of oblong boards, with rounded angles, excepting for the small pieces. Their denominations were the following: *Oho-ban*, "large plate," of

10 ryo; *Goryo-ban*, "5 ryo board;" *Ko-ban*, "small plate," of 1 ryo; *Ni-bu*, "two parts," of $1/2$ ryo; *Itsi-bu*, "one part," of $1/4$ ryo; *Ni-shu*, "two shu," of $1/8$ ryo; *Is-shu*, "one shu," of $1/16$ ryo. The largest were more than $6\frac{1}{2}$ inches in length, and the smallest $3/8$ of an inch. They were stamped with the *Kiri-mon* in round, fan-shaped, or pentagon compartments, severally repeated, the value, the stamp of the mint; and on the small ones is sometimes the date of issue. Besides these stamps, the large coins often bear several punches of the mint-examiner, testifying to their genuineness. Fees used to be charged by the duly appointed officers of the Imperial mint or treasury for certifying the value of the large ones, or *Oho-ban;* and, in order to have these fees paid often, they had recourse to the ingenious device of marking them so that the marks could easily be obliterated, and the plan of writing the requisite signs in Indian ink was adopted; in consequence, the pieces were always wrapped up singly in silk wadding and paper, and the greatest care taken in handling them to prevent the writing being defaced.

CHAPTER X.

MEDALS.

HE ſcience of Numiſmatics has to deal not only with thoſe metallic objects which have actually paſſed current as money, but alſo with the numerous ſpecimens in the precious or other metals which are deſignated medals—ſpecimens, that is to ſay, iſſued to commemorate ſome perſonage or event, but not employed as media of exchange. The application of the word "medal" to this claſs, in contradiſtinction to coins, is a recent one: Italian and French writers of the fifteenth and ſixteenth centuries uſe *medaglie* and *médailles* to ſignify coins which, being no longer in circulation, are preſerved in the cabinets of collectors as curioſities. Even in the laſt century our own word medal was ſo employed. The "medals" of the Roman Emperors, to which Gibbon often alludes in his notes to the *Decline and Fall*, are, of courſe, what we now know as coins; and Addiſon's *Dialogue upon the Uſefulneſs of Medals* is, for the moſt part,

The word "Medal."

a treatise on Roman Imperial coins. The Shilling of Elizabeth, which is made to relate its adventures in the *Spectator*, observes that at the Restoration it came to be "rather looked upon as a medal than an ordinary coin." In the present chapter we shall of course employ the word "medal" in the sense which it has now generally acquired.

An inquiry into the history of the medal need not lead us far back into antiquity. The Greeks had absolutely no distinct class of objects corresponding to our medals, while even their coin-types were only in rare cases of a commemorative character. The coin-types of the Romans, indeed, are often directly allusive to historical events, and the Romans issued a special series of metallic objects not intended for circulation as currency; but even these latter pieces (known to modern numismatists as the "Roman medallions") can hardly be considered as the actual prototypes of the modern medal. Between the latest Roman medallions, which are of the time of Honorius, and the first productions of the famous Italian medallists of the fifteenth century, there is a great chasm, and the medals of the new Italy are in no sense the descendants of the old. The first Italian medals must, indeed, be reckoned as a new artistic product of their time: the processes by which they are made are not those of the older coin or medallion engravers, and they are, at first, entirely unofficial in character. It is only by degrees that the medal becomes more or less official, and is employed to comme-

<small>Italian Medals.</small>

morate important public events. The earlier specimens of Italian workmanship were not intended to commemorate events or even to do honour to illustrious men after their decease; they were destined rather to serve the purpose of the painted portrait or of the modern photograph. The noble families of the time welcomed with a natural eagerness this new art, which not only portrayed their features with all the power of painting, but which rendered them in a material which itself was *aes perenne*, and which was readily available for transmission from friend to friend.

<small>Pisano.</small> First of these great creators of the medal, in time no less than in merit, stands Vittore Pisano of Verona, whose artistic activity in this direction belongs to the ten years 1439-1449. Pisano is known also as a painter (his medals often bear the signature "Opus Pisani pictoris"), and it is, no doubt, a circumstance having an important influence upon the beginnings of modern medallic art that he and most of his fellow-workers were not by profession engravers of coin-dies, but followers of the arts of painting and sculpture. The art of coin-engraving, which had attained to such perfection in the hands of Greek and even of Roman artists, had during the Middle Ages suffered a terrible eclipse. Artistic portraiture was dead, and even the task of producing mere likeness was essayed no longer: the bold relief of Greek coin and Roman medallion was emulated no more, and although in the fourteenth century an ornate and not unpleasing style had begun to

manifest itself on coin-reverses, it never passed the limits of decorative skill.

It was open, of course, to Pisano and his followers to take the processes of die-engraving as they found them—to accomplish what they could within such limitations—to give likeness and life to the conventional heads of the obverse, and employ their taste and invention in improving the designs of the reverse. Trained, however, in the liberal school of painting and sculpture, they hesitated to pour their new wine into the old bottles. These medallists of the fifteenth century are distinguished above all other medallists by the largeness and freedom of their style; they required a yielding substance to work upon, and a broad space wherein to carry out their conceptions. For producing medals of great size and in high relief, the mechanical processes of die-engraving were at that time quite inadequate; and hence it is that all the early medals, and many of those produced in the sixteenth century, are not struck from dies, but cast from moulds. The first Italian medallists made their models from the life in wax—working, in fact, as did the sculptor of bronze who modelled in clay—and from these wax-models they prepared, by a careful and elaborate process, a mould into which the metal was finally poured. To Pisano himself about thirty extant medals have been attributed. They are distinguished (as indeed are all the works of the great medallists of Italy) by their splendid portraiture—portraiture of the highest kind, which

New Process of Casting Medals.

not only reproduces faithfully the features of man or woman, but which alfo reveals character, and which delights efpecially to show character only in its nobler traits.

The medallic art of Pifano (and in an equal or lefs degree that of his contemporaries) is further diftinguifhed by the excellence of its reverfe defigns—defigns remarkable for originality, and for ftrength combined with grace, and which are never chofen at hazard, but felected for their peculiar fitnefs to adorn the circular field of a medal. As characteriftic fpecimens of Pifano's work, let us mention the two famous medals, "Venator intrepidus" and "Liberalitas augufta," each bearing the head of Alfonfo the Magnanimous—"Divus Alphonfus rex triumphator et pacificus"—and having as their reverfe types admirable reprefentations of animals: the one a boar-hunt, the other an eagle furrounded by a vulture and other inferior birds of prey. In the reprefentation of animals Pifano took efpecial delight, and we often find them introduced in the reverfes of his medals. As a rule, he does not attempt elaborate allegorical fubjects; but his reverfes often fhow fome comparatively fimple defign, taken from ordinary life: thus a medal of his of Sigifmondo Pandolfo di Malatefta, which has, as ufual, a portrait of the prince for the obverfe, fhows Malatefta alfo on its reverfe, this time as a full-length figure in armour.

This artift's turn for realifm does not, however, preclude the production of feveral works infpired

Pisano. 241

by pure poetic fancy. A conspicuous instance of this may be found in the medal which he made for Leonello, Marquess of Este, on the occasion of his marriage in 1444. Just as the poet Spenser, when he wrote the *Prothalamion* of the noble Ladies Somerset—" against their bridal day which

ITALIAN. PORTRAIT OF MALATESTA NOVELLO, BY PISANO.

was not long"—imaged, by a charming yet stately fancy, the subjects of his verse as swans, so the artist Pisano, playing on the name Leonello, portrayed his bridegroom as a lion. A little Cupid or winged genius of marriage stands holding out to the lion an unrolled scroll, whereon in musical characters is displayed the lion's marriage-song.

This defign, which to a reader unacquainted with the original might feem too fanciful, is redeemed from being a mere *concetto* by the noble figure of the lion and the graceful grouping. Another of Pifano's reverfe defigns, which fhows the fame qualities of ftately grace and fancy, is that on the medal of Cecilia Gonzaga—" Cicilia virgo filia Johannis Francifci primi marchionis Mantue"—a lady who afterwards became a nun. Cecilia is reprefented fitting amidft a rocky landfcape, with her hand refting on the head of the unicorn who reclines befide her, while above them hangs the crefcent moon. But to dwell at length upon the reverfes of Pifano's medals, or upon his medallic portraits of "many nobles and perfonages renowned in arms or diftinguifhed for learning," we fhould need an entire chapter.

Followers of Pisano.

Matteo Pafti, who worked from 1446, was the firft diftinguifhed medallift who followed in the train of Pifano. He, too, was a native of Verona, and probably a pupil of his great fellow-citizen, whofe influence on his ftyle is traceable. Sperandio, who worked at the end of the fifteenth century, is alfo of the fchool of Vittore. He made numerous medals of the Eftes, and of members of the Bentivoglio family, of Pope Julius II., and others. To the fame century belong Giovanni Boldu, Guacciolotti, Enzola, and Melioli, as well as Lixignolo, Pollajuolo, and others, who have left behind them productions of great merit. After the firft impulfe had been given, the art had, indeed, foon fpread to the northern cities of Italy

—to Mantua, Padua, Milan, Brefcia, etc.—and, fomewhat later, to the cities fouth of the Apennines.

The Italian medallifts of the fixteenth century worthily carry on the work begun by their forerunners of the fifteenth. Though with them fomething of the large treatment of the earlier mafters is loft, we find, on the other hand, the greateft variety in the defigning of reverfes, remarkable fkill and delicacy in the execution of details, as well as abundant examples of excellent portraiture. A difference of a technical kind diftinguifhes the new medallifts from the old; for with the beginning of the fixteenth century there came in the art of ftriking medals from engraved dies, and though all the medals of larger module continued to be caft till the end of the century, the fmaller fpecimens, which then began to multiply, were ftruck by the new procefs. We obferve, indeed, that moft of the medallifts of the fixteenth century were alfo goldfmiths or gem-engravers, and were thus led naturally to the engraving of dies. To fay even a few words of each of the many remarkable medallifts of this century would be impoffible here, but the very names of Pomedello and Spinelli, Cellini and Francia, Romano and Caradoffo, Valerio Belli, Lione Lioni, Paftorino of Siena, and the reft, are full of charm to every lover of Italian medals. Of thefe names, we can only felect but one or two, referring the reader for more detailed notices to the works of Friedlaender, Armand, Heifs

Sixteenth Century Medallists

and others, and to the British Museum *Guide to the Italian Medals*, by Mr. C. F. Keary.

Francia. Francia, who is conspicuous as one of the earliest of this band of medallists, began life, as is well known, as a goldsmith, and acted for some time as director of the mint of Bologna. Vasari has a very interesting passage on his work as a medallist:—" That in which Francia delighted above all else, and in which he was indeed excellent, was in cutting dies for medals; in this he was highly distinguished, and his works are most admirable, as may be judged from some on which is the head of Pope Julius II.—so lifelike that these medals will bear comparison with those of Caradosso. He also struck medals of Signor Giovanni Bentivoglio, which seem to be alive, and of a vast number of princes who, passing through Bologna, made a certain delay when he took their portraits in wax: afterwards, having finished the matrices of the dies, he despatched them to their destination, whereby he obtained not only the immortality of fame, but likewise very handsome presents." Medals by Francia of Julius and Bentivoglio may still be seen in the British Museum. The medals of another renowned goldsmith, Benvenuto Cellini, are not very numerous. He was Master of the Mint to Pope Clement VII., for whom he made two portrait-medals.

Benvenuto Cellini.

Pastorino. In connection with portraiture, the name of Pastorino, who died about 1591, is of especial interest, as he devoted himself with ardour almost entirely to this branch of art, and attained in it wonderful fuccefs. The number of his medals is confiderable, for (as Vafari fays of him) " he has copied all the world, and perfons of all kinds, great nobles, diftinguifhed artifts, and perfons of unknown or of low degree." His delicate and beautiful ftyle makes him efpecially happy in his portraits of women and children. To the reverfe-defigns of the medals of this century we cannot refer in detail; but we muft dwell for a moment upon the reverfe of a medal in the Britifh Mufeum by Annibale Fontana (1540-1587)—a work of fingular charm and beauty, though contrafting ftrongly in its picture-like character with the reverfes of the early medallifts. It reprefents Hercules in the Garden of the Hefperides. The hero is ftanding in calm dignity befide the Tree, his right hand outftretched to pluck its golden apples: its dragon guard he has already flain, and is trampling the carcafe beneath his feet. In the diftance are feen the towers and cities of men in the light of the fetting fun. Fontana.

It muft be added that very few medals in the Italian feries commemorate *events:* their chief ftrength lies in portraiture, and their intereft may be reckoned rather artiftic than hiftorical, although, as has been truly faid, "in this aftonifhing feries of portraits the chief actors in the tragedies and comedies of thofe times pafs before us, their characters written in their faces." After the clofe of the fixteenth century the medals of Italy ceafe to be of high artiftic merit. But we ought not to forget to mention that a continuous Portraits.

series of contemporary Papal portraits, from Nicolas V. onwards, is to be found on the medals. Probably the most interesting piece in this class, from an historical point of view, is the famous medal struck by Gregory XIII. to commemorate the Massacre of St. Bartholomew in 1572. Three specimens of this medal are exhibited in the British Museum; the first in silver, by Federigo Bonzagna, shows as its obverse type the bust of the Pope himself, and on the reverse—*tantum religio potuit*—is represented the Destroying Angel holding sword and cross, while around are men and women wounded, or dead, or flying before her. The legend is "Ugonottorum Strages," and the date 1572. A second example is in bronze, gilt; a third, in bronze and slightly varied, is thought to be of more recent date.

Massacre of St. Bartholomew.

The Italian Renaissance did not fail to make its influence felt in the medallic art of other European countries, and it was from Italy that Germany derived the practice of casting medals, through Peter Fischer, who had studied art beyond the Alps. But although a foreign importation, the German medal soon acquired a distinct and national character. The minute and patient industry which distinguished German workers in other branches of art displayed itself likewise in their medal-work. Their productions are also thoroughly German in their tendency to avoid idealizing any representation; but if they lack the nobility of the Italian masters, they derive true force and artistic value from their

German Medals.

German Medals. 247

naïve and vigorous realifm. Among German medallifts two names are efpecially confpicuous— one, Heinrich Reitz, the goldfmith of Leipzig, who worked for the Electors of Saxony, and in whofe productions has been traced the influence of Lucas Cranach—the other, Friedrich Hagenauer of Augfburg, whofe ftyle is of greater fimplicity than that of Reitz. The medals executed by the goldfmiths of Nuremburg and Augfburg

GERMAN. PORTRAIT OF J. RINGELBERG.

are extremely numerous; moft of them are unfigned, and it is even difficult to feparate the productions of the two great centres, though Nuremburg has a diftinct fuperiority, due to the influence of Albert Dürer Many of the earlier German medals are ftruck, for the Germans had made confiderable improvements in the appliances for ftriking money: thofe fpecimens which are caft have been delicately chafed after the cafting.

The sixteenth century is the period during which the production of German medals attained its higheſt degree of excellence. As an original art, it may be ſaid to have periſhed in the commotions of the Thirty Years' War. Comparatively little attention has been paid to the German ſeries by numiſmatiſts and collectors, but it deſerves much more than it has yet received.

<small>French Medals.</small>

The medallic art in France had a longer leaſe of life than in Germany, and its hiſtory is of conſiderable intereſt. In ſpite of a few early native efforts, this art may be ſaid to have come into exiſtence under the auſpices of Italy. Thus we find that the firſt medal with a French effigy, that of Louis XI., was executed at Aix by an Italian, Franceſco Laurana. Another early medal, repreſenting Charles VIII. and Anne of Brittany, caſt at Lyons in 1494, was the work of a French goldſmith, Louis le Père, who had been inſtructed in the medalliſt's art by Nicolo Spinelli, of Florence. Yet it muſt be obſerved that this medal is French rather than Italian in character, and the medals made by native artiſts under Louis XII., for inſtance thoſe of Louis and Anne of Brittany (1500), and of Philibert le Beau and Margaret of Auſtria (1502), are evidence to prove that a purely French ſchool might have maintained itſelf with very little Italian aſſiſtance. Under François I., however, very diſtinct encouragement is given to Italian artiſts; and Benvenuto Cellini made for this ſovereign a medal with the regal effigy. Another Italian artiſt of merit,

Giacomo Primavera, alfo worked for France, and has left medals of Catherine de Medicis, the Duke of Alençon, the poet Ronfard, and others.

The medals of the latter half of the fixteenth century, partly ftruck and partly caft, are generally unfigned: the feries of large medallions reprefenting Henry II., Catherine de Medicis, Charles IX., and Henry III., has been attributed to Germain Pilon, a medallift who worked for Charles IX. With the acceffion of Henry IV. begins the fine fuite of medals by Guillaume Dupré, an artift whofe productions well continued the traditions of the large caft medals of Italy. He worked both under Henry IV. and Louis XIII., and, like the Italian mafters of the fifteenth century, undertook, and accomplifhed with great fuccefs, the cafting of his own medals. All the more important perfonages among his contemporaries were eager for the privilege of being portrayed by Dupré; and in his medallions, as a French writer has remarked, though with a *foupçon* of exaggeration, he has left pofterity "une galerie iconographique de fon temps, dont la beauté et l'interét égalent ceux des oeuvres analogues de la Renaiffance italienne. Perfonne n'a donné au portrait numifmatique un accent plus vivant et plus vrai; perfonne n'y a mieux rendu la phyfionomie d'une époque." After Dupré, fine medals ftill continued to be produced by the two chief French medallifts of the feventeenth century—Claude Warin, engraver to the mint at Lyons, who died in 1654, and Jean Warin, the Engraver-General of Coins, whofe death took place in 1672. The long series of medals of Louis XIV. is historically interesting, though it too faithfully reflects the pompous and conventional art of his time.

The first medals of Napoleon, struck between 1796 and 1802, are of indifferent execution and design. Under the direction of Denon they gradually improved, and at length attained to some degree of artistic merit; the heads of Napoleon by Andrieu and Droz, from the bust by Chaudet, are interesting portraits touched with ideal beauty, and some of the reverses of the Paris mint medals are not inelegant compositions. Perhaps the most historically important medals of the Napoleon series are those connected with the proposed invasion of England. In May, 1804, Napoleon took the title of Emperor, and in July of the same year he left Paris to visit the camp of Boulogne and the "Army of England." About this time there was struck a medal which is still extant and not uncommon. Its obverse shows the head of Napoleon, and the reverse a male figure squeezing a leopard between his legs while he throttles it with a cord. The legend relates to the flotilla of *prames*, or flat-bottomed boats and gunboats, which was to transport the invading army across the Channel:— "En l'an XII. 2,000 Barques font construites." The invasion being certain to succeed, nothing further was needed but a commemorative medal. There is reason for believing that in this year a die was actually prepared for a medal recording the success of the invasion to be struck in London

when the army arrived there. No specimens *Frappée à Londres.*
struck from this die are now known to be extant, but the British Museum possesses an electrotype which is believed to reproduce the reverse of the original die. Its type and inscriptions have reference to the victorious "Descente en Angleterre." A powerful naked figure has in his grasp a human being whose body ends in a fish's tail. It is the Hercules Napoleon destroying the sea-monster England. In the exergue may be read the modest legend, "Frappée à Londres en 1804." A French medal with a similar type was really issued two years later, but the "Descente" and "Frappée" legends have disappeared thereon in favour of the consolatory Virgilian quotation: "Toto divisos orbe Britannos."

We have yet to speak of the medals of Holland *Dutch Medals.* and of those of our own country. Both the Dutch and English series, which in the seventeenth century run much into one another, are attractive rather because of their historical interest than by reason of their artistic merit. By historical interest we do not, however, mean to imply that the medals furnish us with any very large amount of information not derivable from the documentary sources, but that they have the property of making historical events more vivid and more easily realized. Though medals can be regarded only as a slight and imperfect index to the history of any notable epoch, yet something, at any rate, they do show of its very form and pressure. They are the mirrors which the men of the past delighted to hold up to every momentous event—or to every event which seemed to them momentous; and they are mirrors, moreover, which have the magic power of still retaining the images which they originally reflected.

The Dutch medals of the sixteenth century, though not without occasional picturesqueness, are certainly not the finest of their time; they have, however, much historical interest—a feature which they share with those of the succeeding

DUTCH. PORTRAITS OF C. AND J. DE WITT.

century. In point of art the seventeenth-century pieces are poor, and they convey their political allusions by means of elaborate allegory. Many of the portraits on Dutch medals are noteworthy, especially those of William the Silent, Prince Maurice, the De Witts, Van Tromp, and De Ruyter. In the reign of our William the Third, the Dutch series fills up gaps in the English; indeed, several Dutch medallists worked at different periods for English monarchs.

English Medals.

The medallic feries of England opens in the reign of Henry VIII., and the pieces at firft are commemorative chiefly of perfons, and not of events. Of Henry himfelf there exifts a buft executed after a portrait of Holbein. Another of Henry's medals proclaims his fupremacy over the Church:—"Henricus octavus fidei defenfor et in terra Ecclefiae Angliae et Hiberniae fub Chrifto caput fupremum." The King's fupremacy was confirmed by Parliament in 1534, though this

ENGLISH. PORTRAITS OF PHILIP AND MARY, BY TREZZO.

medal was not made until 1545. The moft interefting portrait medals of this time are thofe of Anne Boleyn, Thomas Cromwell, and Sir Thomas More. More's medal bears the date 1535—the year of his death—and its reverfe typifies him as a cyprefs-tree which has fallen beneath the ftroke of an axe, and derives therefrom a more fragrant odour, "Suavius olet." Thefe early fpecimens, as well as the portrait medals of Edward VI., are caft and highly chafed. Of Mary and her hufband we have, befides other reprefentations, admirable half-length figures on a medal produced at Madrid by the Italian artift Trezzo, while in the fervice of Philip. This medal is the firft figned one in the Englifh feries; and the fact that it is executed by a foreign artift is (unfortunately for the artiftic credit of England) not to be noted as exceptional, but as the rule; for the hiftory of our Englifh medallifts is, as we fhall fee, to a great extent the hiftory of the medallifts of other nations.

Elizabeth. The reign of Elizabeth, efpecially, has to fhow fome excellent portraits by foreign artifts. Chief amongft thefe in beauty and in intereft is the medal of Mary Queen of Scots, made and figned by the Italian Primavera, who worked chiefly in the Netherlands, and, as was noted before, in France. Its date is uncertain, but it was probably produced about the fame time as the Morton portrait, which was painted in 1566-67, during Mary's imprifonment in Lochleven Caftle. Modern cafts of this medal have a reverfe added to them, but the original is merely a copper plaque. Stephen of Holland, who lived for a fhort time in England, executed, chiefly in the year 1562, a number of meritorious portrait-medals (caft and chafed), principally, however, of private perfons. Perfonal medals of the more celebrated men of the Elizabethan era are

Armada Medals. unhappily not very numerous. The lefs important public medals of this reign may well be paffed over in favour of thofe which commemorate the defeat of the Armada. Several of thefe pieces, fomewhat varied in their details, are ftill in exiftence, and as they are of oval form, and furnished with ring and chain for suspension, it is probable that they were distributed at the time as decorations. It is interesting to note that the most important do not bear the signature of any foreign medallist, but are, as it would seem, the work of native artists. Foremost of all the Armada medals must stand the large gold piece with the full-face bust of Elizabeth, encircled by the legend, "Ditior in toto non alter circulus orbe." The obverse of this extraordinary medal, with its high relief, its brilliant colour, its almost barbaric profusion of dress and ornament heaped upon the crowned and sceptred Queen, seems to speak the very euphuism of medallic language, and is wonderfully characteristic of its age. The reverse is conceived in a soberer manner. It represents a bay-tree standing upright and alone upon an island; its leaf also is not withered, nor has the lightning power to scathe it; for, says the legend, "Non ipsa pericula tangunt." The allusion is, perhaps, not merely to the defeat of the Spaniards, but also to the calm which had followed the political complications of the time—"the Queen of Scots was dead; James of Scotland had been conciliated; France and the Vatican were baffled." Upon another medal of this period, England is represented as an ark floating, "saevas tranquilla per undas."

Two other medals of Dutch workmanship, but also referring to the great victory over Spain, have still to be noticed. One of these, which was probably struck by the direction of Prince Maurice, represents the Church ſtanding firm on a rock amid ſtormy waves; the other has a quaintly expreſſed alluſion to the confederation formed againſt Elizabeth by the Pope, the King of Spain, the Emperor, and others. Upon one ſide are ſeen the Kings of the earth and the Rulers taking counſel together, but "Blind"—as the Latin fuperſcription warns them—"Blind are the minds of men, yea, and their hearts are blind;" the floor of their council-chamber is covered with ſpikes, for "Durum eſt contra ſtimulos calcitrare." On the other ſide, the Spaniſh fleet is driven on the rocks, and around are the words of the Pſalmiſt, quoted from the Vulgate: "Thou, O Lord, art great, and doeſt wondrous things; Thou art God alone!"

James I. The medals of James I. are principally Dutch, and for the moſt part commemorative of individuals. It ſhould be noticed that ſeveral of them are ſtruck from dies, and not caſt, for at this period the invention of the ſcrew for ſtriking coins and medals was coming into general uſe. Mechanical improvements of this kind, though very important to the mint-maſter, who naturally wiſhes to turn out his coinage with all poſſible rapidity and neatneſs, will be found both in England and other countries to exerciſe a baneful influence upon the art of medals. The hard and machine-made look of the later ſtruck medals too often contraſts unfavourably with the older ſpecimens produced by caſting and chaſing. To this reign belong the engraved, or, as they ſhould rather be called, the ſtamped medals of

Simon Paffe, the clearnefs and neatnefs of whofe ftyle is very pleafing. Simon, who was the fon of Crifpin Paffe, the artift of Utrecht, refided for about ten years in England, and executed a large number of prints and portraits. His medals are chiefly of James and the royal family. Amongft the few public events commemorated in this reign are the peace with Spain, concluded in 1604; and the alliance of England, France, and the United Provinces againft Spain. Curioufly enough, the Gunpowder Plot, which made fo deep an impreffion on the popular mind, is alluded to only on a fingle medal, and that a Dutch one. This medal fhows a fnake gliding amongft lilies and rofes, and has the legend, "Detectus qui latuit."

The moft noteworthy medals of the early part of the reign of Charles I. are thofe by Nicholas Briot, who, after being chief engraver to the Paris mint, came to England and executed a number of dies and moulds for medals as well as dies for the Englifh coinage. With the outbreak of the Civil Wars there begins in England a period of exceptional medallic intereft. During the lifetime of the King, and under the Protector and Commonwealth, medals continued to be made in extraordinary numbers. Some of thefe record the fucceffes of the contending parties, but moft of them are what are called "badges"—medals, that is to fay, of oval form, furnifhed with a ring for fufpenfion, fo that they could be worn by partifans of either fide. When we reflect that thefe pieces were once worn by the actors in that memorable drama, they can hardly fail to awaken a peculiarly pathetic intereſt; and this intereſt is much enhanced by their frequently preſenting the portraits of the remarkable men of the time. Among the portraits appearing on badges, or on other medals, are thoſe of Eſſex, Fairfax, Waller, Laud, Strafford, and many others. A portrait of Hampden exiſts on a ſmall engraved plate, but it is probably of eighteenth-century work. Of Cromwell and his family there are a conſiderable number of medals, as well as of men conſpicuous among the opponents of the King, ſuch as Ireton, Lilburne, Lambert, and Thurloe. The battle of Dunbar is commemorated by a medal ſhowing on its obverſe a buſt of Cromwell in armour, and, in the diſtance, the battle itſelf, with the inſcription, "*The Lord of Hoſts*—[watch-]word at Dunbar, Septem. y. 3, 1650." The reverſe diſplays the Parliament aſſembled in one Houſe with the Speaker. To the time of the Commonwealth alſo belong ſeveral "Naval Rewards" (1650-1653), eſpecially the fine medals ſtruck by the Parliament in commemoration of Blake's victories over the Dutch, and diſtributed to various officers. A ſpecial medal records the ſaving of the *Triumph*, Blake's flag-ſhip: "For eminent ſervice in ſaving y. Triumph, fiered in fight w^h. y. Duch in July, 1658." Another medal of this time has engraved upon it an Engliſh legend which has a quaint Latin ring about it: "Robt. Blake. *Born* 1598. *Died* 1657. *He fought at once with Ships and Caſtles. He dared the Fury of all the Elements, and left an Example to Poſterity which is incredible; to be imitated.*"

<small>Commonwealth.</small>

<small>Blake Medals.</small>

The continuous and eager demand for medallic badges and memorials at the epoch of the Civil Wars was fortunately well refponded to by three artifts of merit. Two of thefe, the brothers Thomas and Abraham Simon, who employed their talents on the Parliamentary fide, have produced fome of the moft praifeworthy works in the Englifh feries: their place of birth is uncertain, but they may, perhaps, be claimed as Englifhmen. Thomas is efpecially well known, from his connection with the Englifh mint. He it was who made the fplendid coins with the effigy of the Protector, and the famous "Petition Crown" for Charles II. The two brothers produced medals fingly or together: in the cafe of a joint work, it feems that Abraham Simon made the model, while Thomas, a more fkilful engraver, did the after-chafing. The Simons appear to have firft made their models in wax, and then to have caft the medals from moulds in fand. Moft of the medals of Charles I. and the Commonwealth are caft and chafed. Thomas Rawlins, the medallift who worked for the King, and who, after the death of Charles, prepared feveral commemorative medals for the adherents to the royal caufe, cannot be fpoken of fo favourably as the Simons. "His work was above the average, but it failed to attain the fharpnefs and high finifh which characterize that of his two rivals." Thefe three artifts continued to work after the Reftoration; but the chief medallift under Charles II. was John Roettier, the fon of a native of Antwerp. His medals, which are always ſtruck, are ſharply cut, and ſhow good portraits as well as some pictureſque reverſe deſigns. Another medalliſt who worked in Roettier's ſtyle, though with inferior ſkill, was George Bower, or Bowers. Both Roettier and Bower continued to produce medals under James II. and, for a time, under William III.

<small>Charles II.</small> An abundance of loyal medals heralds and inaugurates the Reſtoration. Charles is the ſun juſt riſing from the ſea—the leafleſs branch ſoon to recover greenneſs—the Jupiter deſtroying the proſtrate giants. Many royaliſt badges, with the effigies of the King and his father, probably belong to this time: one intereſting medal was doubtleſs beſtowed upon ſome faithful follower of Charles, for it bears the royal head, and is inſcribed with the words, " Propter ſtrenuitatem et fidelitatem rebus in adverſis." The important engagements between the naval powers of England and Holland receive due illuſtration from medals <small>Popish Plot.</small> —Engliſh, Dutch, and French. The Popiſh Plot, and eſpecially one incident—the murder of Sir Edmund Berry Godfrey—have left curious medallic evidences of themſelves. The medals relating to Godfrey all contain ſome ſatire upon the Jeſuits. On one remarkable ſpecimen in pewter, two monks, ſtyled " Juſtice-killers to his Holineſs," may be ſeen ſtrangling Godfrey, overlooked by the Pope, who is himſelf prompted by the devil. This is " Rome's revenge, or S^r. Edmvndberry Godfrey mvrthered in the pope's ſlaughter-hovs." One other medal of this reign—that ſtruck by Bower

to celebrate the acquittal of Shaftefbury on the charge of high treafon—ought not to be here omitted. Its obverfe has a portrait of the Earl, and the reverfe is a view of London, with the fun appearing from behind a cloud; the legend being "Laetamur: 24 Nov., 1681." This is the piece alluded to with fo much bitternefs in Dryden's fatire called *The Medal*:

> "Five days he fate for every caft and look,
> Four more than God to finifh Adam took;
> But who can tell what effence angels are,
> Or how long Heaven was making Lucifer."

The reign of James II., though brief, has left its traces on a confiderable number of medals. Many of thefe are Dutch, but they are perhaps more full of intereft than the official Englifh medals. The Rebellion of Monmouth is recorded on feveral fpecimens. One, by the Dutch artift Jan Smeltzing, bearing on the obverfe the head of the Duke ("Jacobus infelix Dux Monumethenfis"), has a reverfe of unufual power—the ghaftly decapitated head of the ill-fated leader lying upon the ground, and fpouting blood—"Hunc fanguinem libo Deo Liberatori." The attempt of James to reftore Catholicifm by the repeal of the Teft Act, and the Trial of the Seven Bifhops, receive full illuftration, efpecially the latter event. One well-known medal gives portraits of Archbifhop Sancroft and the Bifhops; another, fhowing feven ftars in the midft of the ftarry heavens, likens the feven prelates to the "fweet influences" of the Pleiades — "Quis reftringet Pleiadum delicias." On yet another specimen, also bearing medallions of the Bishops, a Jesuit and monk are seen vainly endeavouring to undermine the Church, a visible edifice built on a rock, and supported by a hand from Heaven—"The Gates of Hell shall not prevaile!" The other medals of this reign refer chiefly to the flight and abdication of the King, and to the birth of the young prince James. Some of the Dutch medals make very broad hints as to the legitimacy of the youthful heir. On one curious specimen Truth is seen throwing open the door of a cabinet, within which stands a Jesuit, thrusting through a trap a child with pyx and crown. The name of this suppositititious child whom Father Petre or some other papist is thus introducing to the world is inscribed on the cabinet door—"Jacobus Francis Edwardus."

Pretender Medals. The Flight of James to France conducts us naturally to the medals of the Stuart family, of whose members there are several memorials of this kind: many of them, no doubt, were struck for presentation to the faithful adherents who visited the princes in exile, or were issued to awaken interest in the Jacobite cause. One very pleasing medal of this series represents the youthful Charles Edward and his brother Henry; before Prince Charles is seen a star, with the motto "Micat inter omnes." Another medal—clearly, however, not issued by the Stuarts—ridicules the two attempts of the Elder Pretender to recover the English throne in 1708 and 1716; a map of

Great Britain and Ireland, with ships at sea, is displayed, with the dates of the expeditions, and the legend "Bis venit, vidit, non vicit, flensque recessit." A very interesting evidence of the still unsurrendered "right divine" is to be found in the *touch-pieces* of the Stuart family. Previous to the reign of Charles II., the English sovereigns who touched for the cure of the scrofula or "King's evil," distributed to their patients the current gold coin, called the *angel*. Under Charles II., who exerted his healing powers for an enormous number of persons, and under James II., a medalet having types somewhat similar to those of the *angel* was substituted, and hung round the neck of each afflicted person by a white ribbon. The Elder Pretender claimed the power as well as his two sons Charles and Henry, and of all three, touch-pieces are still extant, Henry's bearing the style of Henry IX. The practice of touching was repudiated by William III., and finally abandoned by George I. Between these reigns, however, Anne had been willing to dispense the royal gift of healing, and one child whom she touched (unhappily without result) was Samuel Johnson, whose golden touch-piece, pierced with a hole for suspension, may still be seen in the British Museum. Boswell records that when, on one occasion, Dr. Johnson was asked if he could remember Queen Anne, he answered that he had "a confused, but somehow a solemn, recollection of a lady in diamonds and a long black hood."

The medallic series of William III. and Anne

is due to the efforts of Dutch artists, the most active of whom were the Smeltzings, Luder, Hautsch, Boskam, and Croker, a German. Their medals are in many respects similar to those of John Roettier, but in lower relief; the reverses are generally pictorial and full of minute detail, which is not always ineffective, though their art on the whole is decidedly poor and conventional. The medals of William and Anne form the completest suite in the English series; any attempt, indeed, to give a detailed reference to the events which they commemorate would amount to a repetition of nearly all the best-known events in English history, from the Battle of the Boyne to the Peace of Utrecht. This continuous record is far less satisfactorily kept on the accession of George I. At that time there were few medallists in England, and the Dutch no longer worked for us. The medals of his successor are, however, commemorative of several important events, especially of those connected with the War of the Austrian Succession, the Jacobite Rebellion of '45, and the Conquest of Canada. The long reign of George III. is very fertile in medals, of which a good typical selection, down to the Battle of Waterloo, may be seen in the public exhibition galleries of the British Museum. The greater portion of the medals of this period which are there exhibited relate to "the struggles of England with her American colonists, and to the subsequent wars with France, Spain, and Holland by sea and land. Following these are several pieces commemorating some of the battles of the Peninſular War, and bearing portraits of the principal generals, and a few perſonal medals of ſtateſmen and others."

Some remarks muſt be made on the intereſting claſs of Engliſh *Military and Naval* medals. The Armada medals already mentioned may be regarded as the earlieſt of the claſs, though it is not known that they were iſſued by authority. In 1643 Charles I. granted medals to ſoldiers who diſtinguiſhed themſelves in Forlorn Hopes, and many of the Royaliſt and Parliamentary "badges" were doubtleſs intended as military rewards. Under the Commonwealth were diſtributed the Dunbar medal, and thoſe for Blake's victories over the Dutch, to which we have already alluded. After the Reſtoration, military awards were occaſionally iſſued, though the firſt decorative medal, ſubſequent to the Commonwealth, having a ring for ſuſpenſion, ſeems to be that for the battle of Culloden.

<small>Military and Naval Medals.</small>

"Again a long period elapſes during which no decorative medals appear; and the victories of the Nile and Trafalgar would have remained unrewarded, but for the munificence and patriotiſm of two Engliſhmen, Alexander Daviſon and Matthew Boulton. In 1784 the Eaſt India Company acknowledged the ſervices of its troops by awarding a medal for the campaign in the Weſt of India, an example which originated a cuſtom; and from that time, as long as India remained under the control of the Company, medals were awarded for all ſubſequent wars. The firſt medal

<small>Indian Medals.</small>

issued by authority in England in this century, is that given for the Battle of Waterloo. It was conferred, by order of the Prince Regent, upon every officer and private present at that battle; but no acknowledgment was made of all the brilliant engagements in the Peninsular War till 1847, when a medal was issued for military services between the years 1793-1814. At the same time a corresponding medal for naval services was ordered to be struck for all naval engagements during the same period. Since the accession of her Majesty, medals have been awarded for every campaign, as well as others for 'meritorious service,' 'long service,' etc. Besides the medals issued by the authority of the Crown and those of the East India Company, there are a number of Regimental medals. These were struck at the expense of the officers of the regiments, for distribution among those who served under them; but this custom ceased when a public acknowledgment was made of the services of the army."[1]

The unsatisfactory condition of the medallic art in England—and, indeed, in other European countries—during the present century has been justly lamented; and its productions must too often seem to those acquainted with the best efforts of Greek engravers and Italian medallists to be almost beneath contempt, and beyond the power of criticism to amend. To entertain a very sanguine expectation as to the future of this interesting branch of art would, perhaps, be some-

[1] H. A. Grueber, *Brit. Mus. Guide to Eng. Med.*, p. xv.

what rash; but there is certainly no real ground for denying the possibility of reinstating it in something of its pristine glory. If England cannot at once produce a school of medallists worthy to rank with the Italians of the fifteenth and the sixteenth centuries, her artists may at least begin by shaking themselves free from the trammels in which they have moved so long and so painfully. And, first, there is certainly needed a reform in the present rapid but deadly mechanical processes of producing medals: the old Italian casting and modelling in wax—the old Greek method of striking with the hammer on "blanks" not uniformly flat, must reassert their superiority—especially in the case of medallic portraiture. To create original artists—to breathe a new spirit into medal designs—particularly the reverse designs—is, indeed, a far more difficult task; yet at least it is possible to abandon in part, if not entirely, that classicism, or rather pseudo-classicism, which so long has reigned supreme. To press the inhabitants of Olympus into the service of modern art—to employ the symbolism of that Pagan creed outworn to commemorate a Methodist Conference or a Medical Congress, is in itself a confession of weakness; and though a few artists, such as the Wyons, may in a few instances claim to have imparted congruity and gracefulness to their classical designs, yet in the majority of modern medals these two essential qualities are suggested only by their absence. Modern students of art, and even the ordinary English public, have begun to display an

Classical Designs.

The Wyons.

increasing desire to know and enjoy the remains of classic Art, but it is to the fountain-head that they rightly turn—to Hellas, and not to Rome. It is useless, therefore, at this time of day, for a medallist to hope to conjure with mythological puppets of Hercules and Mars, and well-nigh impossible for him to awaken by classic emblem and divinity the sympathies of an audience for whom the wings of Victory have long lost all their swiftness, and the steeds of Neptune all their animation. Yet it must be observed that already there are signs of better things. Among the medals exhibited to the public at the British Museum will be noticed a series by Professor Legros of large portrait medallions of several eminent Englishmen— Carlyle, Tennyson, Gladstone, and others—which have been in the first instance modelled in wax, and then transferred to metal by casting. This new departure in medallic portraiture is very interesting, and the boldness of style in the medals in question is worthy of praise; but it must be remarked that the heads are treated sketchily, and seem to have little or no affinity to the material in which they are wrought. The Italian artists, on the contrary, even when working in their boldest and largest style, were never sketchy, but paid attention to finish, especially in the details of the hair and eyes, and even in such a minor matter as the lettering of the legend. Professor Legros has not at present essayed what is, perhaps, the still more arduous task of producing original designs suitable for the *reverses* of medals. In the reverse of the Ashantee War medal, designed by Mr. Poynter, we must admire the originality which makes itself independent of the conventional classic reverses—here, at last, we have real negroes, and real English soldiers in their helmets, introduced in a scene which is in itself a genuine artistic expression of the event intended to be commemorated by the medal. Yet even here it must be objected that the artist shows the want of a familiar and practical acquaintance with the material in which his ideas are expressed; and his design, though it would probably expand into an excellent painting, is far too confusedly picturesque for the limits of a small medal, and as a reverse-design cannot therefore be pronounced successful.

Poynter.

1

INDEX.

BBASY Khalifs, 168
'Abbâsy Khalifs of Egypt, 186
'Abd-El-Mejîd, 173
'Abd-El-Melik, 165
Aberystwith mint, 135
Abgarus, 151
Account, money of, 96
Achelous, 23
Addifon, *Dialogue upon Medals*, 30, 236
Adrian I., 80
Adze currency, 200
Aegina, 11, 15
Aelfred, 106
Aelia Capitolina, 155
Aelian, *Var. Hift.*, 12
Aeneas and Anchifes, 54
Aes grave, 43
Aes rude, 42
Aes fignatum, 43
Aefchylus, *Agam.*, 27
Aethelred, 106, 115
African company, 138
Aghlab, Beni-l-, 169
Agnel, 89
Agoniftic types, 22, 27, 28
Agrigentum, 26
Ahfanâbâd, 186
Akbar, 186, 188
Akcheh, 173

'Alam, Shah, 189
Alençon, Duke of, 249
Alexander the Great, 27
Alexander's portrait, 28, 29, 31
Alexander's fucceffors, 143
Alexander II. of Scotland, 114
Alexander III., 114
Alexandrian coinage, 67
Alfonfo VI., 86
Alfonfo the Magnanimous, 240
Alfred. See "Aelfred."
Almohades, 170
Almoravides, 81, 170
Altar, 53
Altun, 173
'Aly, 165
Amphora of Dionyfos, 19
Amphictyonic council, 17
Amyntas, 178
Anatolia, 172
Anchifes, 54
Ancus Marcius, 54
Andalufia, 167
Andrew, St., 115
Andrieu, 250
Angel, 112
Angelots, 112, 120
Anglo-French currency, 111
Animals on Pifano's medals, 240
Anne, 139
Anne Boleyn, 253
Anne of Brittany, 248
Ant coins, 196
Antigonus, 153

Antioch, 150
Antiochus I. and II., 143
Antiochus IV., Epiphanes, 144, 150
Antiochus VII., 153
Antiochus Hierax, 150
Aphrodite (Aegina), 15
Aphrodite Melainis (Thespiae), 19
Apollo and Artemis (Camarina), 24
Apollo (Delphi), 17
Apollo, Didymaean, 15
Apollo (Philip's gold money), 27
Apollo (Tanagra), 19
Apulia, Norman Dukes of, 86, 87
Aquitaine, 111
Arab coinage, 152, 156 *et seq.*
Arab merchants, trade with, 85
Arabia, 151
Arabic currency in the North, 84
Aragon, 86, 109
Ardeshir, 148
Ardit, 111
Aretas, 151
Arethusa, 25
Argenteus, 60
Argos, 11
Ariadne, 22
Ariarathes, 32
Aristophanes, *Birds*, 16
Aristoxenus, artist of Metapontum, 37
Armada medals, 254
Armenia, 150
Arsaces, 144, 146
Arsacidae, 145
Arsames, 150
Art, early Saxon and Irish, 104
  on Charles I.'s coins, 135
  on English coins, 117, 118
  on medals, 237 *et seq.*
  on Mohammadan coins, 156
Artaxerxes or Ardeshir, 148
Artaxias, 151
Artavasdes, 151
Artemis (Ephesus), 21, 40
  (Camarina), 24
Artists' names, Greek, 36

As libralis, 43
Asia, Central, 145
  Minor, 20
  Western, 150
Asiatic divinities, images of, 40
Atâbegs, 169
Athens, 15
  coins copied in Arabia, 152
Atrebates, 102
Attalid Kings of Pergamus, 31
Attambulus, 152
Augsburg medals, 247
Augur, 21
Augustus's new copper coinage, 50
Augustulus to Charlemagne, 77
Aurelian, 151
Aureus, 50, 59, 61
Ayyûbîs, 169
Azes, 178

BABER, 186
Babylonian influence on China, 191
Bacchus, 20
Bactria, 144
Bahmany Kings of Kulbarga, 186
Bak tribes in China, 191
Baliol, John, 114
Barter, 10
Bartholomew Massacre, medal, 246
Base money, 84, 115, 126, 131
Bawbee, or bas pièce, 131
Bean coinage, 232
Beaufort family, 122
Bee (Ephesus), 21
Beeston Castle, 135
Belli, 243
Beneventum, 80
Bentivoglio, 242, 244
Berbers, 170, 172
Berenice, 29
Beybars, 160
Bezant, 81
Billhook currency, 200
Billon, 115, 131
Biot, E., 208
Bird on ear of corn, 23
Bishops, Trial of the Seven, 261

Black Prince, 111
Blancs, 112
Blake, Admiral, 258
Blondeau, 138
Boar of Artemis, 14
Boldu, G., 242
Boeotia, 18
Bonnet pieces, 130
Bonzagna, F., 246
Bordeaux, 111
Boſkam, 264
Bower, G., 260
Boyne, battle of the, 264
Brabant, 108
Bracteates, 84, 90
    ornaments, 103
Brandenburg, Elector of, 94
Briot, Nicholas, 136, 257
Briſtol, 135
Britiſh coins, 100
BRITISH ISLANDS, coins of, 99-140
    Britons, 100
    Roman mints, 102
    Saxons, 102
    Sceat, 103
    Normans, 107
    Groats, 108
    Gold currency, 109
    Anglo-French coinage, 111
    Scottiſh coinage, 113
    Ireland, 115
    Henry VII., 116
    Shilling, 117
    Art on Engliſh coins, 118
    Increaſe of wealth, 119
    Sovereign, 120
    Henry VIII., 120
    Crown, 120
    Wolſey's groat, 122
    Edward VI., 123
    Mary, 123
    Elizabeth, 124
    Eaſt India Company, 125
    Debaſement of coinage, 127
    Tokens, 128
    Scotland, 129
    James I., 131
    Denominations, 133
    Charles I., 134

BRITISH ISLANDS, Siege pieces, 135
    Commonwealth, 136
    Simon's portraits, 137
    Guinea, 138
    James II., Iriſh coins, 139
    Anne's farthing, 140
Broad, 132
Bronze money of James II., 139
Bruce, Robert, 114
Brutus, 52
Buckler of Boeotia, 19
Buddhiſt emblems, 181
    monaſteries and temples, 222
    saints, 179
Bull, human-headed, 21
Bull and Horſeman, 181, 185
Bullion exchange, 10
Buweyhîs, 168
Byzant, 81
Byzantine gold uſed by Arabs, 164
Byzantine iconography, 86
    imitations, 82
    types on Mohammadan coins, 169

CABUL, 178, 181
Caepio, 51
Caeſar, Julius, 50
Calais, 111
Calligraphy, 157, 186
Camarina, 24, 25
Campania, 21, 45, 50
Camulodunum, 102
Canada, conqueſt, 264
Canute, 106
Cappadocia, 32
Caradoſſo, 243
Carauſius, 102
Carliſle, 135
Carlovingian coinage, 82
Caſtile, 86
Caſting medals, new proceſs, 239
Cellini, Benvenuto, 243, 248
Celt, ſhoulder-headed, 201
Centaurs, 20
Cententionalis, 60
Cerberus, 21
Ceylon, 182
Chaiſe, 111

274 Index.

Chamberlain, B. Hall, 226
Characene, 152
Charles I., 134, 257
Charles II., 137, 259, 263
Charles VIII. of France, 248
Charles IX., 249
Charles XII. of Sweden, 94
Charles Edward Stuart, 262
Chefter, 135
Chimaera, 21
CHINA AND JAPAN, coins of, 190-235
  CHINA, 190
    Shell currency, 192
    Earlieft metal currency, 195
    Mines, 197
    Tchou dynafty, 198
    Adze currency, 200
    Ring weights, 202
    Leaf weights, 203
    Period of Contending States, 203
    Knife money of Tfi, 205
    Leaf money, 206
    Gold currency, 207
    State coinage, 208
    Tf'in dynafty, 208
    Han dynafty, 209
    Counterfeiting, 210
    The Shang-lin mint, 212
    Wang Mang, 213
    Revival of knife money, 214
    Han dynafty revived, 215
    Divifion of the Empire, 216
    State of Wei, 216
    State of Wu, 216
    Later Tf'in dynafty, 217
    The Two Empires, 218
    Southern Empire, 218
    Iron money, 219
    Northern Empire, 219
    Sui dynafty, 220
    Tang dynafty, 220
    Limited iffue, 221
    Dearth of metal, 222
    Confifcation of Buddhift treafures, 222

CHINA, Yuen and Ming dynafties, 224
  Mandchu dynafty, 224
JAPAN, 225
  Earlieft iffues, 226
  Imitation of Chinefe money, 227
  Lead currency, 228
  Chinefe coins in Japan, 228
  Ten-fho coinage, 229
  Iron coinage, 231
  Bean coinage, 232
  Silver coinage, 232
  Gold coinage, 233
Chinguiz Khan, 172
Chlovis II., 79
Chohân horfeman, 185
Chriftian Europe, coinage of, 74-98. See "Europe."
Chriftian figures on Mohammadan coins, 169
Chriftian types on Roman coins, 63
Chutiâ Nâgpûr, 201
Cities perfonified on Parthian coins, 147
Cities, views of, 96
Civic coinage of Greece, 14
Clement VII., 244
Cleopatra's portrait, 33
Club of Herakles, 19
Cnut, 106
Colchefter, 102, 135
Commius, 102
Commonwealth, 136, 258
Company, African, 138
  Eaft India, 125, 139, 265
  South Sea, 140
Conftantine, 61
Conftantinople, 173
Confular feries, 48
Contorniates, 69
Contending States in China, 203
Copper coinage in England, 128
  India, 184
  China, 195
Cork, 116, 135
Counterfeiting in China, 210
Cowry currency, 192 et feq.
Cranach, L., 247

Index. 275

Crenides, gold mines, 100
Crescent of Aphrodite, 19
Crimissus, 24
Croker, 264
Cromwell, O., 137, 258
    T., 253
Cross, forms of, 83, 90, 108, 114, 136
Crown, 120
Cubes of gold in China, 198
Culloden medal, 265
Cunipert, 79
Cunobelinus, 102
Curtius, E., 13
Cypraea, 193 et seq.
Cyprus, 142

DAI-KOKO, god of wealth, 232
Daïmios, 229, 231
Damascus, 165, 167
Damietta, conquest of, 160
Danish kings, 106, 107
Dante, *Paradiso*, 88, 126
Daric, 141
Date on English coins, 123
David I. of Scotland, 113
Davison, A., 265
Debasement of coinage in England, 126
    Scotland, 114, 131
    Germany, 84
Declaration type, 134
Decussis, 43
Dehli, 171, 186-189
Dekhan, 186
Delphi, 16
Delphian games, 23
Demeter (Metapontum), 23
Demetrius Poliorcetes, 31
Demi-chaise, 111
Demy, 115
Denarius, 48, 81, 96
Denier, new, 81, 111
Denmark, 85
Denominations of English coins, 133
    Roman coins, 42 et seq.
Denon, 250
Desiderius, 79
Diana, 53
Die-engravers, 36, 119 note

Dînâr, 167
Diocletian's reforms, 60
Diogenes Laertius, vii., 2, 70
Dionysos, 31
    (Thebes), 19
    Hebon, 22
Dioscuri, 50
Dirhem, 167
Divine honours, 29
Dollar, 98
Dolphin of Apollo, 18
    of Syracuse, 25
    of Tarentum, 22
Double hardi, 111
Double sovereigns, 120
Dove of Aphrodite, 14
Drachmas, Attic, 16
Dragon, 211
Dragon's-head coins, 196
Drogheda, 116
Droz, 250
Dryden, *The Medal*, 261
Dublin, 116, 135
Ducats, 87, 97, 130
Dunbar, battle, 258
Dupondius, 43, 50
Dupré, 9, 92, 249
Dürer, A., 93, 247
Durham, 122
Dutch medals, 251, 256, 258, 259, 261

EADWARD THE CONFESSOR, 107
Eagle, two-headed, 169
    on thunderbolt, 50
    of Zeus, 14
Eagles devouring hare, 26
Ear of corn of Demeter, 23
Earth god, 21, 22
East, early coins of, 141
Eckhel's *Doctrina Numorum Veterum*, 1
Economic fallacies, 126
Ecu, 97, 130
Edessa, 151
Edinburgh, 135
Edward I., 108
Edward III., 108, 109
Edward, the Black Prince, 111
Edward IV., 112

Edward VI., 118, 123, 253. See "Eadward."
Egberht of Weffex, 106
Eleazar, 154
Elis, 37
Elizabeth, 124, 254
Elm-leaf money, 209
Eloi, St., 79
Emperors, Roman, portraits, 5
England, portraits, 92, 93. See "Britifh Islands."
England, army of, 250
Engravers, Englifh, 119 *note*
   Greek, 36
Enzola, 242
Epaminondas, 39
Ephefus, 20, 39
Erafmus, 128
Effex, 258
Efte, Leonello, Marquefs of, 241
Eftes, 242
Efterlings, 109
Ethelred. See "Aethelred."
Etruria, 21
Eucratides, 175, 177
EUROPE, CHRISTIAN, coinage of, 75-98
   Divifions of the fubject, 75
   Special intereft of each, 76
   I. Auguftus to Charlemagne, 77
   Lombards, 79
   II. True Mediaeval period, 80
   New Denarius, 81
   France, 82
   Germany and Italy, 83
   Bracteates, 84
   Spain, 85
   Iconography, 86
   III. Return to gold, 87
   Fiorino d'oro, 88
   Fourteenth century, 90
   IV. Renaiffance, 90
   Portraits, 91
   V. Modern coinage, 93
   Sovereigns' portraits, 94
   Medallic character, 95
   Views of cities, 96
   Weights and denominations, 96

Evaenetus, a coin engraver, 36
Exeter, 135
Eybek the Mamlûk, 161

FAIRFAX, 258
Fairs at Delphi, 17
Fallacies, economic, under Tudors, 126
Farthing, 108
Farthings, Queen Anne, 140
Fâtimy Khalifs, 170
Federal currency of Boeotia, 18
Finenefs of Mohammadan coins, 167
Fiorino d'oro, 88
Fifcher, P., 246
Five-guinea piece, 138
Flanders, 108
Fleurs-de-lis on Scottifh coins, 114
Florence, 88, 92
Florin, 88, 97
   in England, 110
Fontana, 245
Forgers, Chinefe, 210
Formulas, religious, 8
France, Englifh coinage in, 111
   Mediaeval coinage, 82
   portraits, 92
Francia, 243, 244
François I., 248
Franconian emperors, 83
Francs, 112
Franks, 78
Frederick II., 87
Frederick the Great, 95
Frederick of Bohemia, 94
French crufade to Egypt, 160

GAMES, sacred, on coins, 41
   Metapontine, 23
   Olympian, 23
   Pythian, 17
   Tarentine, 22
Gaulifh coins, 100
Gelas, 24
Gems, 197
   engravers of, 4
Genealogy on Muflim coins, 159
George I., 139, 263
George II., 139

George III., 139
George noble, 121
German portraits, 93, 246
    reprefentations of Saints, 87
Germany, mediaeval coinage, 83
Gibbon's ufe of the word "medal," 236
Godfrey, Sir Edmund Berry, 260
Gods on coinage, Greek, 14
Gold coins of Rome, 45
Gold cubes and currency in China, 198, 207
Gold currency in England, 109
Gold mines of Crenides, 100
Gold and filver mines of Pangaeum, 20
Gonzaga, Cecilia, medal, 242
Gorgon's head on Etrufcan coins, 21
GREEK COINS, 3, 10-41
    Bullion money, 10
    Invention of coinage, 10
    Methods of coinage, 11
    Scientific value, 12
    Types, 12
    Religious afpect, 12
    Temple coinage, 13
    State coinage, 14
    Aegina, 15
    Delphi, 16
    Boeotia, 18
    Ephefus, 20
    Etruria, 21
    Campania, 21
    Magna Graecia, 22
    Agoniftic types, 22
    Metapontum, 23
    Sicily river gods, 23
    Water nymphs, 25
    Eagles devouring hare, 26
    Philip and Alexander, 27
    Portraiture, 28
    Alexander's fucceffors, 28
    Portraits, Alexander, etc., 30
    Realifm, 31
    Mithradates, 32
    Cleopatra, 33
    Styles of art and fequence, 33
    Die engravers, 36

GREEK COINS, Magiftrate.' names, 38
Greek cities of Afia, 40
    Imperial coinage, 39
    Kings of India, 175
    types on Indian coins, 177
    types in Perfia, 142
Gregory XIII., 246
Griffin, 21, 50
Groats, 89, 108
Gros, 111
Groffi, or gros, 89, 91
Groffus, 97
Grueber, H. A., *Guide to Englifh Medals*, 266
Guacciolotti, 242
Guadaleta, battle, 78, 85
Guienne, 111
Guiennois, 111
Guinea, 138
Gujarat, 181, 186
Gun-metal, 139
Gunpowder Plot medal, 257
Gupta Kings of Kanauj, 180
Guftavus Adolphus, 94

HADES on Etrufcan coins, 21
Hadleye, Robert de, 108
Hadrian, 63
Hagenauer, F., 247
Hainault, 108
Half-crowns, 120
Half-demy, 115
Half-groat, 112
Half-guinea, 138
Half-moon money, 200
Half-plack, 115
Half-quarter-fovereign, 124
Halfpence and farthings, 108
Half-fhekel, 153
Half-fovereigns, 120
Hamdânîs, 168
Hampden, 258
Han dynafty, 195, 196, 209, 215
Hardi, 111
Hare devoured by eagles, 26
Harp of Ireland, 136
Harrington, Lord, 129
Hat, Cardinal's, 122
Hautfch, 264
Heliocles, 177

Helios, 178
Hempen cloth, 192
Henry II., 107
    Irifh coinage, 116
Henry VII., 117
Henry VIII., 118, 120, 253
Henry [IX.] Stuart, 263
Henry II., III., and IV. of France, 249
Heraclius, 164
Herakles, 179, 245
    of Croton, 3
    on Philip's coins, 28
    at Thebes, 19
    fhield of, 19
Heraldic devices on Englifh coins, 121
Heraus, 178
Hermaeus, 178
Herodian family, 154
Herodotus, 11
Hefperides, 245
Hia dynafty, 192
Himyarites, 152
Hindu types, 181
Hipparis, 24
Hippoftratus, 178
Hiftorical value of Mohammadan coins, 158, 161
    Roman money, 5, 6
    Greek coins, 12
Hohenftaufen dynafty, 87
Holbein, 253
Holland, medals, 251, 254, 258
Holy Carpet, 159
Honorius, 103
Hulagu, 187
Huns, 144
Hypfas, 24

ICONOGRAPHY, 64, 86
Ides of March, 53
Idrîsîs, 169
Ikhfhîdîs, 169
Ilkhâns of Perfia, 171
Imitations, 152, 227
Imperial coinage of Rome, 59
Incufe fquare, 11
India, 144
INDIAN COINS, 175-189
    Greek Kings, 175

INDIAN COINS, Scythic Kings 178
    Native Kings, 179
    Guptas, 180
    Sah Kings, 181
    Brahman Kings of Cabul, 181
    Mohammadan coinage, 182
    Copper currency, 184
    Muflim dynafties, 185
    Patâns of Dehli, 186
    Mohammad ibn Taghlak, 187
    Moguls of Dehli, 188
India Company, Eaft, 125, 139, 265
Invention of coinage, 10, 141
Ireland, 115, 127, 139
Ireton, 258
Iron bars, 15
Iron currency in Japan, 231
Italian cities, autonomous, 84
    medals, 237 et feq.
    mediaeval coinage, 83

JAGATAY family, 171
James I. of Scotland, 115
James II. ,, 115
James III. ,, 115
James IV. ,, 130
James V. ,, 130
James VI. of Scotland and I. of England, 130, 256
James II., 139, 261
James [III.] the Pretender, 262
Janus, 44-46
Japan, 225-235. See "China."
Jaunpûr, 186
Jehângîr, 189
Jewifh coins, 153
Joachimfthal, 98
John Baptift, St., 88, 116
John, King, ii., 1, 113
    Irifh coinage, 116
John, St., 86
Johnfon, Samuel, 263
Judaea, 62, 153, 154
Julius II., 242, 244

KADPHISES, 179
Kanerkes, 179
Kanauj, 180

Index.   279

Kashmîr, 182
Keary, C. F., *Guide to Italian Medals*, 244
Khalifs, 164-168, 186
Khorafan, 168
Khubilai Khân, 188
Khutbeh and Sikkeh, 162
Kipchak, 171
Kiri-mon, 234
Knives, 192
Knife money of Tfʻi, 204
Knife money revived, 214
Krim, 171
Kufic character, 157
Kulbarga, 186
Kurds, 169
Kwan-tze, financial reform, 197

L. S. D., 97
Lamb, Paschal, 89, 111
Latten tokens, 128
Laud, Archbishop, 258
Laurana, F., 248
Laurel, 133
Lead currency in Japan, 228
Lead tokens, 128
Leaf money, 206, 209
Leaf weights, 203
Leather tokens, 128
Legros, 268
Leipzig medals, 247
Lenormant, F., 2
Leopard, 111
  on florin, 110
Leovigild, 78
Lex Julia Papiria, 44
Lexignolo, 242
Liang dynasty, 218
Liberty, cap of, 53
Libra, 97
Lima, 140
Limerick, 116
Lion, 115
Lion crest borne by Beybars, 160
Lion noble, 132
Lioni, 243
Local mints, 56, 66
Locust, 23
Lombards, coins of, 79
Londinium, 102
London, 102, 135, 251

"Londres, frappée à," 251
Louis IX., St., deniers, ∞
  Crusade of, 160
Louis XI., 248
Louis XII., 248
Louis XIII., 249
Louis XIV., 94, 250
Louis le Père, 248
Low Countries, 108, 251
Luder, 264
Ludwig of Bavaria, 95
Luther medals, 95
Lycian league, 142
Lydia, 10
Lyons medals, 248, 249
Lyre of Apollo, 14
Lysimachus, 28, 31
Lysippus, statue of Alexander, 31

Maccabees, 153
Macedon, British imitations of, 100
Magadha, 180
Magistrates' names, 38
Magdalen Tower, 136
Magna Graecia, 22
Magnus Maximus, last Imperial coins in Britain, 102
Mahmal, 159
Mahmûd of Ghazny, 180 *et seq.*
Mahmûd II., 173
Maidens, 16
Malatesta, 240
Malayan Peninsula, 201
Malchus, 151
Malwah, 186
Mamerces, 54
Mamlûk Queen, 158
Mamlûks of Egypt, 172, 160
Mandchu dynasty, 224
Manghir, 173
Mannus, 151
Mansûrah, battle of, 160
Mantua, Marquefs of, 242
Maravedis, 81, 170
Marcia gens, 54
Margaret of Austria, 248
Maria Theresa, 95
Mark, 97
  St., 86

Marks, moneyers', 54
Mars, 50
Mary, Queen, 123
Mary Queen of Scots, 130, 254
Maſſalia, trade with, 100
Matthew, St., 86
Maues, 178
Maundy money, 139
Maurice, Prince, 252, 255
Medaglie, 236
Médailles, 236
Medallic art, 6, 70, 91, 95, 236, etc.
Medallions, 68, 237
MEDALS, 236-269
    The word Medal, 236
    Italian medals, 237
    Piſano, 238
    New proceſs of caſting, 239
    Followers of Piſano, 242
    Sixteenth century medalliſts, 243
    Francia, 244
    Benvenuto Cellini, 244
    Paſtorino, 244
    Fontana, 245
    Portraits, 245
    Bartholomew, 246
    German medals, 246
    French medals, 248
    Dupré, 249
    The Warins, 249
    Napoleonic medals, 250
    Frappée à Londres, 251
    Dutch medals, 251
    Engliſh medals, 253
    Armada medals, 254
    James I., 256
    Charles I., 257
    Commonwealth, 258
    Blake medals, 258
    The Simons, 259
    Rawlins, 259
    Charles II., 260
    Popiſh Plot, 260
    James II., 261
    Pretender medals, 262
    William and Mary, and Anne, 264
    Military and Naval medals, 265

MEDALS—
    Indian medals, 266
    Waterloo, 266
    Preſent condition of medallic art, 266
    Claſſical deſigns, 267
    The Wyons, 267
    Profeſſor Legros, 268
    Mr. Poynter, 269
Mediaeval coinage, 6, 74-98
Medicis, Catherine de, 249
Meduſa, 21
Mejîdîeh, 173
Melioli, 242
Meliſſae (Epheſus), 21
Merv, 165
Meſopotamia, 144, 145, 169
Meſſana, pharos, 53.
Metapontum, 23
Methods of coining, 11
Mewar, 186
Michael, St., 79, 112
Middle Ages, coins of, 74-98
Mikado's creſt, 234
Milan, 79
    portraits, 92
Miliarenſis, 61
Military medals, 265
Mill, 94
Millares, 170
Minerva, 44
Mines in China, 197
Ming dynaſty, 224
Mints of Charles I., 134
    provincial Rome, 55, 66
Mints, Scottiſh, 114
Mithradates, 32, 145, 150
Mithras, 179
Modern coins, 7, 93
Moguls of Dehli, 188
Mohammad ibn Taghlak, 187
Mohammad II., 173
MOHAMMADAN COINS, 156-174
    Art on Muſlim coins, 156
    Calligraphy, 156
    Hiſtorical Aſſociations, 158
    A Mamlûk Queen, 158
    Genealogical data, 159
    Cruſade of St. Louis, 160
    Value of numiſmatic evidence, 163

Index. 281

MOHAMMADAN COINS—
  Origin of the coinage, 164
  Religious infcriptions, 166
  Weight and finenefs, 167
  The Khalifate, 167
  Dynaftic coinage, 168
  Chriftian figures, 169
  Mongols, 170
  Mamlûks, 172
  Berbers, 172
  Ottoman Turks, 173
Mohammadan coins of India, 182
Mohammadan dynafties of India, 185
Mommfen, Th., 2, 44
Moneyers, 54
Mongols, 170
Monmouth, rebellion of, 261
Monopoly of copper tokens, 129
Moorifh currency, 81, 167 *et feq.*
More, Thomas, 253
Morocco, 172
Morton's portrait of Mary, 254
Mofes of Khoren, 150
Mofil, 169
Mouton, 111
Murâbitîn, El-, 81, 170
Murfhidabad, 189
Mufa, 148
Mufta'fim, El-, 159
Muwahhidîn, El-, 170
Mythological types, 12
Mythology on Greek coins, 5
  Indian, 179
  Perfian, 141, 142

NABATHEA, 151
Nanaia, 179
Naples, 22, 91
Napoleon I., 96, 250
Naval rewards, 258
  medals, 265
Neptune, 53
Neuantos, artift of Cydonia, 37
Newark, 135
Nien-hao, 217
Nike on Parthian coins, 147
Nile medal, 265
Noble, 110
Normandy, 111

Normans, 107
  of Apulia, 86 *et feq.*
Norfe Kings in Ireland, 106, 115
Norfe Arabic coins, 84
North Africa, 169, 170
Norway, 106
Numerals on Englifh coins, 118 *note*
Nuremberg, 96, 247
Nymphs, 20, 25

ODENATHUS, 151
Offa, King of Mercia, 82, 103
Olive branch of Athena, 16
Olympian games, 23
Ommiade Khalifs, 167
Omphalos, 18
Ooerkes, 179
ORIENTAL COINS, EARLY, 141-155
  Perfia, 141
  Phoenicia, 143
  Succeffors of Alexander, 143
  Satraps, 144
  Central Afia, 145
  Parthians, 145
  Saffanians, 148
  Armenia, 150
  Nabathea, 151
  Palmyra, 151
  Arabia, 151
  Judaea, 153
Oriental invention of coinage, 11, 141
Ormazd, 149
Ortygia, 26
Ofcan coins, 57
Ofroene, 151
Oftrogoths, 78
Ottoman Turks, 172
Owl of Athene, 16
Oxford, 135
Oxford Crown, 136

PADLOCK money, 200
Pallas, 28, 44, 147
Palm-tree (Ephefus), 21
Palmyra, 151
Pangaeum mines, 20
Pantheon, Indian, 179
Parian Chronicle, 10

Parthians, 145
Parvati, 179
Paſſe, Simon, 257
Paſti, Matteo, 242
Paſtorino, 243, 244
Patâns of Dehli, 185
Pavia, 79
Pavillon, 111
Pearls, 197
Pecunia, 10
Pehlvi, 165
Peloponneſus, 15
Peninſular medal, 266
Penny, ſilver, 82, 105
    copied abroad, 108
    degradation of, 109
    gold, of Henry III., 109
    Scottiſh, 131
    etymology, 81 *note*
Pepin the Short, 82
Père, Louis le, 248
Perſephone, 22, 36
Perſia, ancient, 141
    Shahs of, 7, 171
Peter, St., 86
    the Great, 94, 95
Petition Crown, 138, 259
Petra, 151
Petrarch, 6
Pfaffenpfenninge, 84
Pfenning, 81
Pheidias' Zeus, 40
Pheidon, King of Argos, 10
Philetaerus, 31
Philibert le Beau, 248
Philip of Macedon, 27
Philip the Fair, 126
Philip and Mary, 123, 253
Phoenicia, 143
Phraates IV., 148
Phraataces, 148
Phrygian cap, 178
Pilon, G., 249
Piſano V., 6, 238
Piſo, 51
Plack, 115
Plumbei Angliae, 128
Poitou, 111
Pollajualo, 242
Pomedello, 243
Pompeius, Sextus, 53

Pontefract, 135
Popes, portraits of, 92, 242, 244
Portcullis, 125
Portraits, 4, 7, 94
    Greek, 12, 28
    Roman, 72
    Italian, 91, 238 *et ſeq.*
    Engliſh, 117, 253 *et ſeq.*
    Scottiſh, 130
    German, 246
    French, 248
    Dutch, 252, 254, 256, 257, 259
Poſeidon (Haliartus), 19
    (Tarentum), 23
Poſtumia gens, 53
Pound, 97, 132
Poynter, E. J., 269
Prague, 89
Praxiteles' Aphrodite (Cnidus), 40
Prelatical frauds, 126
Pretender medals, 262
Prieſtly colleges, 13
Prieſts, names on coins, 39
Primavera, G., 249, 254
Prinſep, 183
Procurators of Judaea, 154
Provincial mints, 66
Pruſias, King of Bithynia, 31
Ptolemies, 152
Ptolemy Philadelphus, 30
    Soter, 29
Punched coins, 179
Punch-marked coins, 8
Pythian Feſtivals, 17
Python, 25

QUADRANS, 43, 50
Quarter-ſovereign, 124
Quincuſſis, 43
Quinarius, 3, 48

RAJPUT kings, 181
Ram's head of Apollo, 18
Rawlins, T., 136, 259
Realiſm on Greek coins, 31
    on Italian medals, 240
Reformation medals, 95
Regimental medals, 266
Reitz, H., 247
Religious types, 12

Renaissance, 91
  in England, 117
Restoration medals, 260
Restrictions on export of coins, 126
Reuter, de, 252
Revolts, Jewish, 154
Rider, 115
Ring weights, 202
Ringelberg, J., 247
River gods, 23
Robert II., 115
Robert III., 115
Roettier, 138, 259
Roma, head of, 50
ROMAN COINS, 42-73
    Aes rude, signatum, and grave, 42, 43
    Early gold and silver, 45
    Campanian coins, 45
    Reduction of the as libralis, 46
    First Roman silver coins, 48
    Victoriatus, 49
    Uncial as, 49
    Gold coins after, B.C. 269, 50
    Types, 52
    Moneyers' marks, 54
    Mint officers, 55
    Local issues, 56
    Oscan coins, 57
    Imperial coinage, 59
    Argenteus, 60
    Diocletian's reforms, 60
    Solidus, 61
    Imperial types, 61
    Christian types, 63
    Iconographic types, 64
    Local mints, 66
    Alexandrian coinage, 67
    Medallions and tickets, 68
    Medallic art, 70
Roman currency used by barbarians, 77
Roman effigies on Jewish coins, 154
Roman mints, 66, 102
Romano, 243
Ronsard, 249
Rose noble, 112
    ryal, 132

Rose, Tudor, 120
  on sixpence, 124
Runes, 103
Russia, 93, 95, 172
Ryal, 120

SABAZIUS, 20
Sabines, rape of, 54
Sacae, 144, 178
Saddle-money, 206
Sâffarîs, 168
Sah Kings, 181
Saints, 64, 86, 179
Saladin, 169
Sâlih, Es-, 159, 160
Salutes, 112
Sâmânîs, 168
Sancho Ramirez, 86
Saphadin, 160
Sassanians, 148
  silver used by Arabs, 164
Satraps, Greek, 144
Saturn, head of, 52
Satyrs, 20
Saulcy, de, 2
Saurashtran, 181
Sauvaire, H., 158
Saxons, 102
  Emperors, 83
Scandinavian coinage, 85
Scarborough, 135
Sceat, 103
Sceptre piece, 132
Schilling, 96
Schools of coin artists, 4
Schutz-thaler, 95
Scotland, 106, 113, 129
Sculpture compared with coins, Greek, 3
Scylla, 53
Scythic Kings, 178
Seisachtheia, 16
Seistân, 168
Segesta, 24
Selene, 178
Seleucia, 177
Seleucid era, 147
Seleucidae, 143
Seleucus I., 143
Selinus, 24
Seljuks, 169

Index.

Semis, 43, 50
Semrang Sen, 201
Sequence, chronological, of Greek coins, 33
Sequin (Zecchino), 89, 97, 173
Serapis, 179
Servius Tullius, 42
Seſtertius, 48, 50
Sextans, 43
Sextantal as, 47
Shafteſbury, 261
Shahs of Perſia, 171
Shakeſpeare, *Henry VIII.*, 122
    Merchant of Venice, 113
    Merry Wives, 113
Shang dynaſty, 197
Shang-lin mint, 212
Shejer-ed-durr, 158
Shekel, Perſian, 141
    Jewiſh, 153
Shell currency, 192 *et ſeq.*
Sherifs of Morocco, 172
Shield, Engliſh, 120 *et ſeq.*
Shield of Boeotia or Herakles, 18
Shilling, 96, 117
Shrewsbury, 135
Shu King, 199
Sicily, 23
Siege pieces, 135
Sieges-thaler, 95
Sigli or shekels, 141
Signatures of artiſts, 36, 37
Sikkeh rupee, 189
Siliqua, 61
Silk, 192
Silver among the Germans, 104
Silver prevailing in Europe, 81
Simon, Abraham, 136, 259
Simon bar Cochab, 154
Simon the Maccabee, 153
Simon, Thomas, 136, 259
Siva, 179
Sixpence, 123
Skilling, 96
Sluys, battle of, 110
Smeltzing, 261, 264
Solidus, 61, 96
Solon, 15
Sophocles, Trach., 12
South Sea Company, 140

Sovereign, 120
Sovereigns, portraits of, 94
Spade weights, 202
Spain mediaeval coinage, 85, 167
    Armada, 255
Spectator's Shilling, 237
Spenſer, *Prothalamium*, 241
Sperandio, 242
Sphinxes, 21
Spinelli, N., 248
Spur ryal, 132
Stag of Artemis, 14
    Artemis (Epheſus), 21
State coinage of China, 208
    of Greece, 14
Statues, copies of, on coins, 3, 40, 71
Stephen of Holland, 254
Sterlings, 109, 113
Stone age, relic of, 201
Strabo, viii., 6
Strafford, 258
Stuarts, coinage, 134
Study of coins, 1
Styles of art on Greek coins, 33
Styles, ſequence of, 33
Succeſſors of Alexander, 28
Sulla, 50
Sung dynaſty, 218
Sunga Kings of Magadha, 180
Swan of Camarina, 25
Sword dollar, 132
Syracuſan artiſts, 36, 37
Syracuſe, 25
Syro-Greek kingdom, 143

TACITUS, *Germ.*, 5
Taikun, 234
Tai-ping rebellion, 224
Tamerlane, 171, 185
Tanagra, 19
Tankah, 186
Taras, 22
Tarentum, 22
Tarpeia, 54
Tartars, 218 *et ſeq.*
Tch'en dynaſty, 219
Tchou dynaſty, 198
Telephus, 178
Temple coinage, 13

Index. 285

Temples and monasteries, Buddhist, 222
Temples, pictures, and statues, represented on coins, 3, 5, 40, 71
Ten-shilling pieces, 138
Ten-sho period in Japan, 229
Terina, 4
Test Act medal, 261
Thaler, 98
Theodebert, 78
Theodotus of Cydonia, 37
Third-ryal, 131
Thirty-shilling pieces, 132
Thistle dollar, 132
    mark, 132
    noble, 132
Thomas, E., 183, 184, 187
Thrace, 19
Three-halfpenny pieces, 124
Threepenny piece, 124
Thunderbolt, symbol of Zeus, 14
Tiara, Armenian, 150
Tickets, 68
Tigranes, 143, 150
Timur, 171
Tin tokens, 128
Tiraeus, 152
Titus, coins of, 62
Tokens, English, 128
Topa dynasty, 219
Tortoise-shell currency, 193
Tortoise of Aphrodite, 14. 15
Touch-pieces, 263
Tower mint, 136
Towns, names of, 106
Trafalgar medal, 265
Trajan, 63
Transoxiana, 168
Treasures, temple, 14, 222
Tremissis, 79
Trezzo, 253
Trident of Poseidon, 19
Triens, 43, 50
Triental as, 46
Trim, 116
Trinity, Holy (Hand, Cross, and Dove), 86
Trinobantes, 102
Tripod of Apollo, 14
Triumph, the, 258

Tromp, Van, 252
Ts'i, Duke of, 198
    knife money of, 204
Ts'in dynasty, 208
    later, 217
Tudors, 117 *et seq.*
Tûlûn, Beny, 168
Turks, Ottoman, 172
Twenty-shilling piece, 130
Two-guinea piece, 138
Two-penny piece, 124
Two-third ryal, 131
Type, 11
Tyre and Sidon, 143

ULYSSES, 54
Umawy Khalifs, 167
Uncia, 43
Uncial as, 49
Unicorn, 115
Unite or broad, 132
Urtukîs, 169
Utrecht, Peace of, 264

VAGARSHAG, VALARSACES, 150
Vandals, 78
Venice, 89
Verona, artists of, 238, 242
Vespasian, 62, 154
Viceroys of Egypt, 173
Victoriatus, 49
Victory, 28, 46, 63, 147
Views of cities, 96
Vigo Bay Expedition, 139
Vikings, 85, 106
Virgil, *Æneid*, 45
Virgin on Mohammadan coins 169
Virgin and Child, 86
Virgin and Saviour, 64
Visigoths, 78
Vultus Sanctus, 86

WANG MANG, 213
Warin, 92, 249
Water nymphs, 25
Waterloo medal, 264, 266
Waterford, 116
Wealth, increase in England, 119
    god of, 232

Wei, State of, 216
Weights and denominations, 96
Weight of Mohammadan coins, 167
Weights, current, in China, 202
Weſtminſter Abbey, ſhields in, 121
Wexford, 116
Weymouth, 135
Wheel of Apollo, 19
William I. and II., 107
William III., 139, 263
William the Lion, 113
William the Silent, 252
Winecup on Indian coin, 189
Witts, the De, 252
Wolſey's groat, 122
Women on Arabian coins, 152
Worceſter, 135

Wu, State of, 216
Wyon, 267

XERXES, 150

YANG-TCHEU cowries, 193
Yh-King, 192
York, 122, 135
Yu-chi, 178
Yuen dynaſty, 224

ZECCHINO (sequin), 89, 97, 17
Zengy, Beny-, 169
Zenobia, 151
Zeus, chryſelephantine, copied on, 40
  on Philip's ſilver coins, 27
Zion, deliverance of, 153
Zodiacal coins, 8, 189

www.ingramcontent.com/pod-product-compliance
Lightning Source LLC
Chambersburg PA
CBHW032054220426
43664CB00008B/998